Engineering in K–12 Education

UNDERSTANDING THE STATUS AND IMPROVING THE PROSPECTS

Committee on K–12 Engineering Education

Linda Katehi, Greg Pearson, and Michael Feder, *Editors*

NATIONAL ACADEMY OF ENGINEERING *AND*
NATIONAL RESEARCH COUNCIL
OF THE NATIONAL ACADEMIES

THE NATIONAL ACADEMIES PRESS
Washington, D.C.
www.nap.edu

THE NATIONAL ACADEMIES PRESS   500 Fifth Street, N.W.   Washington, DC 20001

NOTICE: The project that is the subject of this report was approved by the Governing Board of the National Research Council, whose members are drawn from the councils of the National Academy of Sciences, the National Academy of Engineering, and the Institute of Medicine. The members of the committee responsible for the report were chosen for their special competences and with regard for appropriate balance.

This study was supported by a grant between the National Academy of Sciences and Stephen D. Bechtel, Jr. Additional support was provided by the National Science Foundation (Contract/Grant No. DRL-0935879) and PTC, Inc. Any opinions, findings, conclusions, or recommendations expressed in this publication are those of the author(s) and do not necessarily reflect the views of the organizations or agencies that provided support for the project.

Library of Congress Cataloging-in-Publication Data

Engineering in K–12 education : understanding the status and improving the prospects / Committee on K–12 Engineering Education ; Linda Katehi, Greg Pearson, and Michael Feder, editors.
    p. cm.
  Includes bibliographical references and index.
  ISBN 978-0-309-13778-2 (pbk.) — ISBN 978-0-309-13779-9 (pdf) 1. Engineering—Study and teaching (Elementary)—United States. 2. Engineering—Study and teaching (Secondary)—United States. I. Katehi, Linda. II. Pearson, Greg. III. Feder, Michael. IV. Committee on K–12 Engineering Education.
  LB1594.E54 2009
  620.0071—dc22

                              2009028717

Copies of this report are available from the National Academies Press, 500 Fifth Street, N.W., Lockbox 285, Washington, DC 20055; (800) 624-6242 or (202) 334-3313 (in the Washington metropolitan area); Internet, http://www.nap.edu

THE NATIONAL ACADEMIES
Advisers to the Nation on Science, Engineering, and Medicine

The **National Academy of Sciences** is a private, nonprofit, self-perpetuating society of distinguished scholars engaged in scientific and engineering research, dedicated to the furtherance of science and technology and to their use for the general welfare. Upon the authority of the charter granted to it by the Congress in 1863, the Academy has a mandate that requires it to advise the federal government on scientific and technical matters. Dr. Ralph J. Cicerone is president of the National Academy of Sciences.

The **National Academy of Engineering** was established in 1964, under the charter of the National Academy of Sciences, as a parallel organization of outstanding engineers. It is autonomous in its administration and in the selection of its members, sharing with the National Academy of Sciences the responsibility for advising the federal government. The National Academy of Engineering also sponsors engineering programs aimed at meeting national needs, encourages education and research, and recognizes the superior achievements of engineers. Dr. Charles M. Vest is president of the National Academy of Engineering.

The **Institute of Medicine** was established in 1970 by the National Academy of Sciences to secure the services of eminent members of appropriate professions in the examination of policy matters pertaining to the health of the public. The Institute acts under the responsibility given to the National Academy of Sciences by its congressional charter to be an adviser to the federal government and, upon its own initiative, to identify issues of medical care, research, and education. Dr. Harvey V. Fineberg is president of the Institute of Medicine.

The **National Research Council** was organized by the National Academy of Sciences in 1916 to associate the broad community of science and technology with the Academy's purposes of furthering knowledge and advising the federal government. Functioning in accordance with general policies determined by the Academy, the Council has become the principal operating agency of both the National Academy of Sciences and the National Academy of Engineering in providing services to the government, the public, and the scientific and engineering communities. The Council is administered jointly by both Academies and the Institute of Medicine. Dr. Ralph J. Cicerone and Dr. Charles M. Vest are chair and vice chair, respectively, of the National Research Council.

www.national-academies.org

Preface

This report is the final product of a two-year study by the Committee on K–12 Engineering Education, a group of experts on diverse subjects under the auspices of the National Academy of Engineering (NAE) and the Board on Science Education at the Center for Education, part of the National Research Council (NRC). The committee's charge was to determine the scope and nature of efforts to teach engineering to the nation's elementary and secondary students. In fulfilling that charge, the committee considered a number of specific questions, such as What types of curricula and teacher professional development have been used? How does engineering education "interact" with science, technology, and mathematics? And what impact—on student learning, interest in engineering, and other outcomes—have various initiatives had?

Engineering education is a relatively new school subject in U.S. K–12 education. Up to this point it has developed in an ad hoc fashion, and its spread into classrooms has been fairly modest. Even so, the presence of engineering in K–12 classrooms is an important phenomenon, because it casts new light on the very important issue of STEM (science, technology, engineering, and mathematics) education. There is broad agreement today among educators, policy makers, and industry leaders that the teaching of STEM subjects in American K–12 schools must be improved. Many of the concerns about STEM education tie to worries about the innovation capacity of the United States and its ability to compete in the global marketplace.

This report will be of special interest to individuals and groups interested in improving the quality of K–12 STEM education in this country. Engineering educators, policy makers, employers, and others concerned about the development of the country's technical workforce will also find much to ponder. The report should prove useful to advocates for greater public understanding of engineering, as well as to those working to boost citizens' technological and scientific literacy. Finally, for educational researchers and cognitive scientists, the document exposes a rich set of questions related to how and under what conditions students come to understand engineering.

The committee met five times, sponsored two data-gathering workshops, and solicited online input from the public midway through the project. The committee also commissioned an analysis of a number of existing K–12 engineering curricula; conducted reviews of the literature on areas of conceptual learning related to engineering, the development of engineering skills, and the impacts of K–12 engineering education initiatives; and collected preliminary information about a few pre-college engineering education programs in other countries. Beyond this data gathering, the report reflects the personal and professional experiences and judgments of committee members.

Linda P.B. Katehi, *Chair*
Committee on K–12 Engineering Education

Acknowledgments

This report has been reviewed in draft form by individuals chosen for their diverse perspectives and technical expertise, in accordance with procedures approved by the NRC's Report Review Committee. The purpose of this independent review is to provide candid and critical comments that will assist the institution in making its published report as sound as possible and to ensure that the report meets institutional standards for objectivity, evidence, and responsiveness to the study charge. The review comments and draft manuscript remain confidential to protect the integrity of the deliberative process. We wish to thank the following individuals for their review of this report:

William F. Bertrand, Bureau of Teaching and Learning Support, Division of Standards and Curriculum, Pennsylvania Department of Education

Lizanne DeStefano, Bureau of Educational Research, College of Education, University of Illinois at Urbana-Champaign

David P. Driscoll, Consultant, Melrose, Massachusetts

Katie M. Dodge, Cooper Upper Elementary, Livonia Public Schools, Livonia, Michigan

Susan Hackwood, Office of the Executive Director, California Council on Science and Technology

Joseph G. Langhauser, Fleet and Commercial Sales, Mobility Program, General Motors Corporation
Karl S. Pister, Department of Civil and Environmental Engineering, University of California, Berkeley
Mark Sanders, Integrative STEM Education, Virginia Tech
Reed Stevens, Cognitive Studies in Education, University of Washington
Carl Truxel, Technology Education Department, Dulaney High School, Baltimore County Public Schools, Baltimore, Maryland
Yannis C. Yortsos, Viterbi School of Engineering, University of Southern California

Although the reviewers listed above have provided many constructive comments and suggestions, they were not asked to endorse the conclusions or recommendations nor did they see the final draft of the report before its release. The review of this report was overseen by William G. Agnew, Retired Director, Programs and Plans, General Motors Corporation, Corrales, New Mexico. Appointed by the NRC, he was responsible for making certain that an independent examination of this report was carried out in accordance with institutional procedures and that all review comments were carefully considered. Responsibility for the final content of this report rests entirely with the authoring committee and the institution.

In addition to the reviewers, many other individuals assisted in the development of this report. Anthony J. Petrosino and Vanessa Svihla, University of Texas at Austin, and Sean Brophy, Purdue University, prepared a commissioned paper examining cognitive science research related to engineering skills; Eli M. Silk and committee member Christian D. Schunn, University of Pittsburgh, prepared a commissioned paper examining cognitive science research related to core concepts in engineering; Vanessa Svihla, Jill Marshall, University of Texas at Austin, and Anthony J. Petrosino prepared a commissioned paper examining the impacts of K–12 engineering education efforts; Jonson Miller, Drexel University, prepared a commissioned paper reviewing the history of engineering and technical education in the United States; and Marc J. de Vries, Eindhoven University of Technology/Delft University of Technology, The Netherlands, prepared a commissioned paper examining pre-college engineering education initiatives outside the United States.

Thanks are also due to the project staff. Maribeth Keitz managed the study's logistical and administrative needs, making sure meetings and workshops ran efficiently and smoothly. Christine Mirzayan Science & Technology Policy Graduate Fellow Carolyn Williams did extensive research on pre-college engineering education programs outside the United States, work that led to the commissioned paper by Marc de Vries. Freelance writer Robert Pool helped write several chapters of the report. NAE Senior Editor Carol R. Arenberg substantially improved the readability of the report. Special thanks are due to Kenneth Welty, University of Wisconsin, Stout, who conducted an extensive analysis of K–12 engineering curricula that substantially informed the committee's work. Michael Feder, at the NRC Board on Science Education, helped guide the project from its inception. Greg Pearson, at the NAE, played a key role in conceptualizing the study and managed the project from start to finish.

Contents

---

*Appendix C is reproduced on the CD (inside back cover) and in the PDF available online at http://www.nap/edu/catalog.php?record_id=12635.

List of Acronyms

AAAS   American Association for the Advancement of Science
ASCE   American Society of Civil Engineers
ASEE   American Society for Engineering Education
AWIM   A World in Motion®

CAD/CAM   computer-aided design/computer-aided manufacturing
CLT   cognitive load theory
CD   compact disk
CO_2 carbon dioxide

DPS   Denver Public Schools
DSST   Denver School of Science and Technology
DVD   digital video disk

EPICS   Engineering Projects in Community Service

FBS   function-behavior-structure
FIRST   For Inspiration and Recognition of Science and Technology

HSCE   Higher School Certificate in Engineering

INSPIRES	INcreasing Student Participation, Interest, and Recruitment in Engineering and Science
ITEA	International Technology Education Association
K–12	kindergarten through grade 12
M/S/T	mathematics/science/technology
MWM	Material World Modules
NAE	National Academy of Engineering
NAEP	National Assessment of Educational Progress
NAGB	National Assessment Governing Board
NCETE	National Center for Engineering and Technology Education
NCLB	No Child Left Behind
NSF	National Science Foundation
PD	professional development
PLTW	Project Lead the Way
SAE	Society of Automotive Engineers
SBF	structure-behavior-function
SMET	science, mathematics, engineering, and technology
STEM	science, technology, engineering, and mathematics
TCNJ	The College of New Jersey
TIMSS	Trends in International Mathematics and Science Study
TISD	Texarkana Independent School District

Summary

Although K–12 engineering education has received little attention from most Americans, including educators and policy makers, it has slowly been making its way into U.S. K–12 classrooms. Today, several dozen different engineering programs and curricula are offered in school districts around the country, and thousands of teachers have attended professional development sessions to teach engineering-related coursework. In the past 15 years, several million K–12 students have experienced some formal engineering education.

The presence of engineering in K–12 classrooms is an important phenomenon, not because of the number of students impacted, which is still small relative to other school subjects, but because of the implications of engineering education for the future of science, technology, engineering, and mathematics (STEM) education more broadly. Specifically, as elaborated in the full report, K–12 engineering education may improve student learning and achievement in science and mathematics; increase awareness of engineering and the work of engineers; boost youth interest in pursuing engineering as a career; and increase the technological literacy of all students. The committee believes engineering education may even act as a catalyst for a more interconnected and effective K–12 STEM education system in the United States. Achieving the latter outcome will require significant rethinking of what STEM education can and should be.

In recent years, educators and policy makers have come to a consensus that the teaching of STEM subjects in U.S. schools must be improved. The focus on STEM topics is closely related to concerns about U.S. competitiveness in the global economy and about the development of a workforce with the knowledge and skills to address technical and technological issues. To date, most efforts to improve STEM education have been concentrated on mathematics and science, but an increasing number of states and school districts have been adding technology education to the mix, and a smaller but significant number have added engineering.

In contrast to science, mathematics, and even technology education, all of which have established learning standards and a long history in the K–12 curriculum, the teaching of engineering in elementary and secondary schools is still very much a work in progress. Not only have no learning standards been developed, little is available in the way of guidance for teacher professional development, and no national or state-level assessments of student accomplishment have been developed. In addition, no single organization or central clearinghouse collects information on K–12 engineering education.

Thus a number of basic questions remain unanswered. How is engineering taught in grades K–12? What types of instructional materials and curricula have been used? How does engineering education "interact" with other STEM subjects? In particular, how has K–12 engineering instruction incorporated science, technology, and mathematics concepts, and how has it used these subjects as a context for exploring engineering concepts? Conversely, how has engineering been used as a context for exploring science, technology, and mathematics concepts? And what impact have various initiatives had? Have they, for instance, improved student achievement in science or mathematics or stimulated interest among students in pursuing careers in engineering?

In 2006 the National Academy of Engineering and National Research Council Center for Education established the Committee on K–12 Engineering Education to begin to address these and other questions. Over a period of two years, the committee held five face-to-face meetings, two of which accompanied information-gathering workshops. The committee also commissioned an analysis of existing K–12 engineering curricula; conducted reviews of the literature on areas of conceptual learning related to engineering, the development of engineering skills, and the impact of K–12 engineering education initiatives; and collected preliminary information about a few pre-college engineering education programs in other countries.

The goal of the project was to provide carefully reasoned guidance to key stakeholders regarding the creation and implementation of K–12 engineering curricula and instructional practices, focusing especially on the connections among science, technology, engineering, and mathematics education. The project had these specific objectives:

- Survey the landscape of current and past efforts to implement engineering-related K–12 instructional materials and curricula in the United States and other nations;
- Review evidence related to the impact of these initiatives, to the extent such information is available;
- Describe the ways in which K–12 engineering content has incorporated science, technology, and mathematics concepts, used these subjects as context to explore engineering concepts, or used engineering as a context to explore science, technology, and mathematics concepts; and
- Report on the intended learning outcomes of K–12 engineering education initiatives, taking into account student age, curriculum focus (e.g., science vs. technology education), program orientation (e.g., general education vs. career/vocational education), and other factors.

In meeting the goal and objectives, the project focused on three key issues and three related guiding questions:

- There are multiple perspectives about the purpose and place of engineering in the K–12 classroom. These points of view lead to emphases on very different outcomes. QUESTION: What are realistic and appropriate learning outcomes for engineering education in K–12?
- There has not been a careful analysis of engineering education within a K–12 environment that looks at possible subject intersections. QUESTION: How might engineering education complement the learning objectives of other content areas, particularly science, technology, and mathematics, and how might these other content areas complement learning objectives in engineering education?
- There has been little if any serious consideration of the systemic changes in the U.S. education system that might be required to enhance K–12 engineering education. QUESTION: What educa-

tional policies, programs, and practice at the local, state, and federal levels might permit meaningful inclusion of engineering at the K–12 level in the United States?

The committee believes this report will be of special interest to individuals and groups interested in improving the quality of K–12 STEM education in this country. But engineering educators, policy makers, employers, and others concerned about the development of the country's technical workforce will also find much to ponder. The report should prove useful to advocates for greater public understanding of engineering, as well as to those working to boost citizens' technological and scientific literacy. Finally, for educational researchers and cognitive scientists, the document exposes a rich set of questions related to how and under what conditions students come to understand engineering.

GENERAL PRINCIPLES FOR K–12 ENGINEERING EDUCATION

The specifics of how engineering is taught vary from school district to school district, and what takes place in classrooms in the name of engineering education does not always align with generally accepted ideas about the discipline and practice of engineering. This is not to suggest that K–12 students should be treated like little engineers, but when a school subject is taught for which there is a professional counterpart, there should be a conceptual connection to post-secondary studies and to the practice of that subject in the real world.

The committee set forth three general principles for K–12 engineering education.

Principle 1. K–12 engineering education should emphasize engineering design.

The design process, the engineering approach to identifying and solving problems, is (1) highly iterative; (2) open to the idea that a problem may have many possible solutions; (3) a meaningful context for learning scientific, mathematical, and technological concepts; and (4) a stimulus to systems thinking, modeling, and analysis. In all of these ways, engineering design is a potentially useful pedagogical strategy.

Principle 2. K–12 engineering education should incorporate important and developmentally appropriate mathematics, science, and technology knowledge and skills.

Certain science concepts as well as the use of scientific inquiry methods can support engineering design activities. Similarly, certain mathematical concepts and computational methods can support engineering design, especially in service of analysis and modeling. Technology and technology concepts can illustrate the outcomes of engineering design, provide opportunities for "reverse engineering" activities, and encourage the consideration of social, environmental, and other impacts of engineering design decisions. Testing and measurement technologies, such as thermometers and oscilloscopes; software for data acquisition and management; computational and visualization tools, such as graphing calculators and CAD/CAM (i.e., computer design) programs; and the Internet should be used, as appropriate, to support engineering design, particularly at the high school level.

Principle 3. K–12 engineering education should promote engineering habits of mind.

Engineering "habits of mind"[1] align with what many believe are essential skills for citizens in the 21st century.[2] These include (1) systems thinking, (2) creativity, (3) optimism, (4) collaboration, (5) communication, and (6) attention to ethical considerations. Systems thinking equips students to recognize essential interconnections in the technological world and to appreciate that systems may have unexpected effects that cannot be predicted from the behavior of individual subsystems. Creativity is inherent in the engineering design process. Optimism reflects a world view in which possibilities and opportunities can be found in every challenge and an understanding that every technology can be improved. Engineering is a "team sport"; collaboration leverages the perspectives, knowledge, and capabilities of team members to address a design challenge. Communication is essential to effective collaboration, to understanding the particular wants and needs of a "customer," and to explaining and justifying the final design solution. Ethical considerations draw attention to the impacts of engineering on people and the environment; ethical considerations include possible unintended consequences

---

[1] The committee has adopted the term "habits of mind," as used by the American Association for the Advancement of Science in *Science for All Americans* (1990), to refer to the values, attitudes, and thinking skills associated with engineering.

[2] See, for example, The Partnership for 21st Century Skills, *www.21stcenturyskills.org.*

of a technology, the potential disproportionate advantages or disadvantages of a technology for certain groups or individuals, and other issues.

These principles, particularly Principle 3, should be considered aspirational rather than a reflection of what is present in current K–12 engineering education efforts or, indeed, in post-secondary engineering education.

THE SCOPE OF K–12 ENGINEERING EDUCATION

No reliable data are available on the precise number of U.S. K–12 students who have been exposed to engineering-related coursework. With a few notable exceptions, the first formal K–12 engineering programs in the United States emerged in the early 1990s. Since that time, fewer than 6 million students have had some kind of formal engineering education. By comparison, the estimated enrollment for grades pre-K–12 for U.S. public and private schools in 2008 was nearly 56 million.

No reliable data are available on the number of teachers involved in K–12 engineering education. The committee estimates that only about 18,000 teachers have received pre- or in-service professional development training to teach engineering-related coursework. The relatively small number of curricular and teacher professional development initiatives for K–12 engineering education were developed independently, often have different goals, and vary in how they treat engineering concepts, engineering design, and relationships among engineering and the other STEM subjects.

Although engineering education represents a relatively small slice of the K–12 educational pie, activity in this arena has increased significantly, from almost no curricula or programs 15 years ago to several dozen today. The future of K–12 engineering education will depend, at least in part, on whether it continues to be taught as a separate subject or whether engineering becomes a catalyst for more interconnected STEM education.

IMPACTS OF K–12 ENGINEERING EDUCATION

A variety of claims have been made for the benefits of teaching engineering to K–12 students, ranging from improved performance in related subjects, such as science and mathematics, and increased technological literacy to improvements in school attendance and retention, a better understanding of what engineers do, and an increase in the number of students who pursue careers in engineering. Only limited reliable data are available to support these claims. The most intriguing possible benefit of K–12 engineering education relates to improved student learning and achievement in mathematics and science, but even here, the paucity and small size of studies and their uneven quality cannot support unqualified claims of impact. For engineering education to become a mainstream component of K–12 education, there will have to be much more, and much higher quality, outcomes-based data.

RECOMMENDATION 1. Foundations and federal agencies with an interest in K–12 engineering education should support long-term research to confirm and refine the findings of earlier studies of the impacts of engineering education on student learning in STEM subjects, student engagement and retention, understanding of engineering, career aspirations, and technological literacy.

RECOMMENDATION 2. Funders of new efforts to develop and implement curricula for K–12 engineering education should include a research component that will provide a basis for analyzing how design ideas and practices develop in students over time and determining the classroom conditions necessary to support this development. After a solid analytic foundation has been established, a rigorous evaluation should be undertaken to determine what works and why.

THE NATURE OF K–12 ENGINEERING EDUCATION

Based on extensive reviews of the research literature and curricular materials, the committee concluded that there is no widely accepted vision of what K–12 engineering education should include or accomplish. This lack of consensus reflects the ad hoc development of educational materials in engineering and that no major effort has been made to define the content of K–12 engineering in a rigorous way.

Curriculum Content

The committee's review of curricula revealed that engineering design, the central activity of engineering, is predominant in most K–12 curricular and professional development programs. The treatment of key ideas in engineering, many closely related to engineering design, is much more uneven and, in some cases, suggests a lack of understanding on the part of curriculum developers. These shortcomings may be the result, at least in part, of the absence of a clear description of which engineering knowledge, skills, and habits of mind are most important, how they relate to and build on one another, and how and when (i.e., at what age) they should be introduced to students. In fact, it seems that no one has attempted to specify age-appropriate learning progressions in a rigorous or systematic way; this lack of specificity or consensus on learning outcomes and progressions goes a long way toward explaining the variability and unevenness in the curricula.

Curriculum Connections

Although there are a number of natural connections between engineering and the three other STEM subjects, existing curricula in K–12 engineering education do not fully explore them. For example, scientific investigation and engineering design are closely related activities that can be mutually reinforcing. Most curricula include some instances in which this connection is exploited (e.g., using scientific inquiry to generate data that can inform engineering design decisions or using engineering design to provide contextualized opportunities for science learning), but the connection is not systematically emphasized to improve learning in both domains. One option, which was evident in several of the curricula we reviewed, is to use engineering as a pedagogical strategy for science laboratory activities.

Similarly, mathematical analysis and modeling are essential to engineering design, but very few curricula or professional development initiatives reviewed by the committee used mathematics in ways that support modeling and analysis. The committee believes that K–12 engineering can contribute to improvements in students' performance and understanding of certain mathematical concepts and skills.

RECOMMENDATION 3. The National Science Foundation and/or U.S. Department of Education should fund research to determine how science inquiry and mathematical reasoning can be connected to engineering design in K–12 curricula and teacher professional development. The research should cover the following specific areas:

- the most important concepts, skills, and habits of mind in science and mathematics that can be taught effectively using an engineering design approach;
- the circumstances under which students learn important science and mathematics concepts, skills, and habits of mind through an

engineering-design approach as well or better than through science or mathematics instruction;

- how engineering design can be used as a pedagogical strategy in science and mathematics instruction; and
- the implications for professional development of using engineering design as a pedagogical tool for supporting science and mathematics learning.

Finally, our review of curricula showed that technology in K–12 engineering education has primarily been used to illustrate the products of engineering and to provide a context for thinking about engineering design. There were few examples of engineering being used to elucidate ideas related to other aspects of technological literacy, such as the nature and history of technology and the cultural, social, economic, and political dimensions of technology development.

Professional Development Programs

Compared with professional development opportunities for teaching other STEM subjects, the opportunities for engineering are few and far between. Nearly all in-service initiatives are associated with a few existing curricula, and many do not have one or more of the characteristics (e.g., activities that last for at least one week, ongoing in-classroom or online support following formal training, and opportunities for continuing education) that have been proven to promote teacher learning.

The committee found no pre-service initiatives that are likely to contribute significantly to the supply of qualified engineering teachers in the near future. Indeed, the "qualifications" for engineering educators at the K–12 level have not even been described. Graduates from a handful of teacher preparation programs have strong backgrounds in STEM subjects, including engineering, but few if any of them teach engineering classes in K–12 schools.

RECOMMENDATION 4. The American Society for Engineering Education (ASEE), through its Division of K–12 and Pre-College Education, should begin a national dialogue on preparing K–12 engineering teachers to address the very different needs and circumstances of elementary and secondary teachers and the pros and cons of establishing a formal credentialing process. Participants in the dialogue should include leaders in K–12 teacher education in mathematics, science, and technology; schools of education and engineering; state departments of education; teacher licensing and certification groups; and STEM program accreditors. ASEE should consult with the National Center for Engineering and Technology Education, which has conducted research on this topic.

Diversity

The lack of diversity in post-secondary engineering education and the engineering workforce in the United States is well documented. Based on evaluation data, analysis of curriculum materials, anecdotal reports, and personal observation, the committee concluded that lack of diversity is probably an issue for K–12 engineering education as well. This problem is manifested in two ways. First, the number of girls and underrepresented minorities who participate in K–12 engineering education initiatives is well below their numbers in the general population. Second, with a few exceptions, curricular materials do not portray engineering in ways that seem likely to excite the interest of students from a variety of ethnic and cultural backgrounds. For K–12 engineering education to yield the many benefits its supporters claim, access and participation will have to be expanded considerably.

RECOMMENDATION 5. Given the demographic trends in the United States and the challenges of attracting girls, African Americans, Hispanics, and some Asian subpopulations to engineering studies, K–12 engineering curricula should be developed with special attention to features which appeal to students from these underrepresented groups, and programs that promote K–12 engineering education should be strategic in their outreach to these populations. Both curriculum developers and outreach organizations should take advantage of recent market research that suggests effective ways of communicating about engineering to the public.

POLICY AND PROGRAM ISSUES

Although many unanswered questions about K–12 engineering education remain, engineering is being taught in K–12 schools around the country, and it appears that the trend is upward. Thus it is imperative that we begin to think about ways to guide and support engineering education in the future. An underlying question for policy makers is how engineering concepts, skills, and habits of mind should be introduced into the school curriculum. There are at least three options—ad hoc infusion, stand-alone courses, and interconnected STEM education. These options vary in terms of ease of implementation:

- Ad hoc infusion, or introduction, of engineering ideas and activities (i.e., design projects) into existing science, mathematics, and technology curricula is the most direct and least complicated option, because implementation requires no significant changes in school structure. The main requirements would be (1) willingness on the part of teachers and (2) access to instructional materials. Ideally, teachers would also have a modicum of engineering pedagogical content knowledge to deliver the new material effectively. The ad hoc option is probably most useful for providing an introductory exposure to engineering ideas rather than a deep understanding of engineering principles and skills.
- Stand-alone courses for engineering, an option required for implementing many of the curricula reviewed for this project, presents considerably more challenges for teachers and schools. In high schools, the new material could be offered as an elective. If that is not possible, it would either have to replace existing classes or content, perhaps a science or technology course, or the school day would have to be reconfigured, perhaps lengthened, to accommodate a new course(s) without eliminating existing curricular material. Stand-alone courses would also require teacher professional development and approval of the program at various levels. This option has the potential advantage of providing a more in-depth exposure to engineering.
- Fully integrated STEM education, that is, using engineering concepts and skills to leverage the natural connections between STEM subjects, would almost certainly require changes in the structure and practices of schools. Research would be necessary to develop and test curricula, assessments, and approaches to teacher professional development. New integrated STEM programs or "pilot schools" might be established to test changes before they are widely adopted.

These three options, as well as others that are not described here, are not mutually exclusive. Indeed, the committee believes that implementation should be flexible, because no single approach is likely to be acceptable or feasible in every district or school.

Whichever options are implemented, planners must take into account the "technical core" of education, that is, what happens in the classroom between the teacher, the student, and the content. One way to access the technical core is to work toward "coherence" by creating educational systems with standards, curricula, professional development, and student assessments and school leadership that supports the need for change.

RECOMMENDATION 6. Philanthropic foundations or federal agencies with an interest in STEM education and school reform should fund research to identify models of implementation for K–12 engineering education that embody the principles of coherence and can guide decision making that will work for widely variable American school systems. The research should explicitly address school populations that do not currently have access to engineering studies.

The need for qualified teachers to teach engineering in K–12 classrooms raises a number of policy and program issues. The current ad hoc approach of mostly in-service training may not be adequate to train enough teachers, if K–12 engineering continues to grow. A variety of traditional and alternative mechanisms should be evaluated as part of the initiative suggested in Recommendation 4.

INTEGRATED STEM EDUCATION

During the course of this project, the committee focused increasingly on the potential of using engineering education as a catalyst for improving STEM education in general, about which serious concerns have been raised among policy makers, educators, and industry managers. So far, the role of either technology education or engineering education has rarely been mentioned in these concerns. The STEM acronym is more often used as shorthand for science or mathematics education; even references to science and mathematics tend to be "siloed," that is, treated largely as separate entities. In other words, as STEM education is currently structured and implemented in U.S. classrooms, it does not reflect the natural connections among the four subjects, which are reflected in the real world of research and technology development.

The committee believes the "siloed" teaching of STEM subjects has impeded efforts to increase student interest and improve performance in science and mathematics. It also inhibits the development of technological and scientific literacy, which are essential to informed citizens in the 21st century. The committee believes that increasing the visibility of technology and, especially, engineering in STEM education in ways that address the interconnections in STEM teaching and learning could be extremely important. Ideally, all K–12 students in the United States should have the option of experiencing some form of formal engineering studies. We are a long way from that situation now.

In the committee's vision for STEM education in U.S. K–12 schools, all students who graduate high school will have a level of STEM literacy sufficient to (1) ensure their successful employment, post-secondary education, or both, and (2) prepare them to be competent, capable citizens in our technology-dependent, democratic society. Because of the natural connections of engineering education to science, mathematics, and technology, it might serve as a catalyst for achieving this vision. The committee was not asked to determine the qualities that characterize a STEM-literate person, but this would be a worthwhile exercise for a future study.

RECOMMENDATION 7. The National Science Foundation and the U.S. Department of Education should support research to characterize, or define, "STEM literacy." Researchers should consider not only core knowledge and skills in science, technology, engineering, and mathematics, but also the "big ideas" that link the four subject areas.

Pursuing the goal of STEM literacy in K–12 schools will require a paradigm shift by students, teachers, administrators, textbook publishers, and policy makers, as well as by the many scientists, technologists, engineers, and mathematicians involved in K–12 education. However, the committee believes that, as a result of that shift, students would be better prepared for life in the 21st century and would have the tools they need to make informed career decisions or pursue post-secondary education. In addition, integrated STEM education could improve teaching and learning in all four STEM subjects by forcing a reevaluation of the currently excessive expectations for STEM teachers and students. The committee is not suggesting a "dumbing-down" process. On the contrary, this is a call for more in-depth knowledge in fewer key STEM areas and for more time to be devoted to the development of a wider range of STEM skills, such as engineering design and scientific inquiry.

Meaningful improvements in the learning and teaching of engineering—and movement toward integrated STEM education—will not come easily or quickly. Progress will be measured in decades, rather than months or years. The necessary changes will only happen with a sustained commitment of financial resources, the support of policy makers and other leaders, and the efforts of many individuals in and outside K–12 schools. Despite these challenges, the committee is hopeful, the potential for enriching and improving K–12 STEM education is real, and engineering education can be the catalyst.

1

Introduction

In the past 15 years a consensus has emerged about the need to improve K–12 education, particularly in science, technology, engineering, and mathematics, the so-called STEM subjects. The lengthening list of groups and agencies calling for improvements includes the National Science Board, U.S. Department of Education, American Association for the Advancement of Science, National Academies, and many, many others (NSB, 2007; DOEd, 2008; AAAS, 1993; NAS, NAE, and IOM, 2007). In response, some legislative action, such as the 2007 America COMPETES Act (P.L. 110-69), has been taken to strengthen K–12 STEM education.

Many concerns about the quality of STEM education are related to the challenges facing the nation in an increasingly interconnected, increasingly competitive world. The general belief is that improving K–12 STEM education can help the country meet those challenges in two important ways. First, it will keep the "pipeline" of students prepared to pursue careers in various scientific and technical fields full. Second, it will raise the level of scientific and technological literacy in the general population. Ultimately, these changes should improve our ability to compete successfully in the global marketplace, defend ourselves against various non-economic threats, and improve our overall quality of life.

Based on those beliefs, a tremendous amount of attention has been paid to the question of how to improve the teaching and learning of science and mathematics in elementary and secondary schools. In fact, this has been the focus of grants by federal agencies, presidential commissions, initiatives by professional organizations, and studies by think tanks. Improving technology education (the "T" in STEM), however, has received significantly less attention.

By contrast, almost no attention has been paid—at least on the national level—to the issue of engineering education (the "E" in STEM) in grades K–12. The goal of this report is to begin to fill that gap by providing an overview of the current state of K–12 engineering education in the United States and a discussion of what we must do in the coming years to make engineering a more effective component of the STEM equation.

CURRENT K–12 STEM EDUCATION

The STEM acronym is a relatively recent innovation (Cavanagh and Trotter, 2008). Until 2001, the common shorthand was SMET, science, mathematics, engineering, and technology. The National Science Foundation (NSF) was the first to begin referring to this collection of subjects as STEM, reflecting a change in philosophy. Up to that point, NSF's K–12 programs had targeted mostly high-achieving students who were the most likely to pursue careers in science, mathematics, and engineering. In the past decade, however, the agency has focused more resources on broad-based programs to appeal to the entire student population.

The STEM acronym has since become ubiquitous, which might lead one to conclude that the four subjects (Box 1-1) represent a well connected system of learning. However, in reality, in most elementary and secondary schools, STEM subjects are taught with little or no connection among them. Students learn mathematics in one classroom, science in another, and technology and engineering—if they learn them at all—in yet other classrooms.

Science and Mathematics

Science and mathematics are the two STEM components with the longest histories in K–12 education. Both subjects have standards, curricula, and assessments, large numbers of textbooks and other teaching materials, and established courses of teacher education and professional development. Every student in every school in the country is expected to have a minimum level of proficiency in science and mathematics by the end of high school.

More important in the context of this report, student proficiency in both science and mathematics is widely recognized as important to individual

---

BOX 1-1
The Four STEM Subjects*

Science is the study of the natural world, including the laws of nature associated with physics, chemistry, and biology and the treatment or application of facts, principles, concepts, or conventions associated with these disciplines. Science is both a body of knowledge that has been accumulated over time and a process—scientific inquiry—that generates new knowledge. Knowledge from science informs the engineering design process.

Technology comprises the entire system of people and organizations, knowledge, processes, and devices that go into creating and operating technological artifacts, as well as the artifacts themselves. Throughout history, humans have created technology to satisfy their wants and needs. Much of modern technology is a product of science and engineering, and technological tools are used in both fields.

Engineering is both a body of knowledge—about the design and creation of human-made products—and a process for solving problems. This process is design under constraint. One constraint in engineering design is the laws of nature, or science. Other constraints include such things as time, money, available materials, ergonomics, environmental regulations, manufacturability, and repairability. Engineering utilizes concepts in science and mathematics as well as technological tools.

Mathematics is the study of patterns and relationships among quantities, numbers, and shapes. Specific branches of mathematics include arithmetic, geometry, algebra, trigonometry, and calculus. Mathematics is used in science and in engineering.

---

*See Chapter 2 for a more detailed discussion of relationships among science, technology, engineering, and mathematics.

---

success and to the success of the country. Thus the relatively poor showing of U.S. students in these subjects on national assessments (Grigg et al., 2006; Lee et al., 2007) and comparative international studies, such as the TIMSS (Trends in International Mathematics and Science Study) assessment of fourth- and eighth-grade students around the world (Martin et al., 2008;

Mullis et al., 2008), has led to numerous calls for improving science and mathematics education.

In 2007, for example, the National Academy of Sciences, National Academy of Engineering, and Institute of Medicine (together called the National Academies) published *Rising Above the Gathering Storm: Energizing and Employing America for a Brighter Economic Future.* The purpose of the report was to determine how the United States could maintain its competitiveness in the global marketplace, and the first recommendation was to "increase America's talent pool by vastly improving K–12 mathematics and science education" (NAS, NAE, and IOM, 2007). A variety of legislative initiatives at the state and federal levels have also addressed the issue. In addition to the recently enacted America COMPETES Act, the No Child Left Behind Act of 2001 (P.L. 107-110) specifically targets student achievement in science and mathematics by, for example, mandating testing in both subjects and providing funding for math and science partnerships between school districts and local colleges and universities (DoEd, 2008).

Technology Education

Although technology education has roots in the manual and industrial arts, over the past two decades the field has broadened to emphasize understanding of technology in its most general sense (Box 1-2). Technology education today is the study of the human-made world, including artifacts, processes, and their underlying principles and concepts, and the overarching goal of technology education is to equip students to participate effectively in our technologically dependent world (e.g., NAE and NRC, 2002).

Some of the specific goals of technology education are described in *Standards for Technological Literacy: Content for the Study of Technology,* a report published in 2000 by the International Technology Education Association (ITEA). To meet those standards, K–12 students must develop competencies in five areas: the nature of technology, technology and society, design, abilities for a technological world, and the designed world. The fourth competency, "abilities for a technological world," requires that students know how to use and maintain everyday technologies and be able to assess the effects of using different technologies on society and the environment. The fifth competency, "the designed world," requires an understanding of technologies in specific areas, such as medicine, agriculture, and information and communications.

Despite a sustained campaign by ITEA and others, technology education is only slowly gaining acceptance. Many people—including many

---

BOX 1-2
A Broad View of Technology

In the broadest sense, technology is the process by which humans modify nature to meet their wants and needs. Most people, however, think of technology in terms of its artifacts: computers and software, aircraft, pesticides, water-treatment plants, birth-control pills, and microwave ovens, to name a few. But technology is more than these tangible products. The knowledge and processes used to create and to operate the artifacts—engineering know-how, manufacturing expertise, various technical skills, and so on—are equally important. Technology also includes all of the infrastructure necessary for the design, manufacture, operation, and repair of technological artifacts, from corporate headquarters and engineering schools to manufacturing plants and maintenance facilities. Technology is a product of engineering and science, and science and technology are tightly coupled. A scientific understanding of the natural world is the basis for much of technological development today. Conversely, technology is the basis for a good part of scientific research. The climate models meteorologists use to study global warming, for example, require supercomputers to run the simulations. Technology is also closely associated with innovation, the transformation of ideas into new and useful products or processes. Innovation requires not only creative people and organizations, but also the availability of technology and science and engineering talent. Technology and innovation are synergistic. The development of gene-sequencing machines, for example, has made the decoding of the human genome possible, and that knowledge is fueling a revolution in diagnostic, therapeutic, and other biomedical innovations.

SOURCE: Adapted from NAE and NRC, 2002.

---

educators—confuse it with classes that train students to use computers. Today, classes in technology education are offered in a minority of school districts around the country, and only 12 states require completion of a technology education course by students graduating high school (Dugger, 2007). Consequently, there are far fewer technology education teachers working in U.S. schools than science or mathematics teachers, and far fewer students taking technology education classes than classes in science and mathematics. Finally, technology education has received very little attention from policy makers. Compared to science and mathematics, technology is still a small blip on the radar screen of STEM education.

Engineering

If technology education is a small blip on the STEM radar screen, engineering education is almost invisible. Few people even think of engineering as a K–12 subject, and nationwide, very few K–12 teachers are engaged in engineering education, and very few schools expose students to engineering ideas and activities. Engineering curricula that have been developed vary widely in focus, content, and requirements for implementation. Their purposes range from encouraging students to pursue careers in engineering to increasing technological literacy and improving student performance in science and mathematics. The conceptual frameworks of these curricula also vary greatly. No standards have been set for engineering education, no state or national assessment has been adopted, and almost no attention has been paid to engineering education by policy makers. In fact, engineering might be called the missing letter in STEM.

Connection among the STEM Subjects

Most K–12 schools in the United States teach STEM subjects as separate disciplines, sometimes called "silos"—a math silo, a science silo, perhaps a technology education silo, and, in rare cases, an engineering silo—with few connections in curriculum, in teaching, or in classroom activities. Thus opportunities for leveraging the benefits of interconnections, such as using science inquiry to support learning of mathematical concepts, are largely lost. Students are left with an implicit message that each discipline stands on its own.

This is a stark contrast to the real world of research and technology development, where scientists, engineers, mathematicians, and technologists—along with social scientists, business managers, and others—work together in teams to solve problems. Each STEM discipline brings unique capabilities and perspectives, but for the team to function effectively, each player must be able to draw on and use knowledge from all four disciplines. In some cutting-edge areas, such as nanotechnology, the line between scientists and engineers has all but disappeared.

Opportunity and Uncertainty

The near absence of engineering education in K–12 classrooms represents both opportunity and uncertainty. The opportunity lies in strengthening the engineering component of STEM education, which data presented in Chapter 3 suggest can simultaneously complement and improve learning in the other three disciplines. The uncertainty arises because there are still a great many unanswered questions about how engineering education should be incorporated into K–12 classrooms, as well as about the value of existing K–12 engineering education.

THE STUDY AND REPORT

The purpose of this study is to address three specific questions:[1]

- What are realistic and appropriate learning outcomes for K–12 engineering education?
- How might engineering education complement the learning objectives of other content areas, particularly science, technology, and mathematics, and how might these other content areas complement learning objectives in engineering education?
- What educational policies, programs, and practices at the local, state, and federal levels might lead to the meaningful inclusion of engineering in K–12 education in the United States?

The Study Committee

To answer these questions, in 2006 the National Academy of Engineering (NAE) and National Research Council Center for Education established the Committee on K–12 Engineering Education. The work of the committee was supported by a grant from NAE member Stephen D. Bechtel, Jr., and additional funds were provided by the Parametric Technology Corporation and NSF.

Study Objectives

The study had four objectives:

- Survey the landscape of current and past efforts to implement engineering-related K–12 instructional materials and curricula in the United States and other nations.

---

[1]The complete statement of task appears in an annex to this chapter.

- Review the available information showing the impact of these initiatives.
- Describe how K–12 engineering content incorporates science, technology, and mathematics concepts, uses these subjects as context for exploring engineering concepts, or uses engineering as a context for exploring science, technology, and mathematics concepts.
- Report on the intended learning outcomes of K–12 engineering education initiatives, taking into account the age of the students, the focus of the curriculum (e.g., science vs. technology education), the orientation of the program (e.g., general education vs. career/vocational education), and other factors.

Although efforts have been made to introduce engineering to K–12 students in a variety of informal (non-school) settings, through websites, contests, after-school programs, and summer programs, this study focused only on formal K–12 activities.

Fact-Finding Process

To meet these objectives and answer the questions listed above, the committee spent two years studying K–12 engineering education in the United States. During this time, the committee held five face-to-face meetings, two of which accompanied information-gathering workshops.

To get a sense of the K–12 engineering "landscape," the committee commissioned an analysis of existing K–12 engineering curricula and reviews of the literature on conceptual learning related to engineering, the development of engineering skills, and evidence of the effectiveness of K–12 engineering education initiatives. Finally, the committee also collected preliminary information about a few pre-college engineering education efforts in other countries.

This report is based on these meetings, workshops, and analyses and reviews, as well as the expertise and experience of committee members.

Report Outline

Chapter 2 of the report addresses the question, "What is engineering?" Although many readers already have a clear idea of engineering, the committee believes that understanding the purposes of and approaches to K–12 engineering education requires understanding not only what engineering is but also the key concepts of engineering (e.g., optimization, systems, the design process) and the relationships between engineering and other disciplines, particularly science and mathematics.

Chapter 3 provides a discussion of the available evidence showing the benefits of K–12 engineering education, such as improving learning in mathematics and science, improving technological literacy, and encouraging young people to consider careers in engineering or other technical fields, and the challenges to teaching engineering to K–12 students. Chapter 4 includes reviews of current K–12 engineering curricula, based largely on the commissioned analyses and reviews. In addition, the chapter reviews teacher education and professional development programs.

Chapter 5 discusses cognitive science research related to how students learn engineering concepts and skills and what this research suggests about the best approaches to teaching engineering in grades K–12. The committee's findings and recommendations are presented in Chapter 6.

Appendix A of the report provides biographical information for committee members; Appendix B contains short descriptive summaries of 19 curriculum projects that did not receive a detailed review by the committee; Appendix C, included on an accompanying CD inside the back cover of the report, contains detailed reviews of another 15 K–12 engineering education curriculum projects.

Intended Audiences

This report will be of special interest to individuals and groups interested in improving the quality of K–12 STEM education in this country. But engineering educators, policy makers, employers, and others concerned about the development of the country's technical workforce will also find much to ponder. The report should prove useful to advocates for greater public understanding of engineering, as well as to those working to boost citizens' technological and scientific literacy. Finally, for educational researchers and cognitive scientists, the document exposes a rich set of questions related to how and under what conditions students come to understand engineering.

REFERENCES

AAAS (American Association for the Advancement of Science). 1993. Benchmarks for Science Literacy. New York: Oxford University Press.

Cavanagh, S., and A. Trotter. 2008. Where's the "T" in STEM? Education Week 27(30):17–19. Also available at *http://www.edweek.org/ew/articles/2008/03/27/30stemtech.h27.html* (accessed May 8, 2008).

DoEd (U.S. Department of Education). 2008. Mathematics and science partnerships. Office of Elementary and Secondary Education. Available online at *http://www.ed.gov/ programs/mathsci/index.html* (accessed December 23, 2008).

Dugger, W.E. Jr. 2007. The status of technology education in the United States: a triennial report of the findings from the states. The Technology Teacher 67(1): 14–21.

Grigg, W.S., M.A. Lauko, and D.M. Brockway. 2006. The Nation's Report Card: Science 2005. Washington, D.C.: U.S. Department of Education, National Center for Education Statistics. Also available online at *http://nces.ed.gov/NAEP/pdf/main2005/2006466. pdf* (accessed December 12, 2008).

Lee, J., W.S. Grigg, and G.S. Dion. 2007. The Nation's Report Card: Mathematics 2007. Washington, D.C.: U.S. Department of Education, National Center for Education Statistics. Also available online at *http://nces.ed.gov/nationsreportcard/pdf/main2007/2007494.pdf* (accessed December 12, 2008).

Martin, M.O., I.V.S. Mullis, P. Foy, J.F. Olson, E. Erberber, C. Preuschoff, and J. Galia. 2008. TIMSS 2007 International Science Report: Findings from IEA's Trends in International Mathematics and Science Study at the Fourth and Eighth Grades. Available online at *http://timss.bc.edu/TIMSS2007/PDF/TIMSS2007_InternationalScienceReport.pdf* (accessed December 12, 2008).

Mullis, I.V.S., M.O. Martin, P. Foy, J.F. Olson, C. Preuschoff, E. Erberber, A. Arora, and J. Galia. 2008. TIMSS 2007 International Mathematics Report: Findings from IEA's Trends in International Mathematics and Science Study at the Fourth and Eighth Grades. Available online at *http://timss.bc.edu/TIMSS2007/PDF/TIMSS2007_ InternationalMathematicsReport.pdf* (accessed December 12, 2008).

NAE and NRC (National Academy of Engineering and National Research Council). 2002. Technically Speaking: Why All Americans Need to Know More about Technology. Washington, D.C.: National Academy Press.

NAS, NAE, and IOM (National Academy of Sciences, National Academy of Engineering, and Institute of Medicine). 2007. Rising Above the Gathering Storm: Energizing and Employing America for a Brighter Economic Future. Washington, D.C.: The National Academies Press.

NSB (National Science Board). 2007. A National Action Plan for Addressing the Critical Needs of the U.S. Science, Technology, Education, and Mathematics Education System. Washington, D.C.: National Science Foundation.

Annex

PROJECT STATEMENT OF TASK

The goal of this project, a collaboration between the National Academy of Engineering and the National Research Council's Center for Education, through its Board on Science Education, is to provide carefully reasoned guidance to key stakeholders regarding the creation and implementation of K–12 engineering curricula and instructional practices, focusing especially on the connections among science, technology, engineering, and mathematics education.

Engineering is defined as "design under constraint," where the constraints include the laws of nature, cost, safety, reliability, environmental impact, manufacturability, and many other factors. While science attempts to discover what is, engineering is concerned with what might be—with extending human capability through modifying the natural world. Indeed, engineering is responsible for many of the most significant improvements in our quality of life. Engineers identify and then solve problems using a highly creative and iterative design process. While engineering requires the application of mathematics and scientific knowledge, it is this design process and the practical nature of the problems tackled that best distinguish engineering. What qualifies as engineering in the K–12 classroom, as contrasted with what engineering education is in post-secondary institutions, is something that this project will attempt to elucidate. In the early grades, "engineering" may be little more than a teacher-directed design activity, such as the construction of a balsa wood bridge, while in the later grades the design project may be considerably more open ended and involve the application of mathematics and science concepts to solve a specific problem.

The project has the following objectives:

1. Survey the landscape of current and past efforts to implement engineering-related K–12 instructional materials and curricula in the United States and other nations.
2. Review evidence related to the impact of these initiatives, to the extent such information is available;
3. Describe the ways in which K–12 engineering content has incorporated science, technology, and mathematics concepts, used these subjects as context to explore engineering concepts, or used engineering as a context to explore science, technology, and mathematics concepts; and
4. Report on the intended learning outcomes of K–12 engineering education initiatives, taking into account student age, curriculum focus (e.g., science vs. technology education), program orientation

(e.g., general education vs. career/vocational education), and other factors.

In meeting the goal and objectives, the project will focus on three key issues and three related guiding questions:

1. There are multiple perspectives about the purpose and place of engineering in the K–12 classroom. These points of view lead to emphases on very different outcomes. QUESTION: What are realistic and appropriate learning outcomes for engineering education in K–12?
2. There has not been a careful analysis of engineering education within a K–12 environment that looks at possible subject intersections. QUESTION: How might engineering education complement the learning objectives of other content areas, particularly science, technology, and mathematics, and how might these other content areas complement learning objectives in engineering education?
3. There has been little if any serious consideration of the systemic changes in the U.S. education system that might be required to enhance K–12 engineering education. QUESTION: What educational policies, programs, and practice at the local, state, and federal levels might permit meaningful inclusion of engineering at the K–12 level in the United States?

Prior to the stage when the committee completes the preparation of its draft report for the institutional report review process, the committee will strive to obtain public inputs on key issues and on directions for the committee to consider in its recommendations.

2

What Is Engineering?

To understand approaches to and the potential benefits of K–12 engineering education, one must first have an understanding of engineering itself. The word engineer is derived from the Medieval Latin verb *ingeniare,* meaning to design or devise (Flexner, 1987). The word *ingeniare* is, in turn, derived from the Latin word for engine, *ingenium,* meaning a clever invention. Thus, a short definition of engineering is the process of designing the human-made world. In contrast, science is derived from the Latin noun *scientia,* meaning knowledge, and is commonly described as the study of the natural world. Whereas scientists ask questions about the world around us—what is out there, how do things work, and what rules can be deduced to explain the patterns we see—engineers modify the world to satisfy people's needs and wants. Of course, in the real world, engineering and science can not be neatly separated. Scientific knowledge informs engineering design, and many scientific advances would not be possible without technological tools developed by engineers.

Usually, engineers do not literally construct artifacts. They develop plans and directions for how artifacts are to be constructed. Some artifacts are small—a hand calculator, for example, or a computer chip—and some are large—a bridge, for example, or an aircraft carrier. Engineers also design processes, ranging from the manufacturing processes used in the chemical and pharmaceutical industries to create chemicals and drugs to procedures for putting components together on an assembly line.

One useful way to think about engineering is as "design under constraint" (Wulf, 1998). One of the constraints is the laws of nature, or science. Engineers designing a solution to a particular problem must, for instance, take into account how physical objects behave while in motion. Other constraints include such things as time, money, available materials, ergonomics, environmental regulations, manufacturability, repairability, and so on.

This somewhat sterile description belies the inherently creative nature of engineering and its contribution to human welfare. As noted in a recent initiative to develop more effective ways of communicating to the public about engineering, engineers "make a world of difference. From new medical equipment and safer drinking water to faster microchips, engineers apply their knowledge to improve people's lives in concrete, meaningful ways" (NAE, 2008).

This introduction to engineering includes a brief history of engineering and its importance to society, a discussion of some defining features of engineering, and descriptions of relationships between engineering, science, and mathematics. Throughout this chapter, the reader should keep in mind that although engineers are crucial to shaping technology, they collaborate with professionals in many other fields, including scientists, craftspeople who build devices, business people who market and sell products, and a variety of technicians and technologists who are responsible for the operation, maintenance, and repair of devices.

A BRIEF HISTORY OF THE ENGINEERING PROFESSION

Engineers have been important in every stage of human history, because people have always designed and built tools and other devices. Today, however, the word engineer is used in a more specific sense to refer to a member of the engineering profession, which has evolved over the past 300 to 400 years.[1]

Origins

Some of the earliest examples of activities we might call engineering can be found in the context of major building projects, such as the construction of the system of aqueducts in and around Rome from the fourth century B.C. to the third century A.D. (Aicher, 1995; Evans, 1994). The aqueducts

---

[1]Much of the following short history of engineering is taken from a commissioned paper by Jonson Miller, Drexel University, a consultant to the project.

carried water from the outskirts of Rome to the city itself via a system of pipes, trenches, bridges, and tunnels.

A project of this sort today would be largely the responsibility of engineers, but the historical records of Rome do not mention anyone who played that particular role. Much of the construction and maintenance of the aqueducts was under the supervision of a *curator aquarum*, or water commissioner, but he (and it was almost certainly a man) seems to have been considered more of an administrator than anything else. The individuals who actually built and maintained the aqueducts were architects, surveyors, craftsmen of various sorts, and manual laborers (generally slaves), but not engineers. The concept of an engineer as we know it today did not yet exist.

Engineering as a Formal Discipline

Engineering first emerged as a formal discipline during the Renaissance, with the design of military fortifications. Historically, artisans had been in charge of both planning and constructing fortifications, but by the middle of the sixteenth century a group of non-artisan specialists had appeared who used geometry and mathematics to design fortifications in a more rational way and who generally let craftsmen take care of the actual construction. These specialized military architects were the first true engineers in the modern sense of the word.

Over time military engineers expanded their purview to include other military work, such as designing siege engines, as well as civilian projects, such as designing and planning transportation systems. Engineering was first formalized and professionalized in France, with the establishment of training programs that required formal examinations in mathematics, drawing, engineering theory, and other subjects (Langins, 2004). The first formal engineering schools were established in the mid-eighteenth century, also in France, and included the École des Ponts et Chaussées (School of Bridges and Roads) and the École Royale du Génie (Royal School of Engineering).

Later, when colonists in the nascent United States needed a corps of military engineers, they looked to France. During the Revolutionary War the Continental Congress established the Corps of Engineers to help design fortifications and artillery. After the war, the corps was given a home at West Point, New York, as director of the new U.S. Military Academy (Reynolds, 1991).

One purpose of the academy was to develop military engineers by providing training in mathematics, as well as in military and civil engineering. During the first half of the nineteenth century a number of individual states, particularly southern states, started their own institutes, such as the Virginia Military Institute founded in 1839, that offered French-style engineering curricula. Most formal engineering training available in the United States up to the time of the Civil War was offered at these military academies.

Engineering as an Artisanal Craft

At the same time as a formal approach to engineering was being pursued in France, the United States and other countries adopted a second, more practical approach. The trend began in Great Britain with the advent of industrialization, when the country's artisans, who had a tradition of apprenticeships and on-the-job training, spearheaded the early design and development of the machinery and machine shops of the industrial age. The British transportation infrastructure was also developed by independent engineers who got their training through apprenticeships.

The apprenticeship tradition was transported to the 13 British colonies that would eventually become the United States, and the engineers who designed the machine shops and mechanized textile mills in the early days of this country had generally been trained in informal settings like those of typical British artisans and engineers (Calhoun, 1960; Reynolds, 1991). Similarly, many of the engineers who worked on road, bridge, and canal projects in the United States in the late 1700s and early 1800s were trained in this tradition—indeed, quite a few of them had learned their trades in Great Britain before coming to this country.

And so throughout much of the nineteenth century, engineers in the United States and elsewhere received their training in one of two very different ways—either a formal, theoretically oriented way that emphasized mathematics, science, and engineering theory, or a practical, hands-on way that favored on-the-job training.

The Rise of Professional Engineers

After the Civil War, engineering programs in the United States increasingly emphasized formal training, although on-the-job training remained important for a variety of engineering disciplines—particularly mechanical engineering—until the middle of the twentieth century. At the same time, in the years following the Civil War a number of engineering professional societies appeared: the American Society of Civil Engineers (ASCE) in 1865, the American Society of Mechanical Engineers in 1880, the American

Institute of Electrical Engineers in 1884, and so forth. These societies had a strong influence on how the various fields of engineering were developed. They influenced education and training programs for engineers, and they developed standards for industry as well as ethical codes for their members (Reynolds, 1991). Professional societies also helped define new fields of engineering, as when mining engineers split from the ASCE in 1871 to form the American Institute of Mining Engineers and when industrial chemists broke away from the American Chemical Society in 1908 to form the American Institute of Chemical Engineering.

The professionalization of engineering continued through much of the twentieth century. One of the most important trends over the past 50 years has been the increasing emphasis on mathematics and science in the education of engineers. When the Soviet Union launched the Sputnik satellite in 1957, the U.S. response included a national effort to increase the number of scientists and engineers coming through the educational pipeline and to emphasize the teaching of science and mathematics. As a result, engineering education began to put much more emphasis on theory and mathematics (Lucena, 2005).

Over the past quarter century, as the national focus has shifted from the perceived Soviet military threat to concerns about globalization and U.S. competitiveness in the world economy, the emphasis in engineering education has shifted again. Today, engineering schools no longer focus exclusively on science, mathematics, and engineering theory. They also emphasize flexibility and being able to respond quickly to emerging challenges (e.g., NAE, 2004). Expectations for engineering students are now likely to include the ability to work well in teams, to communicate ideas effectively, and to understand other cultures and the effects of technology on societies and individuals. In short, as technology has evolved from a collection of mostly isolated devices and structures to a tightly interconnected global system, engineers—as the designers of this technological world—have also evolved. Today, they must be competent in far more than the traditional science- and math-oriented subjects.

Engineering, Industrial Arts, and Technology Education

The advent of formal engineering education with its emphasis on theoretical mathematics and science was accompanied by a growing recognition that aspiring engineers also needed manual skills. As early as 1870, Calvin M. Woodward, dean of the engineering department at Washington University, instituted shop training for his engineering students after he found that they were unable to produce satisfactory wooden models to demonstrate mechanical principles. John D. Runkle, president of the Massachusetts Institute of Technology, introduced a similar program after seeing demonstrations of Russian manual arts training at the 1876 Centennial Exposition in Philadelphia. Both men believed that shop skills were essential for engineers (Sanders, 2008).

In the 1880s, under the leadership of Woodward and Runkle, Washington University and MIT established schools for intermediate and secondary students that provided a combined program of liberal arts and manual training. Other schools, however, emphasized training in specific trades to provide skilled workers for specific industries. Both types of schools grew quickly.

By the early twentieth century, there had been a conceptual shift from "manual training" to "industrial arts." Contrary to what many people assume, industrial arts represented a shift away from vocational training toward general education for all (Herschbach, 2009). Students studied how industry created value from raw materials in the context of the developing industrial society in America. The curriculum required the ability to use industrial tools, equipment, and materials in a laboratory setting, but the "shop experience" was a means to an end, not an end in itself.

By the mid-twentieth century, industrial arts had become a standard component in the public school curriculum. However, it continued to be confused with vocational education, which was also on the rise during this period. By the end of the century, the teaching of industrial arts had expanded to include an understanding of technology in general. In 1985 the Industrial Arts Association of America changed its name to the International Technology Education Association (ITEA).

Since the name change and, especially, since publication of *Standards for Technological Literacy: Content for the Study of Technology* (2000), technology education teachers have increasingly sought to teach engineering concepts and skills to students[2] (Lewis, 2004). But this shift has not been universal, and technology education is still best thought of as a continuum of practice spanning traditional industrial arts ("shop") classes, career-focused indus-

---

[2]The shift is evident in a 2009 ballot measure to change the name of the International Technology Education Association (ITEA) to include the word engineering. A full 65 percent of voting members favored the name change (K. Starkweather, ITEA, personal communication, June 16, 2009). However, the association's bylaws require a 66 percent majority, so the measure did not pass.

trial technology, and technology education programs that include differing degrees of engineering content.

The varied implementation of technology education makes it difficult to clearly distinguish it from "engineering education" at the K–12 level. The distinctions are most apparent between the industrial arts model of technology education, with its emphasis on tool skills and fabrication of technological artifacts, and engineering education that focuses on the engineering design process as an approach to problem solving. Some analysts (McAlister, 2007) have pointed out that pre-service education for most technology teachers includes relatively few mathematics and science courses. Because engineering design, particularly modeling and analysis, relies on mathematics and science concepts, another emerging distinction between educators in technology and those in engineering may be their degree of preparation in science and mathematics.[3]

More broadly, there are indicators of growing interest in understanding and improving the connections between engineering and technology education. For example, the ITEA Council on Technology Teacher Education devoted an entire volume to the topic (CTTE, 2008); from 2004 to 2009, the National Science Foundation funded the nine-university National Center for Engineering and Technology Education (*www.ncete.org*), in part to grow these connections; and in 2004, the American Society for Engineering Education established a Division on K–12 and Pre-College Engineering, and some members of the division are from technology education.

The Demographics of Engineering Today

In 2006, the most recent year for which data are available, the United States had an engineering workforce of about 1.5 million people[4] (BLS, 2008a). About 37 percent of engineering jobs were in manufacturing industries, and 28 percent were in the professional, scientific, and technical services sector, primarily architectural, engineering, and related services. Many engineers also worked in the construction, telecommunications, and wholesale trades. In addition, federal, state, and local governments employed about 12 percent of engineers.

---

[3]The importance of mathematics and science to engineering design is discussed at length in Chapter 4.

[4]This number does not include roughly 27,000 engineering teaching personnel who are employed by engineering schools (ASEE, 2007a, p. 28).

Although this chapter is focused on the history of engineering, it is important to recognize another significant component of the technology workforce, engineering technicians and technologists. Formal engineering technology programs, which were developed in the mid-twentieth century, provide students with a distinctly hands-on, practical education, in contrast to engineering programs, which focus more on theory and design (Grinter, 1984). Today, there are both two- and four-year engineering technology programs in the United States. Graduates of the former are often called engineering technicians; graduates of the latter are called engineering technologists. Engineering technologists typically implement designs created by engineers. They may be involved in making incremental design changes, building and testing products and processes, managing the installation of complex equipment, and developing maintenance procedures. Engineering technicians are primarily operators of technology, but they also have installation and maintenance skills beyond the capabilities of skilled tradesmen. In practice, there may be considerable overlap between engineering technologists and engineering technicians.

In 2006, 511,000 engineering technicians were working in the United States, a third of them electrical and electronics technicians (BLS, 2008b). The U.S. government does not collect employment data on engineering technologists in a separate job classification. However, the Engineering Workforce Commission estimates that there were about 10,000 bachelor's degrees in engineering technology awarded in 2007 (ASEE, 2007b).

Women and minorities are greatly underrepresented in engineering schools (both as students and faculty) and engineering jobs in the United States relative to their proportions in the population at large (Table 2-1). Although their participation has been increasing over the past two decades, the rate of increase has slowed—and for women the upward trend has recently reversed. This situation has many people in the engineering community worried about the future supply of engineers, especially as the U.S. population becomes increasingly diverse.

Some have expressed a concern that other countries—particularly China and India—have been outpacing the United States in the production of engineers. Although it is difficult to make comparisons because of differences in the methods of collecting data and differences in how engineers are defined, the trends are clear. The number of engineering bachelor's degrees awarded in the United States has increased gradually over the past seven years to slightly more than 74,000 in the 2005–2006 school year (ASEE, 2007a). This is a jump of about 20 percent since 1999. In China, by contrast, the number

TABLE 2-1 Selected Data for Women, African Americans, Hispanics, and Native Americans in Engineering

Women

Proportion of U.S. population, 2005 (est.): 50.7 percent
Proportion of students enrolled in degree-granting institutions, 2004: 57.4 percent
Proportion of bachelor's degrees in engineering, 2004: 20.5 percent
Proportion of tenured/tenure-track appointments on U.S. engineering faculties, 2005: 10.6 percent
Proportion employed as engineers, 2003: 11 percent

African Americans

Proportion of U.S. population, 2004: 12.8 percent
Proportion enrolled in degree-granting institutions, 2004: 12.5 percent
Proportion of bachelor's degrees in engineering earned, 2004: 5.3 percent
Proportion of tenured/tenure-track appointments on U.S. engineering faculties, 2005: 2.3 percent
Proportion employed as engineers, 2003: 3.1 percent

Hispanics

Proportion of U.S. population, 2004: 14.1 percent
Proportion enrolled in degree-granting institutions, 2004: 10.5 percent
Proportion of bachelor's degrees in engineering, 2004: 7.4 percent
Proportion of tenured/tenure-track professors on U.S. engineering faculties, 2005: 3.2 percent
Proportion employed as engineers, 2003: 4.9 percent

Native Americans

Proportion of U.S. population, 2004: 1 percent
Proportion enrolled in degree-granting institutions, 2004: 1 percent
Proportion of bachelor's degrees in engineering, 2004: 0.6 percent
Proportion of tenured/tenure-track professors on U.S. engineering faculties, 2005: 0.2 percent
Proportion employed as engineers, 2003: 0.3 percent

SOURCES: NSF, 2005a,b, 2006a,b; U.S. Census Bureau, 2002, 2005; U.S. DOEd 2006a,b.

of students graduating with four-year degrees in engineering, computer science, and information technology more than doubled between 2000 and 2004 (Wadhwa et al., 2007). A similar doubling occurred in India.

The committee did try to ascertain the level of pre-college engineering education in India and China. The various individuals we spoke with, including high-level education and industry officials in both countries, indicated there were no such efforts. We were told that Indian and Chinese students' first exposure to engineering ideas typically occurs in college. However, we could find no reliable evidence to confirm this. [5]

THE ROLE OF ENGINEERING IN MODERN SOCIETY

Over the past 400 years the role of engineers has expanded and diversified from a singular focus on military fortifications and engines to include products that affect almost every aspect of society and people's daily lives. Many of these are well known—engineers design both computers and the software that runs on them, both automobiles and the roads and bridges they travel on, and power plants and the transmission systems that carry power to the people who need it. In other respects, the accomplishments of engineers are not as widely recognized. For example, every piece of medical equipment, from the simplest thermometer to the most complex MRI device, was designed by an engineer, as were machines that are used to manufacture other machines and the equipment scientists rely on for work that often leads to scientific discoveries.

One way to get a sense of the importance of engineering in modern society is to examine the list of 14 grand challenges for engineering produced by the National Academy of Engineering (NAE) in 2008 (Box 2-1). These challenges are major issues confronting society in the twenty-first century, and engineering will be crucial to addressing all of them.

For instance, sustainability is a major theme linking five of the grand challenges. As societies search for ways to maintain themselves in a sustainable way relative to the environment, engineers will have to find ways to provide clean water and economical solar power and energy from fusion and develop ways to remove carbon dioxide from the atmosphere, such as storing it in the Earth's crust. Engineers, working with doctors and medical researchers, can improve human health by developing better ways of storing, analyzing, and communicating health information and by designing more effective drugs. To avoid the misuse of powerful technologies, engineers will find ways to keep terrorists from obtaining and using nuclear materials and technologies and to secure cyberspace. Finally, engineers in the coming century will be crucial to improving human capacities by, for example, advancing personalized learning and engineering the tools that will enable scientific discovery.

---

[5]For a brief review of pre-college engineering efforts in countries other than India and China, see the annex to Chapter 4.

BOX 2-1
Grand Challenges for Engineering

On February 15, 2008, the National Academy of Engineering announced its list of 14 "grand challenges for engineering," examples of the types of challenges confronting societies in the twenty-first century. The solutions to these challenges will all have large engineering components. Although engineers cannot solve these challenges alone, neither can the challenges be solved without engineers.

The fourteen grand challenges are:

- Making solar power economical;
- Providing energy from fusion;
- Developing carbon-sequestration methods;
- Managing the nitrogen cycle;
- Providing access to clean water;
- Restoring and improving urban infrastructure;
- Advancing health informatics;
- Engineering better medicines;
- Reverse-engineering the brain;
- Preventing nuclear terror;
- Securing cyberspace;
- Enhancing virtual reality;
- Advancing personalized learning; and
- Engineering the tools of scientific discovery.

SOURCE: NAE, 2008.

DESIGN AS A PROBLEM-SOLVING PROCESS

Science, mathematics, and engineering all have domains of knowledge, process skills, and ways of looking at the world. Perhaps the most important for engineering is design, the basic engineering approach to solving problems. Using the design process, engineers can integrate various skills and types of thinking—analytical and synthetic thinking; detailed understanding and holistic understanding; planning and building; and implicit, procedural knowledge and explicit, declarative knowledge.

What Is Engineering Design?

Design is a deceptively common word that is used to describe what graphic artists do, what fashion designers do, what landscape architects do, and what flower arrangers do. But in the context of engineering, the word has a specific meaning. Design is the approach engineers use to solve engineering problems—generally, to determine the best way to make a device or process that serves a particular purpose. When electronic engineers design an integrated circuit chip, when transportation engineers design a subway system, when chemical engineers design a chemical processing plant, and when biomedical engineers design an artificial organ, they all use variants of the same basic problem-solving strategy—engineering design.

According to *Standards for Technological Literacy: Content for the Study of Technology* (ITEA, 2000), engineering design has a number of characteristic attributes. First, it is purposeful; a designer begins with an explicit goal that is clearly understood; thus design can be pictured as a journey with a particular destination, rather than a sightseeing trip. Second, designs are shaped by *specifications* and *constraints*. Specifications spell out what the design is intended to accomplish. Constraints are limitations the designer must contend with, such as costs, size requirements, or the physical limitations of the materials used. In addition, the design process is systematic and iterative. Engineering design is also a highly social and collaborative enterprise. Engineers engaged in design activities often work in teams, and communication with clients and others who have a stake in the project is crucial.

Over time, engineers have developed a variety of rules and principles governing the development of a design. Although the rules are not absolute, engineers understand that these principles are based on many years of accumulated experience and that without such rules engineers would be very much like tinkerers or amateur inventors.

Design is not a linear, step-by-step process. It is generally iterative; thus each new version of the design is tested and then modified based on what has been learned up to that point. Finally, there is never just one "correct" solution to a design challenge. Instead, there are a number of possible solutions, and choosing among them inevitably involves personal as well as technical considerations (ITEA, 2000, pp. 91–92).

Although there is no formula for engineering design that specifies step 1, step 2, and so on, there are a number of characteristic steps in a design process. One step, for example, is identifying the problem. As noted above, an explicit goal for a design is what distinguishes it from tinkering. A second step is generating ideas for how to solve the problem. Engineers often use research or brainstorming sessions to come up with a range of design alternatives for further development. Another step is the evaluation of potential solutions by building and testing models or prototypes, which provides valuable data that cannot be obtained in any other way. With data in hand, the engineer can evaluate how well the various solutions meet the specifications and constraints of the design, including considering the trade-offs needed to balance competing or conflicting constraints. Engineers call this process *optimization.*

These steps are repeated as necessary. For example, an engineer may go all the way back to step 1, identifying the problem, if the research and prototypes turn up something unexpected. Usually, however, the results of various tests lead to a round of improvements—complete with brainstorming ideas, testing new prototypes, and so on—and yet another round of improvements, until enough iterations have been performed that the engineer is satisfied with the result. Once the finished product has been tested and approved, it can be produced and marketed (ITEA, 2000, p. 99).

How Design Compares with the Scientific Method

Engineering design is often compared with scientific inquiry, the core problem-solving approach used in science, and, indeed, the two approaches have a number of similar features. But they also differ in significant ways. By identifying the convergences and divergences, one can get a better idea of how the two approaches might fit together in a school curriculum (Lewis, 2006).

The most obvious similarity, or convergence, is that both design and scientific inquiry are reasoning processes used to solve problems, "navigational devices that serve the purpose of bridging the gap between problem and solution" (Lewis, 2006, p. 271). For both scientists and engineers, some problems are relatively straightforward; challenging problems, however, are characterized by high levels of uncertainty that require a great deal of creativity on the part of the problem solver. In searching for solutions, engineers and scientists use similar cognitive tools, such as brainstorming, reasoning by analogy, mental models, and visual representations. And both require testing and evaluation of the product—the engineering design or the scientific hypothesis.

One point of divergence between engineering design and scientific inquiry is the role of constraints, which are common to both processes but are fundamental to engineering design. Budget constraints, for example, can limit scientific inquiry and perhaps even keep scientists from answering a particular question, but they do not affect the answer itself. For engineers, however, budget constraints can determine whether a particular design solution is workable. Another divergence is trade-offs. As Lewis notes (2006), trade-offs are a basic aspect of design but have essentially no part in scientific inquiry.

A related difference is the scientist's emphasis on finding general rules that describe as many phenomena as possible, whereas the engineer's focus is on finding solutions that satisfy particular circumstances. Scientific inquiry begins with a particular, detailed phenomenon and moves toward generalization, while engineering design applies general rules and approaches to zero in on a particular solution. In addition, judgments about the suitability of a design are inevitably shaped by individual and social values; thus the optimal design for one person may not be optimal for another. This is quite different from the scientific method; in the ideal scientific situation, answers are independent of values.

Another way to compare design with the scientific method is to consider the characteristics of the two problem-solving approaches (Box 2-2). *Science*

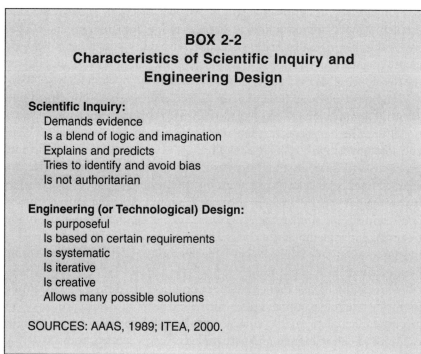

BOX 2-2
Characteristics of Scientific Inquiry and
Engineering Design

Scientific Inquiry:
    Demands evidence
    Is a blend of logic and imagination
    Explains and predicts
    Tries to identify and avoid bias
    Is not authoritarian

Engineering (or Technological) Design:
    Is purposeful
    Is based on certain requirements
    Is systematic
    Is iterative
    Is creative
    Allows many possible solutions

SOURCES: AAAS, 1989; ITEA, 2000.

for All Americans, published by the American Association for the Advancement of Science, identifies five characteristics of scientific inquiry that distinguish it from other modes of inquiry: science demands evidence; science is a blend of logic and imagination; science explains and predicts; scientists try to identify and avoid bias; and science is not authoritarian (AAAS, 1989). At first glance, these rather general statements seem to apply, at least partly, to engineering design. Certainly engineers also demand evidence, for instance, and they use a blend of logic and evidence in their design work. Conversely, there is little doubt that science can be a very creative endeavor, is systematic, and is purposeful. This overlap reflects the many similarities in the ways scientists and engineers go about their work.

Nevertheless, there are also important differences between the scientific method and engineering design. The distinguishing features of engineering design include taking into account specifications and constraints; dependence on iteration; and the embrace of multiple possible solutions. The differences in the two lists reflect the basic differences between science and engineering—scientists investigate and engineers create.

For example, although "purposeful" might describe a characteristic of the scientific method, it would certainly not appear near the top of the list. For engineering design, however, purposefulness is a fundamental characteristic—the first question that must be answered about any design is, "what is its purpose?" For scientists, however, the focus is on the particular questions they are investigating. Scientists may have an underlying purpose for investigating particular questions—for example, a geneticist studying the BCRA gene does so for the purpose of understanding breast cancer—but the day-to-day work of the scientist is driven by the question, not the purpose.

Similarly, specifications and constraints are not essential to answering scientific questions. Not every scientific question has a single "correct" solution, but there is no expectation in the scientific method that the process will inevitably produce multiple answers. These, however, are fundamental characteristics of design that set it apart from the scientific method.

IMPORTANT CONCEPTS IN ENGINEERING

In addition to specifications and constraints, a number of other concepts are key to understanding what engineers do and how they do it. The list may vary depending on who compiles it, but certain concepts will appear on most lists (e.g., AAAS, 1993; Burghardt, 2007; Childress and Rhodes, 2006; Childress and Sanders, 2007; ITEA, 2000; Sneider, 2006).

One crucial idea that appears regularly on the engineering list, but also on the science list and lists for many other areas of study, is the concept of *systems*. In very general terms a system is a collection of interacting pieces. The collection of all trains, planes, and automobiles, along with railways, airports, roads, and everything else involved in getting people and things from one place to another makes up one type of system—the country's transportation system. The various components of an iPod constitute another kind of system. The machines and their operators in an automobile plant make up another kind of system.

In most cases a system is more than the sum of its parts, and understanding a system involves not only understanding the individual parts but also understanding how the parts interact. Most of the "things" engineers design are systems of one kind or another, and in many cases those things function as part of a larger system. Thus engineers must have a good grasp of how systems work and the factors that influence the performance of the system (AAAS, 1993).

Engineers use *modeling* as a way to understand what may happen when an actual artifact or process is used. In the case of a wooden plank used as a footbridge across a stream, for instance, an engineer might be asked to predict the weight of the heaviest person who could cross the plank without breaking it. The engineer creates a *representational model* of the plank, which may consist of drawings or physical, three-dimensional renditions. The model incorporates assumptions about the size and physical properties of the plank and about how it is secured on the banks of the stream.

Using the representational model, the engineer creates a free-body diagram, which shows the various forces that act on the plank, and from the free-body diagram develops a *mathematical model* based on laws of mechanics. By creating the representational models of potential solutions and then mathematically characterizing them, engineers can predict the behavior of technologies before they are built, and the predictions can be tested experimentally. The accuracy of the representational and mathematical models—often calculated with the assistance of computer programs and/or computer simulations—determines the validity of the predictions. This process of *predictive analysis* is another central feature of engineering design.

Very sophisticated software programs have been developed for predicting the performance of integrated circuit chips, for example. Without these programs, it would be essentially impossible to design the highly sophisticated chips that are manufactured today (EDAC, 2008). Because of the importance of mathematical modeling and predictive analysis to engineering design, mathematics is essential to engineering, and engineers must be comfortable using mathematical tools.

As mentioned above, one step in design is understanding the requirements, or *specifications* and *constraints*, of the design. The specifications are key features and elements of the product and what it is supposed to do. Constraints are limitations on the design—physical, financial, social, political, environmental factors, and so on. It is almost never possible to meet all of the specifications and accommodate all of the constraints simultaneously. Determining the best solution to a technical problem requires balancing competing or conflicting factors; this process is called *optimization*. Often different alternatives are better in different ways. One material may be stronger, for instance, but a second material may cost less. Choosing the best solution normally requires *trade-offs*, that is, deciding not to maximize one desirable thing in order to maximize another. Deciding which criteria are the most important is essential to determining the best solution to a problem. The idea is to decide upon a design that comes closest to meeting the specifications, that fits within the constraints, and that has the least number of negative characteristics (AAAS, 1993).

THE RELATIONSHIP OF ENGINEERING TO SCIENCE AND MATHEMATICS

Engineering is intimately related to science and mathematics. Engineers use both science and mathematics in their work, and scientists and mathematicians use the products of engineering in their work. In every field of engineering, an understanding of the relevant science is a prerequisite to doing the job. Chemical engineers must understand chemistry, bioengineers must understand molecular biology, petroleum engineers must understand geology, electronics engineers must understand how electrons behave in various materials, nuclear engineers must understand how the nuclei of atoms behave, and so on. Indeed, science is so fundamental to what engineers do that, in a very real sense, engineering can be thought of as putting science to work.

Mathematics is as fundamental to engineering as science. Engineers use mathematics both to describe data (e.g., graphs showing the strength or other properties of a material under varying conditions) and to analyze them (e.g., the flow rate of fluids through the pipes of a chemical plant). As noted above, engineers use science and mathematics most obviously in building and analyzing models.

Conversely, engineering is essential to science and mathematics. Scientists depend upon the products of engineers—everything from space telescopes to gene sequencers—to perform various manipulations and measurements in exploring the natural world. And although many mathematicians still require little more than chalk and a chalkboard for their studies, a growing number of them now take advantage of increasingly powerful computers—a gift from engineers—to perform mathematical explorations. Thus the relationship between engineering and science and mathematics is a two-way street.

ENGINEERING IN THE TWENTY-FIRST CENTURY

A description of engineering would be incomplete without addressing the challenges the field faces in the coming decades. Of course, looking into the future is always a tricky proposition, but several trends in engineering provide a basis for extrapolating and predicting some things about the future of engineers and engineering.

An Increasingly Diverse Workforce

As shown in Table 2-1, the engineering workforce in the United States today includes relatively few women and minorities compared to the percentages of these groups in the general population and the overall workforce. These numbers indicate that the potential contributions of women and minorities to the engineering workforce are not being realized. Addressing this underrepresentation will be critical to the future of engineering in light of the changing demographics in the United States.

Projections based on current trends indicate that by 2050 minorities will make up almost half of the U.S. population and a corresponding percentage of the U.S. workforce (U.S. Census Bureau, 2002). Thus even if minorities are still underrepresented in the engineering workforce, they will likely account for a much larger percentage of the workforce in coming years. The hope is, of course, that the engineering workforce of the future will be far more diverse and representative than it is today.

Adaptation to a Changing World

The kinds of jobs engineers are being asked to do and the skills they are expected to have are changing (Duderstadt, 2008). A major factor driving changes in the demands on U.S. engineers is increasing global competition. U.S. engineers increasingly find themselves competing for work with engineers from other countries, who are often paid much less—in some countries as much as 80 percent less. To succeed in this environment, U.S. engineers will need not only the analytic skills—high-level design, systems thinking, and creative innovation—that are taught in engineering courses, but also a variety of skills that are often overlooked in engineering education. These include communications and leadership skills, the flexibility to adapt to changing conditions, the ability to work in multicultural environments, an understanding of the business side of engineering, and a commitment to lifelong learning (NAE, 2004).

Implications for K–12 Engineering Education

As noted in Chapter 1 and discussed at greater length later in the report, one of the purposes of at least some K–12 engineering education programs is to encourage more young people to consider engineering as a career pathway. It is unrealistic to expect that the challenges facing U.S. innovation can be addressed solely by boosting the number and diversity of K–12 students interested in technical and scientific fields. But broadening the appeal of engineering and related careers to American pre-college students will almost certainly be part of the solution.

REFERENCES

AAAS (American Association for the Advancement of Science). 1989. Science for All Americans. New York: Oxford University Press.

AAAS. 1993. Benchmarks for Science Literacy. New York: Oxford University Press.

Aicher, P.J. 1995. Guide to the Aqueducts of Ancient Rome. Wauconda, Ill.: Bolchazy-Carducci Publishers.

ASEE (American Society for Engineering Education). 2007a. Profiles of Engineering and Engineering Technology Colleges. ASEE 2006 Edition. Washington, D.C.: ASEE.

ASEE. 2007b. Engineering and Technology Degrees. Engineering Workforce Commission of the American Association of Engineering Societies, Inc. Washington, D.C.: ASEE.

BLS (Bureau of Labor Statistics). 2008a. Occupational Outlook Handbook, 2008–09 Edition, Engineers. Available online at *http://www.bls.gov/oco/ocos027.htm* (accessed November 24, 2008).

BLS. 2008b. Occupational Outlook Handbook, 2008–09 Edition, Engineering Technicians. Available online at *http://www.bls.gov/oco/ocos112.htm* (accessed December 3, 2008).

Burghardt, D. 2007. What is engineering?—Perspectives on K–12 engineering. Paper prepared for the NAE/NRC Committee on K–12 Engineering Education. July 23, 2007. Unpublished.

Calhoun, D.H. 1960. The American Civil Engineer: Origins and Conflict. Cambridge: The Technology Press.

Childress, V., and C. Rhodes. 2006. Engineering Student Outcomes for Grades 9–12. National Center for Engineering and Technology Education, Utah State University, Logan, Utah. Available online at *http://ncete.org/flash/Outcomes.pdf* (accessed September 2, 2008).

Childress, V., and M. Sanders. 2007. Core Engineering Concepts Foundational for the Study of Technology in Grades 6-12. Available online at *http://www.conferences.ilstu. edu/NSA/papers/ChildressSanders.pdf* (accessed September 2, 2008).

CTTE (Council on Technology Teacher Education). 2008. Engineering and Technology Education, 57th Yearbook, R.L. Custer and T.L. Erekson, eds. Woodland Hills, Calif.: Glencoe/McGraw-Hill.

DOEd (United States Department of Education). 2006a. Digest of Education Statistics, 2005 (NCES 2006-030), Table 205. National Center for Education Statistics. Available online at *http://nces.ed.gov/fastfacts/display.asp?id=98* (accessed December 22, 2008).

DOEd. 2006b. Digest of Education Statistics, 2005 (NCES 2006-030), Table 170. National Center for Education Statistics. Available online at *http://nces.ed.gov/programs/digest/ d05/tables/dt05_170.asp* (accessed December 22, 2008).

Duderstadt, J. J. 2008. Engineering for a Changing World: A Roadmap to the Future of Engineering Practice, Research, and Education. The Millennium Project. Available online at *http://milproj.ummu.umich.edu/publications/EngFlex%20report/download/ EngFlex%20Report.pdf* (accessed December 19, 2008).

EDAC (Electronic Design Automation Consortium). 2008. EDA Industry. What is EDA? Available online at *http://www.edac.org/industry_what_is_eda.jsp* (December 23, 2008.)

Evans, H.B. 1994. Water Distribution in Ancient Rome: The Evidence of Frontinus. Ann Arbor, Mich.: University of Michigan Press.

Flexner, S.B. 1987. The Random House Dictionary of the English Language, Second Edition—Unabridged. New York: Random House.

Grinter, L.E. 1984. Engineering and engineering technology education. Journal of Engineering Technology 1(1): 6–8.

Herschbach, D.R. 2009. Technology Education—Foundations and Perspectives. Homewood, Ill.: American Technical Publishers, Inc.

ITEA (International Technology Education Association). 2000. Standards for Technological Literacy: Content for the Study of Technology. Reston, Va.: ITEA.

Langins, J. 2004. Conserving the Enlightenment: French Military Engineering from Vauban to the Revolution. Cambridge, Mass.: MIT Press.

Lewis, T. 2004. A Turn to Engineering: The continuing struggle of technology education for legitimization as a school subject. Journal of Technology Education 16(1): 21-39. Available online at: *http://scholar.lib.vt.edu/ejournals/JTE/v16n1/pdf/lewis.pdf* (accessed May 29, 2009).

Lewis, T. 2006. Design and inquiry: Bases for an accommodation between science and technology education in the curriculum? Journal of Research in Science Teaching 43(3): 255–281.

Lucena, J.C. 2005. Defending the Nation: U.S. Policymaking to Create Scientists and Engineers from Sputnik to the 'War against Terrorism.' New York: University Press of America.

McAlister, B. 2005. Are Technology Education Teachers Prepared to Teach Engineering Design and Analytical Methods? Paper presented at the International Technology Education Association Conference, Session IV: Technology Education and Engineering, Kansas City, Missouri, April 4, 2005.

Miller, J. 2008. Overview of Engineering and Technical Education and Work in the United States. Paper prepared for the NAE/NRC Committee on K–12 Engineering Education. May 13, 2008. Unpublished.

NAE (National Academy of Engineering). 2004. The Engineer of 2020—Visions of Engineering in the New Century. Washington, D.C.: The National Academies Press.

NAE. 2008. Changing the Conversation: Messages for Improving Public Understanding of Engineering. Washington, D.C.: The National Academies Press.

NSF (National Science Foundation). 2005a. Science and Engineering Degrees: 1966–2004. Table 47: Engineering degrees awarded, by degree level and sex of recipient, 1966–2004. Available online at *http://www.nsf.gov/statistics/nsf07307/pdf/tab47.pdf* (accessed January 4, 2008).

NSF. 2005b. Women, Minorities, and Persons with Disabilities in Science and Engineering. Table C-7: Racial/ethnic distribution of S&E bachelor's degrees awarded to U.S. citizens and permanent residents, by field: 1995–2005. Available online at *http://www.nsf.gov/statistics/wmpd/pdf/tabc-7.pdf* (accessed January 4, 2008).

NSF. 2006a. Science and Engineering Indicators 2006. Appendix Table 2-26: Earned bachelor's degrees, by field and sex: Selected years, 1983–2002. Available online at *http://nsf.gov/statistics/seind06/append/c2/at02-26.xls* (accessed September 18, 2007).

NSF. 2006b. Science and Engineering Indicators 2006. Figure 3-26: Women as proportion of employment in S&E occupations, by broad occupation: 1983 and 2003. Available online at *http://www.nsf.gov/statistics/seind06/c3/c3s1.htm#c3s1ll1* (accessed January 4, 2008).

Reynolds, T.S. 1991. The Engineer in 19th-Century America. Pp. 7,8,13 in The Engineer in America: A Historical Anthology from Technology and Culture, edited by T.S. Reynolds. Chicago, Ill.: Chicago University Press.

Sanders, M. 2008. The Nature of Technology Education in the United States. Paper presented at the Annual Conference of the American Society of Engineering Education, Pittsburgh, Pa., June 25, 2008.

Sneider, C. 2006. Draft Learning Progression for Engineering Design. Boston Museum of Science, November 12, 2006. Unpublished.

U.S. Census Bureau. 2002. Current Population Reports: Population Projections of the United States by Age, Sex, Race, and Hispanic Origin: 1995 to 2050. Table J. Available online at *http://www.census.gov/prod/1/pop/p25-1130.pdf* (accessed September 18, 2007).

U.S. Census Bureau. 2005. Race and Hispanic Origin in 2005. Population Profile of the United States: Dynamic Version. Available online at *http://www.census.gov/population/pop-profile/dynamic/RACEHO.pdf* (accessed October 26, 2007).

Wadhwa, V., G. Gereffi, B. Rissing, and R. Ong. 2007. Where the engineers are. Issues in Science and Technology (Spring): 73–84.

Wulf, W.A. 1998. The image of engineering. Issues in Science and Technology. Winter. Available online at *www.issues.org/15.2/wulf.htm* (accessed May 16, 2009).

3

The Case for K–12 Engineering Education

Proponents have put forth a number of reasons for adding K–12 engineering education to the school curriculum (Box 3-1). Their arguments are similar to arguments for improving STEM education. Both cases are based on changes in the world—increasing complexity, interconnectivity, competitiveness, and technology dependence—that pose new challenges for individuals and for nations that cannot be met by continuing education as usual. We will need a steady supply of well-trained engineers, scientists, and other technical workers, as well as a technologically and scientifically literate general public, to succeed and prosper in the twenty-first century (Augustine, 2007; BSCS, 2007).

In this chapter, we present a detailed discussion of the case for K–12 engineering education, focusing on various aspects of the argument and on supporting data.

THE BENEFITS OF K–12 ENGINEERING EDUCATION

The potential benefits to students of including engineering education in K–12 schools can be grouped into five areas:

- improved learning and achievement in science and mathematics;
- increased awareness of engineering and the work of engineers;
- understanding of and the ability to engage in engineering design;

BOX 3-1
Statements from Selected K–12
Engineering Education Programs

The "Engineering by Design"™ Program is a model used by schools developing themes in the STEM and IT Clusters that are seeking to increase all students' achievement in technology, science, mathematics, and English through authentic learning.

ITEA
http://www.iteaconnect.org/EbD/ebd.htm

"The Infinity Project" is helping close the gap between the number of engineering graduates we currently produce in the United States and the large need for high-quality engineering graduates in the near future. For our next generation of college graduates to be competitive in the global world of technology, we need to take steps now to encourage more young students to pursue engineering.

Southern Methodist University
http://www.infinity-project.org/infinity/infinity_hist.html

The "Engineering is Elementary" project aims to foster engineering and technological literacy among children.

Boston Museum of Science
http://www.mos.org/eie/index.php

- interest in pursuing engineering as a career; and
- increased technological literacy.

Although only a small percentage of students has had an opportunity to study engineering in elementary and secondary schools in the United States, a number of curricula for teaching engineering have been developed—many of which are described in Chapter 4. Curriculum developers, cognitive scientists, and others have studied the effects of these curricula and other K–12 engineering initiatives on student learning, interests, and attitudes. Based on their research, it is possible to assess the evidence for these benefits.

The remainder of this chapter provides the highlights and key findings of a commissioned review of the relevant research literature, which includes articles published in peer-reviewed journals, conference papers, program evaluations, and unpublished documents such as dissertations (Svihla et al., unpublished).

Overall, the review turned up limited evidence for many of the benefits predicted or claimed for K–12 engineering education. This does not mean that the benefits do not exist, but it does confirm that relatively few well-designed, carefully executed studies have been conducted on this subject. This issue is discussed in greater detail at the end of this chapter and in Chapter 6.

Improved Learning and Achievement in Science and Mathematics

One of the claims most often made about K–12 engineering education is that it improves learning and achievement in science and mathematics. This is a particularly compelling claim because, for the past two decades, many concerted efforts have been made to improve K–12 science and mathematics education in the United States. By most accounts those efforts have had relatively unimpressive results (Box 3-2).

How might engineering education improve learning in science and mathematics? In theory, if students are taught science and mathematics concepts and skills while solving engineering or engineering-like problems, they will be able to grasp these concepts and learn these skills more easily and retain them better, because the engineering design approach can provide real-world context to what are otherwise very abstract concepts.

Preliminary evidence supports this theory. For example, students who took courses developed by "Project Lead the Way" (PLTW) scored significantly higher on science and mathematics in the NAEP than students in a random, stratified comparison group (Bottoms and Anthony, 2005; Bottoms and Uhn, 2007). Research using a state achievement test as the basis of comparison has found more mixed results. PLTW students from schools serving a high proportion of low-income families showed less improvement in mathematics scores from grade 8 to 10 and no statistical difference in science achievement scores over that period, compared with a control group (Tran and Nathan, In press). And PLTW students attending schools serving predominantly affluent families exhibited small gains in mathematics achievement but no improvement in science achievement, compared with a control sample (Tran and Nathan, In press).

Students who had taken the "Engineering Our Future New Jersey" course, which is offered in 32 elementary, middle, and high schools in the state, demonstrated significant improvements in scores on both science and

---

BOX 3-2
The Push to Improve K–12
Science and Mathematics Education

In 1990, the Department of Education National Education Goals Panel released a report detailing necessary improvements in U.S. education. In that report, science and mathematics were the only subjects addressed specifically. Goal 5 was, "By the year 2000, United States students will be first in the world in mathematics and science achievement" (DOEd, 1989). Eleven years later, when the department published a definitive study of science and mathematics teaching in the United States, the conclusion was that little progress had been made toward reaching that goal (DOEd, 2000).

In the past few years, many studies, such as *Rising Above the Gathering Storm: Energizing and Employing America for a Brighter Economic Future,* have argued that improving science and mathematics education will require substantial reform (NAS et al., 2007). Many of these reports include data from the National Assessment of Educational Progress (NAEP) and two ongoing international comparative assessments, the Trends in International Mathematics and Science Study (TIMSS) and the Programme for International Student Assessment (PISA), to support the contention that U.S. K–12 students, particularly secondary students, simply do not measure up. Although TIMSS and PISA data are often used as indicators, some have argued that most interpretations of these data overstate the U.S. achievement problem, in part because they do not account for differences in the educational systems of the participating countries (Lowell and Salzman, 2007).

In 2007, the Department of Education published a review of all federally funded programs with a math or science education focus, looking at their effectiveness and at ways to integrate and coordinate them. The report focused on 115 programs that it considered to have the best evaluations and concluded that there was very little hard evidence as to which programs were effective and which were not (DOEd, 2007).

---

mathematics achievement tests[1] (Hotaling et al., 2007). Statistically significant gains in science and mathematics scores have also been reported by the

---

[1]In this study, the results were not disaggregated, and no measure of variance was provided. Thus we cannot know if the gains were uniform or if some subgroups were more or less impacted.

Center for Innovation in Engineering and Science Education at Stevens Institute of Technology, which has created a variety of online, problem-based K–12 engineering curricula (McKay and McGrath, 2007). Students who had participated in "Engineering is Elementary," a program developed by the Boston Museum of Science that integrates engineering with science content for elementary students, showed improvement in a post-test measuring science and engineering knowledge (Lachapelle and Cunningham, 2007). Unfortunately, there was no control group for comparison in this study.

Engineering design has been shown to encourage mathematical thinking. Akins and Burghardt (2006) studied teams of middle and high school students who applied mathematical reasoning to solve problems in a design challenge. Pre-test results were used to disaggregate students into quartiles, and all quartiles showed improvement on math and science tests. (No tests of significance were conducted, but post-test scores were 21 percent to 125 percent higher than pre-test scores.) The authors noted that the lowest scoring teams had the highest score gains, which suggests that engineering design has the potential to narrow achievement gaps; this possibility was not noted by the researchers, however.

In some cases, standardized test scores were not impacted by student participation in engineering activities, but other measures, such as the ability to explain, analyze, predict, or reason about science, mathematics, or technology, demonstrate that the students had learned a great deal. For example, a program at one inner-city school involved designing remote-control vehicles. Although the scores of students who participated in the program did not show improvements on district-wide physics achievement tests, pre-post measures showed that the students had a better understanding of the physics related to their vehicles (Barnett, 2005).

In the "Integrated Mathematics, Science, and Technology" (IMaST) curriculum project, participating students and non-IMaST students had similar gains on state mathematics and science achievement tests, but IMaST students scored higher on TIMSS math items than students in a control group (Satchwell and Loepp, 2002). Notably, IMaST students scored higher on measures related to "process" (i.e., mathematical problem solving and science inquiry) whereas the control students scored higher on measures related to "knowing" (i.e., understanding routine mathematics operations and scientific information).

A few studies have been done on the potential of K–12 engineering to differentially affect math and science achievement among girls and underrepresented minorities. In a middle-school study of modules in which engineering design and science were integrated, pre-post data showed that the achievement gap for African American and Latino/a students was narrowed, but the achievement gap for girls was increased (Cantrel et al., 2006). It is not clear in this case whether the students engaged in a truly iterative design process, which has been shown to encourage science learning for girls and students from families of low socio-economic status (SES) (Kolodner et al., 2003). Barnett (2005) reported on a study of inner-city, low SES, predominantly ethnic-minority high school students that included a significant population of English language learners and many students with disabilities. All of these students had participated in a project that involved designing remotely operated vehicles. Pre-post data revealed that, overall, the students' understanding of physics had improved. However, the improvement did not translate to higher scores on a district-wide final exam in physics.

So-called challenge-based environments can mimic design or motivate students to solve problems in order to learn engineering, science, and mathematics content. In a three-year study of this approach, "legacy cycles," Klein and Sherwood (2005) found that students in the experimental group had statistically larger gains in measures of relevant science knowledge and concepts. Although most of the modules did not involve design, they did require problem solving in the context of engineering and had many design elements. The researchers argue that design challenges embedded in science activities increase the likelihood that students will explore variables rather than stopping their inquiries as soon as the design criteria have been satisfied. The "Math out of the Box" program uses a modified legacy cycle in which engineering provides a context for learning applied mathematics (Diaz and King, 2007). This program has been implemented in several schools; the ones that have continued to use it have found that achievement scores in mathematics have risen, particularly for low-SES and African American students. The schools that discontinued the program found that mathematics scores fell.

Qualitative research in the learning sciences provides some insights into how and why science and mathematics learning may be impacted by participation in engineering activities, particularly design activities. Fortus et al. (2004) recorded significant increases in science knowledge among ninth graders engaged in the "Designed-Based Science" curriculum. The researchers suggest that this effect can be explained in part by students' personal ownership of science content as compared with consensus-driven ownership in other forms of inquiry. Students using this curriculum were also able to transfer their understanding of a concept from the original context to a different context (Fortus et al., 2005), which the researchers attribute to the way the design activity is structured to support learning for understanding in the context of solving a problem. Roth (2001) suggests that design activities, which present distributed representations of ideas, can stimulate discussions about science concepts. Ideas represented through design can then be inspected and tested.

Penner et al. (1998) explored how the design by elementary students of a physical model of an elbow can support science and mathematics learning related to the mechanics of motion. The success of the project depended on students having multiple opportunities to engage in and discuss their design experiences, teachers' use of analogies, and sense-making based on data collection and interpretation. Redesign gives students a chance to explore connections between science and design, to test their ideas, and to decide how to correct their designs and then adjust the corresponding understanding of the relevant scientific principle or concept (Sadler et al., 2000).

In summary, the available evidence suggests that under certain circumstances, engineering education can boost learning and achievement in science and mathematics. These effects may be more significant for certain populations, particularly underrepresented minority students. However, the positive effects are not universal and research has not clearly established the causal mechanism(s) to explain such benefits when they occur.

Increased Awareness of Engineering and the Work of Engineers

This goal, improving students' awareness of engineering and the work of engineers, can be of great benefit to a society, because engineering is central to technology development, and technology influences the well-being of everyone. Conversely, a lack of awareness of engineering and misconceptions or ignorance about what engineers do can be detrimental to a society. On a practical level, young people who believe engineers drive trains or repair car engines or who have negative stereotypes of the profession are unlikely ever to consider studying engineering or pursuing it as a career. If enough youngsters feel this way, it may become increasingly difficult to attract and retain a technically proficient workforce. Generally, individuals who do not have a basic idea of what engineers do are unlikely to appreciate how engineering and science contribute to economic development, quality of life, national security, and health care; such awareness is one aspect of technological literacy (NAE and NRC, 2006).

The engineering community, including engineering professional societies, schools of engineering, and firms that depend heavily on engineering talent, have spent hundreds of millions of dollars annually on initiatives to raise the level of the public understanding of engineering (NAE, 2002), for the most part unsuccessfully. For example, researchers have found that K–12 teachers and students generally have a poor understanding of what engineers do (Cunningham and Knight, 2004; Cunningham et al., 2005; Oware et al., 2007). Survey data suggest that many adults in the United States believe that engineers, as compared with scientists, are not as responsive to societal and community concerns and are not as important in saving lives (Harris Interactive, 2004).

This widespread misconception reveals a lack of awareness of the many ways engineering has dramatically improved the human condition (e.g., *www.greatachievements.org*). Teens and adults strongly associate engineering with skills in mathematics and science, according to recent online polling, but much more rarely with creativity, rewarding work, or a positive effect on the world (NAE, 2008).

Findings like these have prompted advocates of K–12 engineering education to argue for the importance of young people having opportunities to learn about engineers, engineering, and technology. Research has shown that participation in engineering education activities can provide those opportunities. For example, assessments showed that students who participated in the "Engineering Our Future New Jersey" program were able to name significantly more types of engineers and to describe types of engineering activities (Hirsch et al., 2005). These students were also able to recognize technology and the work of engineers (Hotaling et al., 2007).

Teachers, too, may be more aware of engineering career options after leading engineering design activities with students (McGrath et al., 2008). Pre-post tests found that young children who took part in the "Engineering is Elementary" program had a significantly broader conception of what technology is and were able to identify activities undertaken by engineers (Lachapelle and Cunningham, 2007). According to a study by graduate teaching fellows in K–12 education funded by the National Science Foundation, such changes in students' awareness of engineers and engineering can be sustained over time (Lyons and Thompson, 2006).

Understanding of and the Ability to Engage in Engineering Design

The iterative, open-ended, problem-solving method known as engineering design is the central activity of engineers. For this reason, a good deal of K–12, as well as post-secondary, engineering education is spent on developing students' understanding and capabilities in this area. In addition, as was mentioned above, design activities provide a real-world focus for abstract concepts, which may have a positive impact on learning not only in engineering, but also in other subjects, such as mathematics and science. In this section, we consider the evidence related to how well students learn to understand and engage in engineering design.

Data from a number of studies suggest that engineering design as practiced by engineers is neither quickly learned by students nor easily taught by teachers. Issues common to novice design, such as using trial-and-error methods (rather than a systematic approach) and spending too much time on defining the problem, have been well documented (e.g., Hill and Smith, 1998; Ressler and Ressler, 2004). Unless the teacher explicitly encourages a systematic approach, the design process can be overwhelmed by student excitement about hands-on activities (Seiler et al., 2001).

Specific concepts integral to engineering design also pose challenges to students. For example, in a project in which undergraduate engineering and education students developed design activities for students in the seventh through twelfth grades, Bergin et al. (2007) found that the K–12 students had difficulty understanding the idea of constraints. Penner et al. (1997) found that elementary students struggled to use modeling in a way that reflects engineering practice. In this study, student pairs were asked to design a functional model of an elbow. At first, the children tended to see models as small versions of the thing itself, and their first design iterations copied the form of an elbow but could not perform the functions of an elbow. After some discussion, it was clear that students had not isolated the motion of the elbow but had inferred a great range of motion based on the pivot of the shoulder. After experimenting with real elbow movements, they began a second iteration of modeling. This time the models incorporated constraints but also included nonfunctional but physically similar details, such as a representation of veins.

Interest in Pursuing Engineering as a Career

As many reports and commentators have noted, the economic competitiveness of the United States depends in large part on our ability to attract, train, and retain a large corps of highly qualified, creative engineers in a variety of fields (e.g., NAS et al., 2007). Unfortunately, many students who are capable of becoming engineers never even enter the educational pipeline leading to an engineering career because they either do not understand what engineers do or they believe that they do not have the necessary aptitude or interests to become engineers. This is particularly common for females and students from certain minorities, who are greatly underrepresented in engineering schools and in engineering practice (see Table 2-1) (Chang, 2002).

Up to now, the primary strategy for ensuring that the engineering pipeline is filled has been to insist that high school graduates have a good grounding in science and mathematics. Thus students are not exposed to engineering until they enter college, frequently not until their junior year. K–12 engineering programs offer a different strategy. By introducing students to engineering in K–12 programs—in theory, at least—more of them, from a wider variety of backgrounds, will be attracted to the field.

Although keeping the engineering pipeline flowing is an explicit goal of only a handful of the curricula we examined, the idea that exposure to engineering thinking, particularly design experiences, will attract more students to the pursuit of engineering or technology-related studies and careers seems intuitively sound. In this section, we examine the evidence for how K–12 engineering education affects student interest in engineering and related factors, such as school attendance, retention, and persistence.

Research has shown that students who choose to participate in engineering-related activities and coursework may become more interested in pursuing careers in engineering. For instance, both girls and boys who attended the "Discover Engineering" summer camp at Ryerson University in Canada reported an increased interest in engineering as a career (Anderson and Northwood, 2002). A follow-up study showed that approximately one-third of camp participants actually went on to pursue engineering degrees (Anderson et al., 2005). However, without a comparison group we cannot know if this group of students was representative of the general population.

Not all students respond the same way to educational interventions. Thus it is important to determine how specific groups tend to respond. For instance, in an engineering enrichment program for gifted students, participants completed small design projects as part of reaching a larger design goal (Bayles et al., 2007). Following the experience, 11 percent of students indicated that they felt less confident about their ability to become engineers, and 41 percent said they felt more confident. In a survey of students entering the "Discover Engineering" outreach program, Anderson and Gilbride (2003a) found that boys were significantly more interested than girls in pursuing engineering careers. Boys who claimed to have more knowledge of engineering were more interested than less-knowledgeable boys, but girls who claimed to be more knowledgeable were not more interested than their less knowledgeable peers. An assessment of student interest in engineering following participation in the program showed an increase in interest among both boys and girls, but girls' interest did not rise to parity (Anderson and Gilbride, 2003b). In a study of a different program, both boys and girls reported gains in confidence about engineering as a career after participating in engineering design activities, and girls and boys had equal scores (Zarske et al., 2007). An investigation of why the two studies produced different results could be potentially informative.

Some evidence suggests that engineering activities have coincided with higher school attendance, perhaps a reflection of increased interest. Barnett (2005) reported that attendance increased for a group of inner-city high school science students (largely from low-SES ethnic minorities) who were randomly assigned to classes in which the major focus was on engineering design projects, compared to their peers who were taught the standard science curriculum.

Studies have also been done on retention levels and persistence in engineering, primarily for students already interested in engineering. Most high school students who took an introductory engineering-design course based on a course for first-year college students, for example, went on to pursue engineering degrees in college (Bayles, 2005). Students who take courses from PLTW, a four-year college preparatory program, tend to take more advanced science and math courses and to consider them important to their future (Bottoms and Anthony, 2005; Bottoms and Uhn, 2007). Most PLTW students say they plan to attend college (Walcerz, 2007), although this cannot definitively be attributed to participation in PLTW because this is a self-selected group. The same students reported feeling confident about their career choices (mostly engineering and technology) because of the courses they took in high school. In addition, participation in PLTW has been shown to reduce attrition rates in college engineering programs and to increase the percentage of degrees attained (Taylor et al., 2006). These findings are positive, but the students who choose to take such courses cannot be considered a general population.

In a study of the long-term impact of a two-week engineering camp for middle schoolers, participating students were likelier than a control group to take STEM courses (Hubelbank et al., 2007). This finding is significant because both groups had applied to attend the camp, and the participants were selected by lottery. The camp experience did not affect students' interest in college-level engineering, however. Students in the control and experimental groups were equally likely to pursue engineering degrees.

Participation in K–12 engineering education programs may correlate with an increase in applications to engineering colleges. Zarske et al. (2007) found this to be true for a K–12 program in Colorado. However, although the number of applications increased, many applicants had not completed the coursework necessary for acceptance into the college program. One way of supporting these students is to provide a bridge program. Anderson-Rowland et al. (1999) demonstrated a significantly higher level of retention for students who attended the Summer Bridging Program (SBP) at Arizona State University, a program for entering minority freshmen. However, the effects of SBP were difficult to determine because participants were also required to enroll in an Academic Success Seminar during their freshman year.

Increased Technological Literacy

Many have argued that K–12 engineering classes improve students' technological literacy. Although this argument might not have been compelling 20 years ago, there is a growing appreciation today of the importance of technological literacy to individuals and to society as a whole. As defined in *Technically Speaking: Why All Americans Need to Know More About Technology,* "technological literacy combines basic knowledge about the various technologies in our world with the ability to think critically about technology and to make well-informed decisions about technological issues" (NAE and NRC, 2006).

A technologically literate person understands the essential characteristics of technology and how it influences society and the factors that shape technology, including engineering. Concepts central to engineering, such as systems, trade-offs, and intended and unintended consequences, provide a foundation for making informed decisions in a technologically dependent society like ours.

In *Technically Speaking,* the case for technological literacy is spelled out in detail. A technologically literate person can make informed decisions about his or her use of personal technologies, for example. Technologically literate citizens can be effective participants in decision-making processes involving technology—for instance, whether a city should support the building of a coal-fired power plant. In a society with a growing number of jobs that require technological skills and savvy, employers are more likely to find technologically competent workers if the general population is technologically literate.

In K–12 schools, technological literacy is largely the purview of technology education teachers. In the United States, 25,000 to 35,000 such teachers work in K–12 schools, mostly middle schools and high schools (Dugger, 2007). In 2000, the International Technology Education Association (ITEA) published *Standards for Technological Literacy: Content for the Study of Technology*, which accelerated an ongoing shift in the field of technology education away from its beginnings in industrial arts toward an emphasis on a broad understanding of the concept of technology. The standards in the ITEA document, developed with input from the National Academy of Engineering and National Research Council, include benchmarks related to engineering design (Box 3-3). ITEA and others have also produced curricular materials (e.g., "Engineering by Design," "Engineering is Elementary") that attempt to meet the learning goals spelled out in the standards.

Research shows that many Americans—children and adults—have a narrow, sometimes incorrect, view of technology. In one study, students

---

BOX 3-3
Selected Engineering-Design-Related Benchmarks,
by Grade Band

To comprehend engineering design, students should learn that:

The engineering design process includes identifying a problem, looking for ideas, developing solutions, and sharing solutions with others. (Grades K–2)

Models are used to communicate and test design ideas and processes. (Grades 3–5)

Design involves a series of steps, which can be performed in different sequences and repeated as necessary. (Grades 6–8)

Engineering design is influenced by personal characteristics, such as creativity, resourcefulness, and the ability to visualize and think abstractly. (Grades 9–12)

SOURCE: ITEA, 2000.

in lower elementary grades associated technology mostly with things that require electricity (they conflated technology with lightning) (Cunningham, et al., 2005). Only a few children recognized bridges and bandages, for example, as technologies. First graders identified parrots as a technology nearly as often as they did cups. Surveys of adults have shown that the vast majority associate technology primarily with computers (ITEA, 2004). Several studies have shown that students who have been exposed to engineering education have a broader conception of technology and have corrected some misconceptions (Hotaling et al., 2007; Lachapelle and Cunningham, 2007). Being able to recognize technology is a basic prerequisite for technological literacy.

The committee did not find any published research that explicitly ties K–12 engineering education to improvements in other aspects of technological literacy. One reason may be that technological literacy, unlike science literacy, is a relatively new idea in education. In addition, there are significant challenges associated with the development of assessments of technological literacy. In an extended discussion of the latter problem, *Tech Tally: Approaches to Assessing Technological Literacy* (NAE and NRC, 2006) pointed out that the "capabilities" dimension of technological literacy may be especially difficult to measure. In that report the study committee reviewed 28 existing assessment instruments for measuring some aspect of technological literacy, even if they were not designed for that purpose. The committee found that none of these instruments was completely adequate for measuring technological literacy and that only two explicitly targeted engineering learning; one was developed for students in "The Infinity Project," and the other was an achievement test for fifth, eighth, and tenth graders in Massachusetts.

Interest on the national level in the technological literacy of K–12 students and improvements in measuring instruments, such as assessments, may increase in coming years. For example, when a revised version of the science portion of NAEP is administered for the first time in 2009, 10 percent of test items will focus on technological design (NAGB, 2008a). In addition, the National Assessment Governing Board, which oversees NAEP, has recently funded a feasibility study for an assessment of technological literacy (NAGB, 2008b). If the study, which runs until 2012, finds that technological literacy can be validly and reliably measured, NAGB may add an assessment of technological literacy to its portfolio of tests.

LIMITATIONS OF THE DATA

Besides the relatively small number of studies on the impacts of teaching engineering concepts and skills to K–12 students, our review of the literature revealed a number of weaknesses in the methodologies used in some studies. Several of these are highlighted below in hopes that they will be addressed in future research on the impacts of this emerging area of education.

An overarching concern with the data is that assessments of whether these well-intentioned initiatives achieve their desired goals frequently appear to be an afterthought. Assessments require advanced planning and viable pre-tests. Although pre- and post-tests cannot replace longitudinal data, they do indicate changes over time. Follow-up surveys can be used to determine the persistence of these changes.

Another problem is that the data are not "generalizable." For example, students who participate in engineering camps, clubs, and courses have chosen to do so. Thus the findings about the effectiveness of these activities cannot be generalized to students who do not choose to participate in these programs. This issue involves not only methodology. Because the findings do not provide information about the specific impacts on women and under-represented minorities or on students who are not initially interested in learning about engineering, these assessments tell us little or nothing about the effectiveness of engineering education on general student populations. This can be a serious problem, because a goal of many of these programs is to increase the number of women and underrepresented minorities in engineering classes and ultimately in engineering practice.

When data on K–12 engineering education initiatives are collected, they often indicate only if participants enjoyed the program and include self-reported changes. It is known that participants in studies sometimes report positive results simply because they are in a study, the so-called Hawthorne effect (Landsberger, 1958). This methodological weakness could be addressed by measuring learning on pre-and post-tests.

Most of the studies we reviewed did not assess the impact of engineering education on student subgroups. The problem arises because in presenting data, it is critical to provide measures of central tendency and distribution. For example, the same average may be found for tightly clustered data, indicating that most respondents have similar scores, or for widely distributed data, indicating that approximately equal numbers of people had scores above and below the mean. The critical factor is the meaning of the spread. For instance, did minority students or students who most need to learn fall below the mean? The simple solution is to disaggregate data. This is only viable, of course, if the number of subgroup members in the study is sufficient to permit statistically valid comparisons.

These problems are not limited to studies of engineering education. In fact, definitive data about the impacts of educational interventions in most subjects are hard to come by. Even for the best-studied areas, such as reading and mathematics, little convincing evidence is available about the effectiveness of teaching approaches. In 2007, for example, the U.S. Department of Education published a review of all federally funded programs with a math or science education focus with the intent of determining their effectiveness as a basis for integrating and coordinating them. The report focused on 115 programs, 24 of them K–12 programs for which the "best" evaluations were done (DOEd, 2007).

> [D]espite decades of significant federal investment in science and math education, there is a general dearth of evidence of effective practices and activities in STEM education. Even the 10 well-designed studies [that the review identified] would require replication and validation to be used as the basis for decisions about education policy or classroom practice.

In short, the lack of a strong evidence base for the benefits of K–12 engineering education is consistent with the situation for much educational research in the STEM arena. This is another reason, if any were needed, for those who promote K–12 engineering education to pursue empirical, methodologically sound impact studies.

REFERENCES

Akins, L., and D. Burghardt. 2006. Work in Progress: Improving K–12 Mathematics Understanding with Engineering Design Projects. Pp. 13–14 in Frontiers in Education Conference, 36th Annual. New York: Institute of Electrical and Electronics Engineers.

Anderson, L.S., and K.A. Gilbride. 2003a. Bringing Engineering to K–12 Classrooms: Initiatives and Results. Proceedings of the 2003 American Society for Engineering Education Annual Conference, Nashville, Tennessee, June 22–25, 2003. Available online at *http://soa.asee.org/paper/conference/paper-view.cfm?id=18386* (accessed January 16, 2009).

Anderson, L.S., and K.A. Gilbride. 2003b. Pre-university Outreach: Encouraging Students to Consider Engineering Careers. Paper presented at 3rd Global Congress on Engineering Education, Glasgow, Scotland, June 30–July 5, 2002. Available online at *http://www.discoverengineering.ryerson.ca/publications/2002UICEE.pdf* (accessed January 16, 2009).

Anderson, L.S., and D.O. Northwood. 2002. Recruitment and Retention Strategies to Increase Diversity in Engineering. Paper presented at the International Conference on Engineering Education ICEE, Manchester, U.K., August 18–21, 2002. Available online at *http://www.ineer.org/Events/ICEE2002/Proceedings/Papers/Index/O065-O070/O069.pdf* (accessed January 14, 2009).

Anderson, L.S., K.A. Gilbride, and N. Bajaj. 2005. Discover Engineering Follow-up Surveys: Assessment/Evaluation of Recruitment Programs. Paper presented at the WEPAN/ NAMEPA Joint Conference, Las Vegas, Nevada, April 11, 2005. Available online at *http://www.x-cd.com/wepan05/24.pdf* (accessed January 13, 2009).

Anderson-Rowland, M.R., S.L. Blaisdell, S.L. Fletcher, P.A. Fussell, M.A. McCartney, M.A. Reyes, et al. 1999. A collaborative effort to recruit and retain underrepresented engineering students. Journal of Women and Minorities in Science and Engineering 5(4): 323–349.

Augustine, N.R. 2007. Is America Falling off the Flat Earth? Washington, D.C.: The National Academies Press. Also available online at *http://www.nap.edu/catalog.php?record_ id=12021* (accessed May 2, 2008).

Barnett, M. 2005. Engaging inner city students in learning through designing remote operated vehicles. Journal of Science Education and Technology 14(1): 87–100.

Bayles, T.M. 2005. Project-Based Learning Design Projects for Introduction to Engineering Design Courses. Paper presented at the American Society for Engineering Education Annual Conference and Exposition Portland, Oregon, June 12–15, 2005. Available online at *http://soa.asee.org/paper/conference/paper-view.cfm?id=21005* (accessed January 14, 2009).

Bayles, T.M., J. Rice, G. Russ, and T. Monterastelli. 2007. High School Outreach: A Look at Renewable Energy. Paper presented at the American Society for Engineering Education, Honolulu, Hawaii, June 27, 2007. Available online at *http://soa.asee.org/paper/ conference/paper-view.cfm?id=4795* (accessed January 14, 2009).

Bergin, D., S.K. Khanna, and J. Lynch. 2007. Infusing design into the G7–12 curriculum: two example cases. International Journal of Engineering Education 23(1): 43–49.

Bottoms, G., and K. Anthony. 2005. Project Lead the Way: A Pre-Engineering Curriculum That Works. Southern Regional Education Board. Available online at *http://www.sreb. org/programs/hstw/publications/briefs/05V08_Research_PLTW.pdf* (accessed May 9, 2008).

Bottoms, G., and J. Uhn. 2007. Project Lead the Way Works: A New Type of Career and Technical Program. Southern Educational Review Board. Available online at *http:// www.sreb.org/programs/hstw/publications/2007pubs/07V29_Research_Brief_PLTW.pdf* (accessed January 15, 2009).

BSCS (Biological Sciences Curriculum Study). 2007. A Decade of Action: Sustaining Global Competitiveness. Colorado Springs, Colo.: BSCS.

Cantrell, P., G. Pekcan, A. Itani, and N. Velasquez-Bryant. 2006. The effects of engineering modules on student learning in middle school science classrooms. Journal of Engineering Education 95(4): 301–310.

Chang, J.C. 2002. Women and Minorities in the Science, Mathematics, and Engineering Pipeline. ERIC Digest. Available online at *http://eric.ed.gov/ERICDocs/data/ericdocs2sql/ content_storage_01/0000019b/80/1a/52/ec.pdf* (accessed May 13, 2008).

Cunningham, C., and M. Knight. 2004. Draw an Engineer Test: Development of a Tool to Investigate Students' Ideas about Engineers and Engineering. Paper presented at the American Society for Engineering Education Annual Conference and Exposition. Salt Lake City, Utah, June 20–23, 2004. Available online at *http://soa.asee.org/paper/ conference/paper-view.cfm?id=19444* (accessed January 16, 2009).

Cunningham, C., C. Lachapelle, and A. Lindgren-Streicher. 2005. Assessing Elementary School Students' Conceptions of Engineering and Technology. Paper presented at the American Society for Engineering Education Annual Conference and Exposition, Portland, Oregon, June 12–15, 2005. Available online at *http://soa.asee.org/paper/ conference/paper-view.cfm?id=21451* (accessed January 16, 2009).

Diaz, D. and P. King. 2007. Adapting a Post-Secondary STEM Instructional Model to K–5 Mathematics Instruction. Paper presented at the American Society of Engineering Education Annual Conference and Exposition, Honolulu, Hawaii, June 24–27, 2007. Available online at *http://www.mathoutofthebox.org/aseepaperdiaz.pdf* (accessed January 15, 2009).

DOEd (U.S. Department of Education). 1989. Report of the National Education Goals Panel. Washington, D.C.: DOEd.

DOEd. 2000. Before It's Too Late: A Report to the Nation from the National Commission on Mathematics and Science Teaching for the 21st Century. Washington, D.C.: DOEd. Also available online at *http://www.ed.gov/inits/Math/glenn/report.pdf* (accessed May 2, 2008).

DOEd. 2007. Report of the Academic Competitiveness Council. Washington, D.C.: DOEd. Also available at *http://www.ed.gov/about/inits/ed/competitiveness/acc-mathscience/ index.html* (accessed April 15, 2008).

Dugger, W.E., Jr. 2007. The status of technology education in the United States: a triennial finding of the findings from the states. The Technology Teacher 67(1): 14–21.

Fortus, D., R.C. Dershimer, J.S. Krajcik, R.W. Marx, and R. Mamlok-Naaman. 2004. Design-based science and student learning. Journal of Research in Science Teaching 41(10): 1081–1110.

Fortus, D., J.S. Krajcik, R.C. Dershimer, R.W. Marx, and R. Mamlok-Naaman. 2005. Design-based science and real-world problem-solving. International Journal of Science Education, 27(7): 855–879.

Harris Interactive. 2004. American Perspectives on Engineers and Engineering. Poll conducted for the American Association of Engineering Societies. Final report, February 13, 2004. Available online at *http://www.aaes.org/harris_2004_files/frame.htm* (accessed July 6, 2007).

Hill, A.M., and H. Smith. 1998. Practice meets theory in technology education: a case of authentic learning in the high school setting. Journal of Technology Education 9(2): 29–45.

Hirsch, L.S., H. Kimmel, R. Rockland, and J. Bloom. 2005. Implementing Pre-engineering Curricula in High School Science and Mathematics. Paper presented at the 35th Annual Frontiers in Education Conference, Indianapolis, Indiana, October 19–22, 2005. Available online at *http://fie-conference.org/fie2005/index.htm* (accessed January 15, 2009).

Hotaling, L., B. McGrath, M. McKay, C. Shields, S. Lowes, C.M. Cunningham, et al. 2007. Engineering Our Future New Jersey. Paper presented at the American Society for Engineering Education Annual Conference and Exposition Proceedings, Honolulu, Hawaii, June 24–27, 2007. Available online at *http://soa.asee.org/paper/conference/ paper-view.cfm?id=4611* (accessed January 15, 2009).

Hubelbank, J., C. Demetry, S.E. Nicholson, S. Blaisdell, P. Quinn, E. Rosenthal, et al. 2007. Long-Term Effects of a Middle School Engineering Outreach Program for Girls: A

Controlled Study. Paper presented at the American Society for Engineering Education, Honolulu, Hawaii, June 24–27, 2007. Available online at *http://soa.asee.org/paper/ conference/paper-view.cfm?id=4368* (accessed January 15, 2009).

ITEA (International Technology Education Association). 2000. Standards for Technological Literacy: Content for the Study of Technology. Reston, Va.: ITEA.

ITEA. 2004. The Second Installment of the ITEA/Gallup Poll and What It Reveals as to How Americans Think about Technology: A Report of the Second Survey Conducted by the Gallup Organization for the International Technology Education Association. Available online at *http://www.iteaconnect.org/TAA/PDFs/GallupPoll2004.pdf* (accessed December 22, 2008).

Klein, S., and R.D. Sherwood. 2005. Biomedical engineering and cognitive science as the basis for secondary science curriculum development: a three year study. School Science and Mathematics 105(8): 384–401.

Kolodner, J.L., P.J. Camp, D. Crismond, B. Fasse, J. Gray, and J. Holbrook. 2003. Problem-based learning meets case-based reasoning in the science classroom: putting learning-by-design into practice. Journal of the Learning Sciences 12(4): 495–547.

Lachapelle, C.P., and C.M. Cunningham. 2007. Engineering is Elementary: Children's Changing Understandings of Science and Engineering. Paper presented at the American Society for Engineering Education Annual Conference and Exposition, Honolulu, Hawaii, June 24–27, 2007. Available online at *http://soa.asee.org/paper/conference/ paper-view.cfm?id=3247* (accessed January 15, 2009).

Landsberger, H.A. 1958. Hawthorne Revisited, Management and the Worker: Its Critics, and Developments in Human Relations in Industry. Ithaca, N.Y.: Cornell University Press.

Lowell, L.B., and H. Salzman. 2007. Into the Eye of the Storm: Assessing the Evidence on Science and Engineering Education, Quality, and Workforce Demand. October 2007. Washington, D.C.: The Urban Institute.

Lyons, J., and S. Thompson. 2006. Investigating the Long-Term Impact of an Engineering-Based GK–12 Program on Students' Perceptions of Engineering. 2006 ASEE Annual Conference and Exposition: Excellence in Education, Chicago, Illinois, June 18–21, 2006. Available online at *http://soa.asee.org/paper/conference/paper-view.cfm?id=2184* (accessed January 15, 2009).

McGrath, B., J. Sayres, S. Lowes, and P. Lin. 2008. Underwater LEGO Robotics as the Vehicle to Engage Students in STEM: The BUILD IT Project's First Year of Classroom Implementation. Paper presented at the fall 2008 American Society for Engineering Education Mid-Atlantic Conference, October 18, 2008, Stevens Institute of Technology, Hoboken, N.J. Available online at *http://www.stevens.edu/asee/fileadmin/asee/pdf/Mc-Grath_-_final.pdf* (accessed January 15, 2009).

McKay, M., and B. McGrath. 2007. Real-world problem-solving using real-time data. International Journal of Engineering Education 23(1): 36–42.

NAE (National Academy of Engineering). 2002. Technically Speaking: Why All Americans Need to Know More About Technology. Washington, D.C.: National Academy Press. Also available online at *http://www.nap.edu/openbook.php?record_id=10250* (accessed May 7, 2008).

NAE. 2008. Changing the Conversation: Messages for Improving Public Understanding of Engineering. Washington, D.C.: The National Academies Press.

NAE and NRC (National Research Council). 2006. Tech Tally: Approaches to Assessing Technological Literacy. Washington, D.C.: The National Academies Press.

NAGB. (National Assessment Governing Board). 2008a. Science Framework for the 2009 National Assessment of Educational Progress. September 2008, Exhibit 18. Distribution of items by science practice and grade, p. 113. Available online at *http://www.nagb.org/frameworks/science-09.pdf* (accessed September 19, 2008).

NAGB. 2008b. Conducting a Special Study in Technological Literacy for the 2012 National Assessment of Educational Progress. Solicitation ED-08-R-0032. Available online at *https://www.fbo.gov/download/a0d/a0dd95e5669a97e35fd90eedcc609428/TECH_LIT_RFP.pdf* (accessed September 19, 2008).

NAS, NAE, and IOM (National Academy of Sciences, National Academy of Engineering, and Institute of Medicine). 2007. Rising Above the Gathering Storm: Energizing and Employing America for a Brighter Economic Future. Washington, D.C.: The National Academies Press.

Oware, E., B. Capobianco, and H. Diefes-Dux. 2007. Gifted Students' Perceptions of Engineers? A Study of Students in a Summer Outreach Program. Paper presented at the American Society of Engineering Education Annual Conference and Exposition, Honolulu, Hawaii, June 24–27, 2007. Available online at *http://soa.asee.org/paper/conference/paper-view.cfm?id=5401* (accessed January 15, 2009).

Penner, D.E., N.D. Giles, R. Lehrer, and L. Schauble. 1997. Building functional models: designing an elbow. Journal of Research in Science Teaching 34(2): 125–143.

Penner, D.E., R. Lehrer, and L. Schauble. 1998. From physical models to biomechanics: a design-based modeling approach. Journal of the Learning Sciences 7(3-4): 429–449.

Ressler, S.J., and E.K. Ressler. 2004. Using a nationwide Internet-based bridge design contest as a vehicle for engineering outreach. Journal of Engineering Education 93(2): 117-128.

Roth, W.M. 2001. Learning science through technological design. Journal of Research in Science Teaching 38(7): 768–790.

Sadler, P.M., H.P. Coyle, and M. Schwartz. 2000. Engineering competitions in the middle school classroom: key elements in developing effective design challenges. Journal of the Learning Sciences 9(3): 299–327.

Satchwell, R.E., and F.L. Loepp. 2002. Designing and implementing an integrated mathematics, science, and technology curriculum for the middle school. Journal of Industrial Teacher Education 39(3): 41–66.

Seiler, G., K. Tobin, and J. Sokolic. 2001. Design, technology, and science: sites for learning, resistance, and social reproduction in urban schools. Journal of Research in Science Teaching 38(7): 746–767.

Svihla, V., J. Marshall, and A.J. Petrosino. Unpublished. K–12 Engineering Education Impacts. Paper prepared for the National Academy of Engineering and National Research Council Committee on K–12 Engineering Education.

Taylor, K.D., G.N. Foster, and M.M. Ratcliff. 2006. Project Lead the Way: Raising the Technical Literacy of High School Graduates. Paper presented at the 9th International Conference on Engineering Education, San Juan, Puerto Rico, June 27–July 1, 2006. Available online at *http://www.icee.usm.edu/icee/conferences/icee2006/papers/3603.pdf* (accessed January 16, 2009).

Tran, N., and M. Nathan. In press. An investigation of the relationship between pre-college engineering studies and student achievement in science and mathematics. Journal of Engineering Education.

Tran, N., and M. Nathan. In press. Effects of pre-college engineering studies on mathematics and science achievements for high school students. International Journal of Engineering Education (Special Issue on Applications of Engineering Education Research).

Walcerz, D. 2007. Report on the Third Year of Implementation of the TrueOutcomes Assessment System for Project Lead the Way. Available online at *http://www.pltw.org/pdfs/AnnualReport-2007-Public-Release.pdf* (accessed January 16, 2009).

Zarske, M., J.L. Yowell, J.F. Sullivan, D. Knight, and D. Wiant. 2007. The TEAMS Program: A Study of a Grades 3–12 Engineering Continuum. Paper presented at the American Society of Engineering Education Annual Conference and Exposition, Honolulu, Hawaii, June 24–27, 2007. Available online at *http://www.pltw.org/pdfs/AnnualReport-2007-Public-Release.pdf* (accessed January 16, 2009).

4

The Current State of K–12 Engineering Education

A major goal of this project was to determine the scope and nature of current efforts to teach engineering to K–12 students in the United States. How many programs are there, who developed them, and which students have they reached? What purposes do they serve? How do they present engineering and engineering design? How do they relate to science, mathematics, and technology? What pedagogical strategies do teachers use? Have outcomes data been collected, and how good are these data? We approached this task in two ways: (1) by reviewing curricula for teaching engineering concepts and skills in K–12 classrooms and (2) by reviewing relevant professional-development initiatives for teachers.

As it turns out, the curriculum landscape is extremely varied; in fact, no two curricula occupy the same "ecological" niche. This is not surprising, given the diverse origins of these materials and points of view of their creators. In addition, because there is no widespread agreement on what a K–12 engineering curriculum should include, the committee decided not to compare programs directly but to identify areas of relative emphasis and notable omissions. This approach revealed certain cross-cutting themes, which are discussed in detail later in this chapter.

Developing a curriculum does not guarantee that engineering education in K–12 will be successful. A critical factor is whether teachers—from elementary generalists to middle school and high school specialists—understand basic engineering concepts and are comfortable engaging in, and teaching, engineering design. For this, teachers must either have appropriate background in mathematics, science, and technology, or they must collaborate with teachers who have this background. We held two data-gathering workshops to explore the professional-development situation for K–12 engineering educators. Information from those workshops is also included in this chapter.

Although the emphasis in this report is on engineering education in this country, the charge to the committee included a directive to find examples of pre-college engineering education in other nations, on the grounds that efforts elsewhere to introduce pre-college students to engineering might influence decisions here. The few initiatives we found are described briefly in an annex to this chapter.

Finally, we recognize that numerous efforts have been made to introduce engineering to K–12 students outside of formal school settings, through websites, contests, after-school programs, and summer programs. The committee charge did not require us to examine these informal K–12 activities. We note, however, that some of these initiatives appear to have increased students' awareness of and stimulated their interest in engineering (e.g., Melchior et al., 2005; TexPREP, 2003).

REVIEW OF CURRICULA

To identify K–12 engineering curricula, the committee relied on the joint efforts of committee members, Prof. Kenneth Welty,[1] University of Wisconsin-Stout, and project staff. The methods included reviews of websites of professional organizations, government agencies, and corporations with an interest in engineering education; searches of online curriculum clearinghouses and libraries; and direct communication with engineering educators, technology teachers, supervisors of state departments of education, and principal investigators of known K–12 engineering education programs and projects. In May 2008, the committee solicited public comments on a project summary, which brought several additional curricula to our attention.

Overall, the committee collected more than 10,000 pages of material, including lengthy narratives downloaded off the Web, material stored on compact disks, material assembled in three-ring binders, and material bound into textbooks. The materials ranged from 425 pages on a single

---

[1]The committee chose Prof. Welty because of his expertise in curriculum analysis, as well as his capacity as a co-principal investigator at the National Center for Engineering and Technology Education (NCETE) funded by the National Science Foundation. NCETE's research agenda complements the overall goals of this project.

topic—gliders—to just 46 pages on the huge topic of biotechnology. To ensure that patterns would be identified and meaningful conclusions drawn, the committee reviewed roughly equal numbers of curricula for each major K–12 grade band (i.e., elementary, middle, and high school).

Because of limitations on time and funding, as well as practical difficulties in locating some more obscure products, this curriculum review cannot be considered comprehensive. Nevertheless, the committee believes nearly all major initiatives and many less-prominent ones are included, thus providing a reasonable overview of the current state of K–12 engineering education in the United States. We are aware that there are individual courses not part of larger curricula that address engineering concepts and skills to varying degrees. These courses, typically developed and taught by technology educators, are not treated in our analysis, however.

Selection Criteria

To bound the analysis, the committee developed criteria to guide the selection of curricula that reflect the committee's consensus that design is the distinguishing characteristic of engineering. To be included in the study, therefore, curricula had to meet the following specifications:

- The curriculum must engage students in the engineering-design process or require that students analyze past solutions to engineering-design problems.
- The curriculum must explore certain concepts (e.g., systems, constraints, analysis, modeling, optimization) that are central to engineering thinking.
- The curriculum must include meaningful instances of mathematics, science, and technology.
- The curriculum must present engineering as relevant to individuals, society at large, or both.
- The curriculum must be of sufficient scale, maturity, and rigor to justify the time and resources required to conduct an analysis.[2]

---

[2]Specifically, each initiative had to be designed to be used by people and organizations outside the group responsible for its initial development. It also had to include at least one salient piece that had undergone field testing and subsequent revision and was no longer identified as a "draft." Finally, during the development of the initiative, it had to include some form of review of the initial concept, pilot or field testing, iterations based on feedback, an external evaluation, or a combination of these.

Review Process

The review process was overseen by Prof. Welty with the help of graduate fellows at NCETE. The committee initially underestimated the challenges of conducting in-depth reviews, such as the unique content, point of view, and organization of each curriculum and, often, their large size, which required many more hours of analysis than had been originally budgeted. As a result, the plan for reviews had to be modified midway through the project. Ultimately, we conducted two types of reviews: in-depth content analyses and descriptive summaries.

In-depth reviews were conducted on curricula that (1) appeared to be widely used in schools, (2) appeared to have longevity, or (3) had other special characteristics that merited close examination. The in-depth reviews covered all three grade bands (Table 4-1).

TABLE 4-1 Curricula Included in the Study[a]

Title	Developer
Pre-K	
1. Young Scientist Series—Building Structures	Educational Development Center
Elementary School	
2. The Academy of Engineering (also for middle school and high school)	PCS Edventures!
3. Children Designing and Engineering	The College of New Jersey
4. City Technology/Stuff That Works	City College of New York
5. Engineering is Elementary	Boston Museum of Science
6. Full Option Science System	Lawrence Hall of Science
7. Insights (Structures Unit)	Education Development Center
8. Invention, Innovation, and Inquiry	International Technology Education Association
9. A World in Motion	Society for Automotive Engineers
Middle School	
10. Building Math	Boston Museum of Science
11. Design and Discovery	Intel Corporation
12. Gateway to Technology	Project Lead the Way
13. The Infinity Project (Middle School)	Southern Methodist University
14. Learning by Design	Georgia Institute of Technology
15 LEGO® Engineering	Tufts University
16. TECH-Know	Technology Student Association

continued

TABLE 4-1 Continued

Title	Developer
17. Technology Education: Learning by Design	Hofstra University
18. A World in Motion	Society for Automotive Engineers

High School

19. Designing for Tomorrow	Ford Partnership for Advanced Studies
20. DTEACh	University of Texas at Austin
21. Engineering: An Introduction for High School	Arizona State University/CK12 Foundation
22. Engineering by Design	International Technology Education Association
23. Engineering the Future	Boston Museum of Science
24. Engineering Your Future	Gomez, Oakes, Leone/Great Lakes Press
25. Engineers of the Future	(Curriculum based on design and technology courses developed in the United Kingdom)
26. Exploring Design and Engineering	The College of New Jersey
27. The Infinity Project	Southern Methodist University
28. INSPIRES	University of Maryland Baltimore County
29. Introduction to Engineering Design	Project Lead the Way
30. Material World Modules	Northwestern University
31. Principles of Engineering	New York State Dept. of Education/Hofstra
32. What is Engineering?	Johns Hopkins University
33. A World in Motion	Society of Automotive Engineers

Other

34. TeachEngineering.org	Five-university collaboration (part of the National Science Digital Library)

[a]Curricula shaded in gray received in-depth reviews.

Each in-depth review included a detailed inventory of the content of the curriculum that addressed concepts and skills related to engineering, technology, mathematics, and science. The research team also identified stated goals, pedagogical strategies, prominent activities, and treatment (if any) of content standards. If available, the team also documented how extensively the curriculum had been implemented and findings related to its impact. The authors of the curriculum were contacted, as needed, to provide background information, clarify details, or confirm researchers' findings. Detailed written reports for each in-depth review were read and discussed by the committee. Descriptive summaries were prepared for the other curricular documents.

The descriptive summaries can be found in Appendix B and the in-depth reviews in Appendix C, included on the CD in the back cover of the report.

CONCEPTUAL MODEL OF ENGINEERING CURRICULA

The search for K–12 engineering education curricula turned up a wide variety of products from many different sources. Each curriculum had its own personality, and no two were completely alike in mission, content, format, or pedagogy. To deal with this complexity, Prof. Welty developed a "beads-and-threads" model (Figure 4-1) that enabled us to analyze the curricula in a systematic way using a manageable set of key variables.

The beads represent the "packaging" in which the engineering content of the curriculum is delivered to students. Most of the curricular materials used interesting technologies to package content into manageable chunks. For example, "The Infinity Project" focused on technologies likely to be of interest to students, such as the Internet and cell phones, digital video and movie special effects, and electronic music. Other developers organized materials around hands-on learning activities familiar to and popular with many students and teachers. For example, the middle school program of "Project Lead the Way," *Gateway to Technology*, includes activities for making and testing CO_2-powered dragsters, magnetic-levitation vehicles, water-bottle rockets, model rockets, and Rube Goldberg devices.

The content of several curricula was organized around the design process. For example, the "Design and Discovery" curriculum, by Intel Corporation, features lessons and learning activities for identifying problems, gathering information, brainstorming solutions, drawing plans, making models, building prototypes, and making presentations. Prominent local or regional industries, such as Ocean Spray Cranberries, Inc., were used as examples in interdisciplinary thematic units in the "Children Designing and Engineering" materials, developed at The College of New Jersey. The material in one curriculum, "Engineering is Elementary," was organized around traditional fields of engineering (e.g., civil, environmental, electrical, agricultural, and mechanical engineering).

In the conceptual model, the threads, which run through the beads, represent the core concepts and basic skills a curriculum is designed to impart, independent of the particular packaging. Three threads, mathematics, science, and technology, represent domain knowledge in these subjects that is used in engineering design. A fourth thread represents the engineering design process. The design thread incorporates a number of spe-

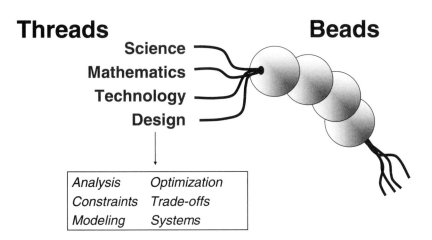

FIGURE 4-1 A beads-and-threads model of K–12 engineering curricula.

cific attributes of engineering design, such as analysis, constraints, modeling, optimization, and systems. The sections below describe of how these threads play out in the curricula.

The Mathematics Thread

We defined mathematics as patterns and relationships among quantities, numbers, and shapes. Specific branches of mathematics include arithmetic, geometry, algebra, trigonometry, and calculus. Our analysis suggests that mathematics is a thin thread running through the beads in most of the K–12 engineering curricula.[3] The thinness of the thread reflects the limited role of mathematics in the objectives, learning activities, and assessment tools of the curricula.

The mathematics used in the curricular materials reviewed by the committee involved mostly gathering, organizing, analyzing, interpreting, and presenting data. For example, in the "A World in Motion" curriculum, students build and test small vehicles (e.g., gliders, motorized cars, balloon-

---

[3]A separate analysis of curriculum, assessment, and professional development materials for three Project Lead the Way courses found explicit integration of mathematics "was apparent, but weakly so" (Prevost et al., 2009).

powered cars, wind-propelled skimmers). The testing involves measuring speed, distance, direction, and duration in conjunction with the systematic manipulation of key variables that affect vehicle performance (e.g., balloon inflation, sail size and shape, gear ratios, wing placement, nose weight). The data are organized into tables or graphs to see if they reveal patterns and relationships among the variables. The conclusions based on the data are then used to inform the design of subsequent vehicles.

Similar instances of gathering and using data for vehicle design were found in the *Models and Designs* unit in the "Full Option Science System" and the *Gateway to Technology* unit of "Project Lead the Way." Other materials engage students in counting and measuring, completing tables, drawing graphs, and making inferences, such as evaluating pump dispensers, conducting surveys, and testing materials.

Engineers often use mathematical equations and formulas to solve for unknowns. Young people can learn about the utility of this application of math in various ways, such as by calculating the amount of current in a circuit based on known values for voltage and resistance or determining the output force of a mechanism based on a given input force and a known gear ratio. Several instances of this kind were found in the "Engineering the Future" curriculum. In one activity, students calculate the weight of a proposed product (an organizer) based on three different materials prior to prototyping. Another requires that students calculate the mechanical advantage of a lever to determine how much force is required to test the strength of concrete.

However, most of the mathematics in the "Engineering the Future" curriculum is used to teach science concepts by illustrating relationships between variables, rather than to assist in solving design problems. For example, simple algebraic equations are used to represent the relationship between the cross-section of a pipe and its resistance to fluid flow, to calculate the output pressure of a hydraulic pump, and to determine the power produced by an electrical circuit. In these cases, mathematics is used to build domain knowledge in much the same way mathematics is used in science classes.

Several projects (e.g., "A World in Motion," "Building Math," *Gateway to Technology*, "Design and Discovery," "Designing for Tomorrow") introduce and require the application of basic geometry principles in conjunction with the development of technical drawings. For example, "Engineering the Future" includes lessons dealing with the concepts of scale and X, Y, and Z axes in the context of making orthographic, isometric, oblique, and perspective drawings. *Introduction to Engineering Design*, a unit in "Project

Lead the Way," addresses basic geometry in some detail in conjunction with the exploration of the modeling of solids using computer-aided design software. In this curriculum, students identify geometric shapes (e.g., ellipses, triangles, polygons), calculate surface area and volume, use Cartesian coordinates, and use addition and subtraction to create geometric shapes.

One strategy for increasing the mathematics content in some curricula was to include mathematical concepts in supplementary materials as enrichment activities. This approach might be characterized as a thread along the outside of the beads. The peripheral placement of the thread indicates that enrichment activities are optional, rather than integral to the unit but complement or extend instruction.

This approach was found in materials associated with projects in "Children Designing and Engineering," "Models and Designs," "Material World Modules," and "A World in Motion." For example, in an "extension activity" in "Models and Designs," students are asked to determine how long it took them to make an electrical device called a "hum dinger" (e.g., fastest time, slowest time, average time, total time). In an optional mathematics assignment in the *Gliders* unit of "A World in Motion," students determine the mathematical properties of different wing shapes (e.g., area, mean chord length, aspect ratio). At the high school level, the "Materials World Modules" invites teachers to engage students in using the formula for Young's modulus to determine the deflection of a fishing pole made out of drinking straws.

Mathematics is a dominant thread in "The Infinity Project" and "Building Math." The latter is designed to teach students how principles learned in middle school algebra can be used in the context of engineering challenges. For example, in the *Amazon Mission* unit, students design an insulated carrier for transporting malaria medicine, a filtration system for removing mercury from water, and an intervention plan for containing the spread of a flu virus. Like most of the other curricula reviewed, "Building Math" also requires that students collect data, make graphs, and interpret patterns, related to, for example, the insulating properties of materials; the flow of water through holes of different sizes; the deflection of materials based on their length, thickness, and shape; and the effect of angles on the speed of an object sliding down a string. A major goal of the "Building Math" curriculum is to teach students that engineers use mathematics to minimize guesswork in designing solutions to problems.

"The Infinity Project" is one of the few initiatives in which advanced algebra and trigonometry are introduced in engineering contexts. This curriculum encourages students to uncover, examine, and apply basic mathematical principles that underlie common digital communication and information technologies. Binary numbers, matrix operations, polynomials, and other forms of mathematics are presented as essential content for synthesizing music, compressing video, and encrypting data, and mathematical concepts and equations are presented as tools used by engineers to create or improve a given digital technology or system. In addition, the laboratory activities require that students use mathematics and mathematical reasoning to design, simulate, and explore digital communication and information technologies.

Engineers often develop mathematical models featuring the key variables in a process, system, or device. The variables include forces that act on a structure, the length of time required for a process, or the distance an object moves. The relationships between variables are represented by equations that can be used to test ideas, predict performance, and inform design decisions. However, our review of curricula did not find any projects or units in which students were instructed to develop and use mathematical models to assist them in designing solutions to problems.

The Science Thread

We defined "science" as the study of the natural world, including the laws of nature associated with physics, chemistry, and biology and the treatment or application of facts, principles, concepts, or conventions associated with these disciplines. Our analysis suggests that science is a moderately thick thread composed of two strands, (1) science concepts related to engineering topics and problems and (2) scientific modes of inquiry that build knowledge and inform design decisions.

The First Strand

The most common science topics in the first strand found in K–12 engineering curricula relate to materials, mechanisms, electricity, energy, and structures and typically involve concepts such as force, work, motion, torque, friction, voltage, current, and resistance. In the curricula, most of these concepts are presented in the form of encyclopedia-like explanations that are subsequently reinforced in laboratory activities.

"Engineering is Elementary" includes concepts related to water, sound, plants, and organisms. At the high school level, "Material World Modules" address natural degradation processes, bioluminescence and chemiluminescence, thermal and electrical conductivity, compressive and tensile forces on atoms, the relationship between molecular weight and viscosity, and the absorption and release of energy by molecular bonds.

The Second Strand

The second strand, scientific inquiry, is a major theme in several curricula, mostly to explore the interface between science and technology. For example, in the unit on *Composites* in "Material World Modules," students make and test foam beams laminated with varying amounts of paper to determine the strength and stiffness of composite materials. Similar experiments related to materials, structures, electrical circuits, and mechanisms are included in "A World in Motion," *Building Structures with Young Children*, a unit in the "Young Scientist Series," "Children Designing and Engineering," "City Technology," "Design and Discovery," "Engineering is Elementary," and "Engineering the Future." The results of these investigations are often applied in subsequent design activities.

Another way scientific inquiry is used in the curricula is related to the collection of data to inform engineering design decisions. For example, the second challenge in "A World in Motion" requires that students conduct investigations to determine the effect of different gear ratios on the speed and torque of a motorized toy vehicle. In some cases, scientific inquiry is used to discover, illuminate, or validate a law of nature, as might be done in a science classroom. For example, in *Gateway to Technology*, students experience Newton's Third Law by sitting on a scooter pointed in one direction, throwing a medicine ball in the opposite direction, and noting the direction and velocity of the scooter in relation to the direction and force used to throw the ball.

Many curricula engage students in scientific inquiry and inquiry-based learning in a symbiotic way. Several curricula introduce students to the basic principles of scientific investigation under the auspices of doing science. For example, "City Technology," "Material World Modules," and "A World in Motion" all stress the importance of manipulating one variable at a time while keeping the other variables constant. Learning activities in these programs include investigations that apply this principle in the contexts of packaging, structures, materials, and flight. In addition to teaching students about scientific investigations, they engage students in the generation, testing, revision, and validation of their ideas about protecting goods, making things stronger, and making models fly. In this sense, these curricula use scientific inquiry as a pedagogical strategy for building student knowledge of engineering design.

The Technology Thread

We defined "technology" as the study of the human-made world, specifically the knowledge, techniques, systems, and artifacts created by humans to satisfy their wants and needs. Our analysis suggests that technology in K–12 engineering curricula is a thick thread that often runs alongside the beads, rather than through them.

In most cases, the study of technology in K–12 curricula is used to build domain knowledge and develop a vocabulary for describing, discussing, and explaining a given technology. The emphasis on technical content is apparent in materials developed for "Project Lead the Way" and "The Infinity Project," both of which feature detailed treatments of specific technologies, such as digital electronics, digital communication and information technologies, automation, computer-aided design, and computer-aided manufacturing.

In some curricula, technologies are presented as concrete examples of scientific principles, especially in curricular materials that use engineering ideas or contexts to enrich science and mathematics learning. For example, a unit on composite materials in "Material World Modules" features discussions on technologies ranging from ancient bricks and clay pots to modern tennis rackets and automobile tires.

Some curricular materials are designed, at least in part, to improve technological literacy. For example, the central focus of the books written for "City Technology" is to "engage elementary children with the core ideas and processes of technology (or engineering, if you prefer)." The goal of "Engineering is Elementary" is to "tap into children's natural curiosity to promote [the] learning of engineering and technology concepts." "Exploring Design and Engineering" "help[s] youngsters discover the 'human-made world,' its design and development." "Engineering the Future" is intended to "help . . . high school students understand the ways in which they will engineer the world of the future—whether or not they pursue technical careers." "Invention, Innovation, and Inquiry" was created to "provide professional support for teachers interested in technological literacy in education."

The Design Thread

We defined "engineering design" as a purposeful, iterative process with an explicit goal governed by specifications and constraints. Our analysis suggests that design in K–12 engineering curricula is a strong, thick thread.

Virtually all of the curricula present a paradigm for designing solutions to problems that include a cyclical pattern of steps. Although the words and phrases used to describe the design process vary from one curriculum to another, the basic approaches are analogous. For example, on the elementary level in "A World in Motion," the design process is organized around themes, such as setting goals, building knowledge, designing, building, testing, and presenting. Similarly, in a project in the "Children Designing and Engineering"curriculum, student design teams are instructed to "know the problem, explore ideas, plan and develop, test, and present."

The patterns are similar in curricula on the middle school and high school levels. For example, in "The Infinity Project," the design process includes the following steps:

- Identify the problem or objective.
- Define goals and identify the constraints.
- Research and gather information.
- Create potential design solutions.
- Analyze the viability of solutions.
- Choose the most appropriate solution.
- Build and implement the design.
- Test and evaluate the design.
- Repeat all steps as necessary.

Analysis

We defined "analysis" as a systematic, detailed examination intended to (1) define or clarify problems, (2) inform design decisions, (3) predict or assess performance, (4) determine economic feasibility, (5) evaluate alternatives, or (6) investigate failures. Our analysis revealed isolated instances of the first three applications of analysis and even fewer instances of the next three. Overall, analysis was rarely an explicit, recurring theme in a design process. Thus in our model, analysis is characterized as a fragment of thread attached to the design thread.

In most of the curricula, the first step in a design activity is to pose a problem or define a task. For example, the first three challenges in "A World in Motion" are framed in the context of designing toy vehicles for a fictitious company. In all three, the challenge to elementary and middle school students is to analyze the contents of a letter or request for proposals to identify the problem and specifications of a successful solution. Similar problem scenarios appear in the *Building Structure with Young Children* unit in the "Young Scientists Series," "Building Math," "Children Designing and Engineering," "Engineering is Elementary," *Gateway to Technology*, and "Intro-duction to Engineering Design." All of these scenarios require basic reading comprehension but very little in the way of engineering analysis.

"City Technology" is one of the few curricula that engages students in a robust analysis to identify and define a problem. In one unit, *Designed Environments: Places, Practices, Plans*, elementary students monitor class-room procedures, identify problems, design and implement new procedures, evaluate the new procedures based on data, and use the findings of the evalu-ation to redesign the procedures as needed. A similar analysis is conducted to identify problems and develop design criteria to improve the configuration of the classroom.

Some of the materials engage students in a detailed analysis of everyday products using a process of reverse engineering. This is the predominant approach in materials in the "Design and Discovery," "City Technology," and "Designing for Tomorrow" curricula. For example, in a lesson in "Designing for Tomorrow," high school students analyze hand-powered can openers in terms of their primary and secondary functions, usability in different con-texts, aesthetic qualities, and salient features. In the "Design and Discovery" curriculum, students dissect digital and mechanical alarm clocks to iden-tify basic components and determine the relationships between form and function. The goals of these analyses are to understand how things work, to appreciate attention to detail, and to identify the strengths and shortcomings of given designs.

Engaging students in redesigning an existing product, rather than developing an original design, is also a major strategy in "City Technology," "Design and Discovery," and "Designing for Tomorrow." Students first analyze the performance of simple devices from a user's point of view. For example, in one "City Technology" unit, elementary students examine paper and plastic bags. In the "Design and Discovery" curriculum, middle school students study backpacks, toothpaste caps, and water bottles. In the "Design-ing for Tomorrow" curriculum, high school students investigate kitchen tools and training cups for toddlers. The analyses are then used to identify prob-lems and/or opportunities for improving the design of the objects.

Most of the curricula include steps for assessing the performance of the final design, a type of analysis that includes both qualitative and quantita-tive techniques to determine how well the final design solves the original design problem. Examples of this kind of analysis can be found in "A World in Motion," "City Technology," "Design and Discovery," "Engineering is Elementary," and "Material World Modules."

Prior to implementing a design, engineers make decisions based on evidence that a given design will work; they rarely rely on trial and error. The evidence is often based on an analysis that predicts performance for a given configuration of variables. In several curricular projects, students are required to manipulate and test variables in various configurations to discover the patterns that can inform or optimize a design. This form of analysis is found in "A World in Motion," "City Technology," "Engineering is Elementary," and "Material World Modules." One of the richest treatments of this kind of analysis was in the *Glider* unit in "A World in Motion."

In contrast to engineering practice, the curricula provide few opportunities for analysis of the economic feasibility of a given design or of the relative feasibility of competing designs. However, economic factors that can influence design are addressed in "Building Math," "Design and Discovery," and "Engineering the Future." For example, in "Building Math," middle school students perform a variety of mathematical computations to design optimal interventions to contain the spread of a virus in a village in the Amazon rain forest on a budget of $10,000. In the "Design and Discovery" curriculum, students compare the costs and trade-offs associated with using different materials for beverage containers (e.g., aluminum, glass, plastic). In an exercise in "Engineering the Future" students perform simple calculations to estimate the cost of materials and production, project a retail price, and estimate the competitiveness of a product in the marketplace.

Many curricular materials encourage students to evaluate alternative design options. These analyses typically involve unstructured discussion among students working in a group about the perceived merits of each option to arrive at a consensus about which option should be further developed. For example, in "Building Math," middle school students design an insulated container of medicine that will maintain a temperature of 59°F to 86°F for a minimum of two hours. After gathering data about the insulating properties of various materials, each member of the design team sketches an idea for a container, describes it to the other members of his or her team, and then, "as a group," they "decide on one 'best' solution." None of the curricula include procedures or expectations for conducting a formal analysis of alternative solutions, such as a trade-off matrix for making quantitative comparisons of the strengths and weaknesses of competing designs (Garmire, 2002).

Investigating failure as a specific line of analysis appears in only a few curriculum projects. A good example, from the *Packaging and Other Structures* unit in the "City Technology" curriculum, requires elementary students to fill paper and plastic bags with containers of water until they fail. The broken bags are then studied in detail to determine the nature and location of the failures, and the results of the analyses are used to develop proposals for improving the performance of the bags.

Constraints

We defined "constraints" as the physical, economical, legal, political, social, ethical, aesthetic, and time limitations inherent to or imposed upon the design of a solution to a technical problem. Our analysis suggests that constraints are a frayed fragment of thread running through some of the beads. The frayed nature of the thread indicates the ambiguities of the concept of constraints and the many ways it is interpreted.

In engineering practice, constraints frame the problem to be addressed by defining the salient conditions under which it must be solved. These conditions can include budget limitations, government regulations, patent laws, and project deadlines, among others. In the curricular initiatives that address this concept at all, constraints were presented as "things"—usually time, money, and materials—that limit the design process. However, "City Technology" includes rules and regulations among constraints on the design process. *Gateway to Technology* includes aesthetic considerations and the limits of human capabilities in its definition. A module on *Reverse Engineering* in the "Designing for Tomorrow" curriculum introduces the idea of constraints as limitations in materials properties and manufacturing processes.

Other factors in addition to constraints that can help define a problem include design specifications (i.e., features of the final solution, without which the design will not solve the problem) and design criteria (i.e., the parameters that must be tested to evaluate the suitability of final product). In the curricula, the terms constraints, specifications, and criteria are usually used interchangeably.

The confusion is most apparent in the learning activities. For example, in a design unit, *Power and Energy: The Whispers of the Willing Wind* from the "Invention, Innovation, and Inquiry" curriculum, constraints for the design and construction of a working model of a windmill are outlined. The "constraints" stipulate that the tower must be no more than 12 inches high, that the side of the base must not exceed 6 inches, and that the turbine must be less than 5 inches in diameter. The reasons for these specifications are not disclosed, but they do not appear to have a relationship to the problem being addressed or to reflect engineering design practices. Their purpose seems to be to direct student behavior to ensure success, limit the amount of resources for the project, and make the teacher's management of the activity easier. This treatment of "constraints" is typical of many curricula we reviewed.

Modeling

We defined "modeling" as any graphical, physical, or mathematical representation of the essential features of a system or process that facilitates engineering design. Our analysis suggests that modeling is represented by a thin, varicolored thread running through most of the beads. The colors represent the different uses of modeling in engineering activities and in the teaching and learning process.

Engineers use models to help visualize potential solutions to design problems and/or as an interim step in the development of working prototypes. In many of the curricula, modeling is defined the same way. For example, in one unit in the "Engineering is Elementary" curriculum, a model is defined as "a small representation, usually built to scale, that serves as a plan." In the "Design and Discovery" materials, a model is defined as a "visual representation of a total design (or some aspect of the design) that is nonfunctional." In those same materials, a prototype is defined as a "working model used to demonstrate and test some aspect of the design or the design as a whole." In the *Gateway to Technology* unit of the "Project Lead the Way" curriculum, modeling is defined as "the process of creating three-dimensional representations of design solutions." Computer modeling is defined as "the use of computer software applications that allows the user to visualize an idea in a three-dimensional format."

As these characterizations suggest, most of the curricula engage students in making things, usually from everyday materials, to help them visualize their designs and present them to others. For example, in *Building Structures with Young Children*, students construct towers and enclosures using building blocks. In "Children Designing and Engineering," elementary students construct models of lighthouses and habitats for koalas. "Engineering is Elementary" projects engage students building models of windmills, water filters, paper bridges, alarm systems, and other objects. In "A World in Motion" projects, students construct and test toy vehicles (e.g., motorized cars, gliders). *Gateway to Technology* involves modeling cranes, magnetic-levitation trains, automated devices, airfoils, and rockets. "Material World Modules" involve the construction and testing of models of concrete roofing tiles, composite fishing poles, and humidity sensors. In "The Infinity Project" activities, students use simulation software to model sound-effect generators, video systems, and computer networks.

In engineering practice, physical and mathematical models are also used to obtain data as a basis for making informed decisions during the design process. An example of this can be found in *Challenge Number 3*, a unit of "A World in Motion," in which eighth graders collect and graph data relating the center of gravity of a model glider to where the wing is placed and to the amount of weight in the nose of the glider. Based on the graphs, students predict optimal flight performance by determining the nose weight that locates the center of gravity closest to the centerline of the wing. Thus this curriculum has students use a physical model, the toy glider, to generate data for a simple mathematical model that represents the relationship between key variables that affect flight. The model is then used to adjust the design of the glider to achieve desired flight behavior. In a "Gateway to Technology" project, students use simulations posted on the Internet to model the effects of changing variables on the performance of rockets. Although the students interact with a mathematical model through the graphical model, the instructional materials do not call attention to the mathematical modeling.

For the most part, models are not used to represent key variables in the early stages of the design process but are presented as steps in the later stage of the design process for refining a relatively mature design solution to a problem. Thus models are used to visualize a design, take it to a higher level of refinement, and communicate its features to others. In many ways, this use of modeling is representative of industrial design rather than engineering design. Industrial design is the professional service of creating and developing concepts and specifications that optimize the function, value, and appearance of products and systems for the mutual benefit of both user and manufacturer (IDSA, 2008).

However, the reader should keep in mind that the pedagogical role of modeling is independent of its role in engineering design. Strategies to engage students in cooperative learning, such as Socratic dialogue, inquiry and design, and reflection and debriefing, typically involve making, testing, and presenting models. Modeling requires that students generate ideas, translate them into concrete form, and assess their validity. In the process, they must re-examine their assumptions, identify misconceptions and failures, refine their thinking, and develop and implement new ideas. Ultimately, models are embodiments of thought processes, insights, and discoveries in a form that communicates them to others.

Optimization

We defined "optimization" as the pursuit of the best possible solution to a technical problem in which trade-offs are necessary to balance competing or conflicting constraints. Our analysis suggests that optimization is a thin, translucent thread that is often obscured by other threads.

Most of the curricula do not explicitly address the concept of optimization. More often than not, optimization is embedded in lessons rather than called out as a key concept in objectives, laboratory activities, or assessment instruments. Optimization is most often embedded in the concepts of iteration (i.e., making incremental refinements during the development of a design) and redesign (i.e., analyzing an existing design to identify deficiencies or opportunities for improvement). In both cases, the goal is to improve a design. However, improving a design is not always synonymous with making trade-offs.

In most of the curricular materials, optimization is equated with "think harder" and "make it even better" as part of iteration and redesign. Improvements are often based on brainstorming rather than analysis, and little, if any, attention is paid to trade-offs. None of the curricula address the potential of using mathematics, especially for optimizing designs that are subject to economic constraints.

Trade-Offs

We defined "trade-offs" as decisions made to relinquish or reduce one attribute of a design in order to maximize another attribute. Our analysis suggests trade-offs are, like optimization, a thin, translucent thread.

The *Skimmer Design Challenge*, a unit in "A World in Motion," challenges students to make informed decisions about the size, shape, and position of a sail on a paper sled that skims across a tabletop pushed by a fan. In this exercise, students must make trade-offs among the size of the sail and the speed, distance, and stability of the sled. They must also determine the proper relationship between the weight of the sled and speed, distance, and stability. Finally, they must determine the orientation of the sail on the mast and the location of the mast on the hull.

In the *JetToy Design Challenge* in the same curriculum, students must determine the optimal relationship between inflation of a balloon, the diameter of the nozzle, and the duration and amount of propulsive force. They must also find the optimal weight of the vehicle in relation to its speed and the distance it can travel. This "tuning process" is informed by data describing how each variable (nozzle size, balloon inflation, vehicle weight, and friction) affects vehicle performance (speed and distance).

Another example of trade-offs is embedded in the *Models and Designs* unit in the "Full Option Science System" curriculum. In the course of making and modifying a rubber-band-powered cart, the students are likely to engage in optimization because each challenge inevitably introduces unanticipated cause-and-effect relationships. For example, the size of the wheels affects how far the go-cart travels. If the wheels are bigger, the amount of force required to propel the go-cart may have to be increased. If more tension is applied to the rubber bands to propel the cart a greater distance, traction is likely to become an issue. The increase in tension is also likely to exacerbate the problem of friction. Each of these adjustments introduces the need for trade-offs. However, neither the concept of trade-offs nor the concept of making trade-offs in the interest of optimization is addressed directly in the curricular materials.

The unit on *Inquiry: The Ultimate School Bag* in the "Invention, Innovation, and Inquiry" curriculum includes the redesign and improvement of a backpack for carrying schoolbooks and personal items. Redesign intrinsically involves optimization, although the concept is not addressed directly here, either.

Some references are made to the concept of trade-offs in the *Building Structure with Young Children* unit in the "Young Scientist Series." Teachers are encouraged to prepare and ask questions about the advantages and disadvantages of different design options. For example, in the context of building a model house, teachers are encouraged to entertain ideas such as making the roof out of a lightweight material that requires less support but is not likely to be strong. If children chose to make a strong roof, they might also have to build in more support.

In the "Gateway to Technology" curriculum, trade-off is defined as "an exchange of one thing in return for another, especially relinquishment of one benefit or advantage for another regarded as more desirable." Although several assignments involve identifying the positive and negative impacts of various technologies, students do not directly address the balance between competing factors. For example, from a student's point of view, the main goal of an activity involving the building a compressed-air dragster is to design the fastest vehicle possible. In this exercise, speed is a function of the vehicle's mass, assuming that the propulsive force remains constant. Even though mass also affects the stability of the vehicle, the instructional materials do not require that students directly confront the trade-offs between mass, stability, and speed.

Systems

We defined a "system" as any organized collection of discrete elements (e.g., parts, processes, people) designed to work together in interdependent ways to fulfill one or more functions. Our analysis suggests that systems and systems thinking are fragments of thread interwoven with other, more continuous threads. By this, we meant that systems and systems thinking do not permeate any single curriculum. Both concepts are used selectively, often to help students analyze or explain how a technology works.

The committee's definition of systems is consistent with the definitions in the curricular materials that addressed systems in some manner. For example, "City Technology" explained systems as "a collection of interconnected parts functioning together in a way that make the whole greater than the sum of its parts." In "Engineering is Elementary," a system is defined as "a group of parts that interact to create a product"; in one unit it is defined as "a group of steps that interact to create a process." In the *Models and Designs* unit of the "Full Option Science Systems" curriculum, system is defined as "two or more objects that work together in a meaningful way."

The concept of systems is treated most directly in curriculum initiatives focused on domain knowledge. In these cases, systems thinking is often an undercurrent in the storyline of how a specific technology works. The same is true in "The Infinity Project for Middle School," which stresses that most technological systems follow a pattern of inputs, processes, and outputs. The materials provide illustrations of sophisticated systems in the form of simple flow charts that accompany explanations in the text of how the systems work; the illustrations are also organizers for laboratory activities related to such things as digital music, digital images, and data encryption.

The "Engineering is Elementary" and "Design and Discovery" curricula introduce the idea that systems can be divided into subsystems and that subsystems can be further divided into components. In the "Design and Discovery" curriculum, a laboratory activity is focused on analyzing bicycles in terms of systems, subsystems, components, and parts.

Several curricula featured units or lessons in which reverse engineering is used to engage students in studying simple devices from a systems perspective. These activities involve identifying parts, determining their function, uncovering relationships, discovering how they work together as a system, and identifying ways to improve their performance. This kind of systems thinking was the part of lessons in the "City Technology," "Design and Discovery," and "Designing for Tomorrow" curricula that ultimately engaged students in exploring opportunities for redesigning products.

In rare cases, systems and systems thinking are used to analyze the reasons a technology fails. One example is a module on *Reverse Engineering* in "Designing for Tomorrow." This module begins with a case study of failures associated with the space shuttle *Challenger* disaster. Through a simplified form of reverse engineering, the students, in theory, discover that the accident was caused by systems breakdowns in the NASA organization, as well as a failure in the space shuttle technology.

Reasons for Teaching Engineering

We were not surprised that the reasons for including engineering content in these curricula are as diverse as the materials themselves. It is surprising, however, that teaching engineering is not always a first-order objective. In most cases, the primary reason for including engineering is to enhance the study of science, mathematics, or both subjects. For example, the "Building Math" program uses examples from engineering to demonstrate "how math is used as a discipline of study and a career path." The materials in "A World in Motion" facilitate an "exploration of physical science while addressing essential mathematic and scientific concepts and skills." The "Insights (Structures Unit)" provides "students with exciting science experiences that extend their natural fascination with the world and help them learn the science skills and concepts they will need in later schooling and in life." Engineering materials in "The Infinity Project" provide "an innovative approach to applying fundamental science and mathematics concepts to solving contemporary engineering problems."

The materials designed to intensify learning in math and science and other core-curriculum subjects capitalize on the hands-on, interdisciplinary nature of engineering. For example, the goal of "Children Designing and Engineering" is to "develop innovative and unique contextual learning units that challenge students to think, act and share." Similarly, "Designing for Tomorrow" provides high school students with "high-quality interdisciplinary learning experiences that challenge them academically and develop their problem-solving, critical-thinking, and communication skills."

Sometimes the goal of enhancing the study of science and mathematics is more explicit. For example, *Building Structures with Young Children* makes "science the work and play of exploring materials and phenomena, while providing opportunities for children to learn from that experience." The "Building Math" program uses the study of engineering to demonstrate "how math is used as a discipline of study and a career path . . . [through]

... standards-based activities that integrate algebra and engineering using a hands-on, problem-solving, and cooperative-learning approach." The materials in "A World in Motion" are designed to facilitate an "exploration of physical science while addressing essential mathematic and scientific concepts and skills." The "Insights," "Material World Modules," and "The Infinity Project are all designed to improve science education and show how fundamental science and mathematics concepts can be applied to solve engineering problems.

Other curricula include engineering content to address the technological literacy needs of students. In the "City Technology" curriculum, the central purpose is to "engage elementary children with the core ideas and processes of technology (or engineering, if you prefer)." The goal of the "Engineering is Elementary" curriculum is "to harness children's natural curiosity to promote [the] learning of engineering and technology concepts." Similarly, the primary objective of the "Exploring Design and Engineering" initiative is to "help youngsters discover the 'human-made world,' its design and development." The "Invention, Innovation, and Inquiry" curriculum was created to "provide professional support for teachers interested in technological literacy in education."

Another more general goal of engineering curricula is to improve students' critical thinking. For instance, the goal of one "Gateway to Technology" unit is "to show . . . students how technology is used in engineering to solve everyday problems." "Engineering is Elementary" develops "interesting problems and contexts and then invite[s] children to have fun as they use their knowledge of science and engineering to design, create, and improve solutions." "Design and Discovery" "engages students in hands-on engineering and design activities intended to foster knowledge, skill development, and problem solving in the areas of science and engineering."

Only a few curricula define their objective as teaching engineering concepts and skills to prepare young people for further education and, ultimately, engineering careers. The Ford Partnership for Advanced Studies curriculum, "Designing for Tomorrow," encourages and prepares students "for success in college and professional careers in fields such as business, engineering, and technology." One of the central goals of "The Infinity Project" is to "help close the gap between the number of engineering graduates we currently produce in the United States, and the large need for high-quality engineering graduates in the near future." And PLTW materials "provide students with the rigorous, relevant, reality-based knowledge necessary to pursue engineering or engineering technology programs in college."

In interviews, many curriculum developers stated that teaching engineering knowledge and skills was not their primary objective. Their reasons for including engineering content included reversing poor test scores in mathematics and science, engaging students in more scientific inquiry, and showing students that mathematics has practical applications.

Several developers deliberately passed up opportunities to address engineering concepts and skills to focus on other problems or opportunities. Some explained that their projects were required to include enough science content to be considered part of science education, and that too much emphasis on engineering design, constraints, modeling, optimization, and technological systems could tip the scale toward engineering. They had to maintain a delicate balance, they said, with a modest bias toward science, to improve the chances that their materials would be accepted and implemented. Other developers said their materials were required to have enough mathematics content to be approved for elective credit in mathematics. Finally, some noted that in the current No Child Left Behind climate of accountability for student achievement in core subjects, there isn't much room for engineering content in the school curriculum.

Another factor that had to be taken into consideration was the comfort level (sometimes the discomfort level) of elementary, science, and mathematics teachers. Elementary teachers, for example, must have a deep understanding of child development coupled with skills in teaching reading, writing, and mathematics, but teaching about engineering is largely uncharted territory. Consequently, in several curricula, materials were configured to capitalize on teachers' strengths and teaching responsibilities by introducing engineering in conjunction with language arts, social science, and natural science instruction.

At the secondary level, many teachers are specialists with teaching assignments based on their training in a given discipline. Because engineering is often outside their areas of expertise, teaching engineering concepts and skills would require learning new content to implement new lessons, learning activities, and assessment methods.

Diffusion of Materials

The curriculum materials reviewed for this study range in maturity from more than 20 years old to just off the press, and they range in sophistication from units of instruction that can be downloaded from the Internet at no cost to programs featuring courses of study that span multiple grade levels

and involve formal commitments, professional development, and investments of large amounts of time, resources, and human capital. Much of the
data on diffusion of these materials is limited to reports from curriculum
pilot- and field-test sites, records of sales or dissemination of materials, and
the number of teachers participating in professional development activities.
However, none of these is a valid indicator of how widely a curriculum is
used or whether it has been adopted by schools or school districts. Several
developers of curriculum initiatives have entered into formal partnerships
with participating schools and thus have mechanisms for structuring, supporting, monitoring, and assessing implementation. Table 4-2 summarizes
what we have learned about the dissemination of these curricula.

Implementation and Costs

The costs for curricular materials range from $1,100 for a series of eight
three-ring binders to no charge at all for a half-dozen large boxes of curricular
and laboratory materials. The contents range from major curricular initiatives
with no single objective to modest projects with more than 60. Some curricula
can be implemented with everyday items at very little cost; others require large
capital investments for specific, elaborate pieces of laboratory equipment.

Project Lead the Way (PLTW) has the most formal and systematic
implementation process. For a school district to obtain and implement the
curriculum, it must make a significant commitment to the program. This
involves first submitting an application to become a PLTW site, then signing
an agreement or memorandum of understanding that outlines the terms
for participating in the program. The school district agrees to initiate a
minimum of four courses within four years at the high school level, purchase
required software through PLTW Inc., serve as a model program for other
school districts, adhere to PLTW's implementation guidelines, ensure that
teachers and guidance counselors complete PLTW's three-phase training
program, establish an advisory committee or "Partnership Team," purchase
equipment and supplies approved by PLTW, and participate in PLTW's systematic evaluation process.

Under this agreement, participating high schools must be certified by
their second year in the program and recertified every five years thereafter.
Certification, which is a requirement for participating in the PLTW testing
process for earning college credit, includes a self-assessment, a site visit, and
a classroom and portfolio review. Schools must demonstrate that they meet
PLTW's quality standards for the professional development of teachers and

TABLE 4-2 Diffusion of Curriculum Materials (for selected programs)[a]

Curriculum	Diffusion	Comments
Project Lead the Way	The PLTW curriculum is used in all 50 states and the District of Columbia in 2,700 schools (2,000 high schools and 700 middle schools). About 600 high schools have completed PLTW's program certification process, and 34 middle schools have been recognized by PLTW's "School of Excellence Recognition Program." PLTW estimates that 225,000 students are currently enrolled in PLTW classes and that more than half a million students have taken at least one PLTW course.	
Materials World Modules	This curriculum has been used in about 500 schools in 48 states by some 35,000 middle shool and high school students. The U.S. Department of Defense uses MWM modules in 13 schools associated with military bases overseas. MWM materials are also used in 35 schools by 120 teachers and 1,200 students in seven cities and towns in Chihuahua, Mexico.	
Infinity Project	The high school course has been used in 350 schools in 37 states and some schools in several other countries. The materials are being used as an introductory engineering course at Southern Methodist University and DeVry University. A new set of middle school modules is being used in 20 schools in Texas.	The modules on robotics, sound engineering, rocketry, the engineering design process, and environmental engineering have been incorporated into mathematics, science, and technology classes.

Designing for Tomorrow	This curriculum, developed by Ford Partnership for Advanced Studies, is used in more than 300 schools in 26 states.	This program has been implemented in comprehensive high schools in urban and suburban settings, career and technical-education programs, freshman engineering courses at the college level, and historically black colleges and universities.
A World in Motion	This curriculum is used in all 50 states and in 10 Canadian provinces/territories. More than 65,000 AWIM kits have been shipped to more than 16,000 schools since 1990. The developer (Society of Automotive Engineers) estimates that more than 4 million students in North America have participated in AWIM activities (based on the assumption that the curriculum kits are reused an average of 2.6 times in classes averaging 24 students).	More than 17,000 engineers have volunteered in AWIM programs.
Engineering is Elementary	This curriculum is used in about 850 schools in 46 states and the District of Columbia. Based on sales figures and teacher participation in professional development workshops, the developer (Boston Museum of Sciences) estimates that about 15,000 elementary school teachers are using their materials. Approximately 1 million students have been exposed to the EiE curriculum since its inception.	Many fewer than 15,000 teachers—about 5,500—have received formal professional development to teach the EiE curriculum. The difference reflects estimates of teachers using the curriculum without having participated in an EiE PD program.

a These data are presented as reported by the curriculum developers.

counselors; the implementation of curriculum using required equipment and software; the formation and use of a Partnership Team, and more. The financial demands associated with implementing the program add up to tens of thousands of dollars over the course of several years, depending on course selection and existing laboratory resources. ("The Infinity Project" and "Designing for Tomorrow" have similar, but less formal requirements on a smaller scale.)

Several curriculum projects at the elementary and middle school levels offer resources to support implementation. The most comprehensive support is provided by "A World in Motion," "Children Designing and Engineering," "Engineering is Elementary," "Full Option Science System," and "Material World Modules." Implementation for these programs begins with the purchase of the instructional materials for the units of interest. These materials typically include teacher guides and, sometimes, videos or DVDs to support implementation. Student materials are presented as separate publications or reproducible master copies embedded in the teacher materials. "A World in Motion" requires participating teachers to involve a practicing engineer (a volunteer) in the delivery of the curriculum. The Society of Automotive Engineers (2009), which developed the curriculum, estimates that 17,000 engineer volunteers have participated since the program's inception.

Teacher materials typically cost $40 to $130, and classroom sets of student materials cost approximately $200. In addition, these programs offer kits of tools, supplies, and materials to facilitate the learning activities. The kits, which usually come in 4- or 5-cubic-foot containers that fit on a shelf or in a storage cabinet, cost $200 to $750, depending on the topic. "A World in Motion" provides the curriculum materials and kits free upon request, after a simple partnership agreement has been signed. Several projects also offer "refill packs" to replenish the consumables in the kits; these cost $20 to $250, depending on the nature of the materials.

Most of these curriculum projects maintain websites that can be used to purchase materials and kits, exchange ideas with other teachers, and tap into additional resources, such as lesson plans, links to relevant websites, a list of books and references, duplicate master copies, curriculum updates, safety data sheets, preparatory videos, discussion boards, additional learning activities, and professional develop materials.

Implementation of "City Technology," "Designing for Tomorrow," and "Invention, Innovation, and Inquiry" programs require purchasing one or more books and obtaining project-related tools and materials, which are available from popular suppliers, such as home stores, office supply stores, discount stores, and vendors for science and technology education. Several recommend that tools and simple mechanical devices for analysis activities be obtained from garage sales or flea markets. Although these programs do not require large capital investments, they do require significant amounts of a teacher's time and energy. The tools, materials, and supplies necessary to implement these curricula must be located, purchased, counted, labeled, organized, and stored. Despite their low cost and simplicity, assembling these materials for laboratory activities is a time-consuming process that requires thoughtful preparation to minimize problems during instruction.

Pedagogy

To get some sense of how the curricula envision the teaching of K–12 engineering, our analysis included an effort to tease out the materials' pedagogical approaches. Of course, neither we nor our consultant, Prof. Welty, was able to spend time observing teachers teach or attending teacher professional development sessions. Thus what we present below reflects pedagogy inferred from the written materials rather than a firsthand account of what actually is occurring in classrooms.

Most of the curricular materials the committee reviewed rely on time-honored teaching strategies for facilitating learning. These strategies include beginning lessons with an anticipator set, activating prior knowledge, presenting new concepts, using questions to promote thinking, providing firsthand experiences, posing authentic problems for students to solve, debriefing students about their experiences, and engaging students in reflection.

All of the curricula emphasize hands-on learning activities that involve the application of concepts and skills being investigated. Most learning activities also focus on solving real-world problems (i.e., problems in contexts beyond the school walls). For example, the "Young Scientist Series" includes a unit titled *Building Structures with Young Children,* in which students use building blocks to erect enclosures to provide shelter for a toy animal. In the "Engineering is Elementary" curriculum, students build and test models that address problems related to harnessing wind power, filtering water, moving materials in a factory, building a footbridge that spans a stream, and more. In the "Building Math" curriculum, middle school students address problems related to keeping medicine cool in a tropical environment, collecting rainwater in the absence of fresh water, and designing insulated clothing that allows for easy movement. In "The Infinity Project," high school students use simulation software to develop and test a system that counts the animals entering and leaving a given area in a refuge. Some curricula, however, do focus on problems that arise in schools. For example, the "City Technology" curriculum engages students in studying and addressing problems related to classroom interruptions, procedures, and layout.

In most of the curricula, teachers use a Socratic approach in conjunction with hands-on learning to actively engage students in learning. Questions are often used to reintroduce prior knowledge and experiences, solicit preconceptions that can be reassessed, launch and guide investigations, build and check for understanding, debrief students about their experiences, and facilitate reflection.

Some of the instructional materials are designed to follow a specific instructional model. For example, all of the units in "Engineering is Elementary" follow a sequence of lessons built on one another. The first lesson provides introductory activities that prepare students for the unit. The second lesson uses a fictional engineering story as an advanced organizer for the rest of the unit. The lesson that follows the reading is designed to orient students to a specific field of engineering (e.g., mechanical engineering, civil engineering, and agricultural engineering). The fourth lesson engages students in hands-on activities that address relationships between science, math, and engineering. All of the units end with engineering design problems consistent with the ones presented in the fictional account.

"Material World Modules" at the middle school and high school levels follow a similar pattern. Each module has three basic elements. Instruction begins with an introductory activity designed to stimulate interest in the topic at hand; this activity requires that students formulate a hypothesis about a cause-and-effect relationship. Second, students engage in four or five hands-on learning activities that introduce key principles, ideas, and methods related to the topic; these activities are framed in the context of one or more design problems. Third, students participate in a design project to develop a prototype product, applying the previously introduced science concepts and skills.

A prominent feature in several curricula is an emphasis on people and storytelling. For example, the "Design and Discovery" curriculum features stories about the history of the paper clip, the development of Kevlar™ by Stephanie Kwolek, the design of a bicycle for women by Georgina Terry, and so on. The textbook for "Engineering the Future" reads like transcripts of talks by a series of guest speakers who tell personal stories about their interest in engineering and their work. "Designing for Tomorrow," includes case studies of the development of the S.C. Johnson Administration Build designed by Frank Lloyd Wright, the space shuttle *Challenger* disaster, and so on. "Models and Design" includes stories about Henry Ford's Model T, the cartoonist Rube Goldberg, and NASA's use of simulation technology.

Evidence of Diversity

Gender and ethnicity play an important role in the development of a person's self-efficacy, identity, approach to learning, and career aspirations (see, for example, Bandura et al., 1999; Maple and Stage, 1991). As noted in Chapter 2, engineers in the United States have historically been predominantly white males; and women, African Americans, and Hispanics are still significantly underrepresented in the profession. Exposing students to images of engineers who look like them and to engineering-related activities that resonate with their personal and cultural experiences may not only improve their understanding of engineering but may also make engineering more appealing as a possible career (EWEP, 2005; NAE, 2008).

Efforts have been made in several curricula to portray engineering as an interesting and accessible career for individuals from diverse backgrounds. For example, the textbook for "Engineering the Future" features 31 stories (or chapters) written by engineers, designers, architects, technologists, and technicians, almost half of them women and a third members of minority groups. Similarly, "Design and Discovery" includes vignettes that enable students to "meet engineers," half of whom are women. Every unit in the "Engineering is Elementary" curriculum features a story about a child who uses basic engineering principles to solve a problem. The main characters in four of the nine units are female, and all of the characters come from different ethnic backgrounds. In addition, several stories include adult females as mentors and advisors.

In contrast, stories in the "Models and Designs" unit of the Full Option Science System curriculum are dominated by male inventors, scientists, engineers, and industrialists (e.g., Stephen Hawkings, Dick Covey, Rube Goldberg, Henry Ford, Eli Whitney). In addition, almost all of the photographs of people engaged in scientific and engineering pursuits are male.

Several curricula focus on topics and projects that research suggests are more likely to appeal to boys than to girls.[4] For example, "A World in Motion," "Gateway to Technology," and "Models and Designs" include

---

[4]There is an extensive literature on gender preferences related to technology and engineering (e.g., Weber and Custer, 2005) that suggests, among other things, that girls are more interested in socially relevant technologies, while boys are more interested in how technologies work, and that girls prefer collaborative work, while boys are more motivated by competition.

major learning activities that involve designing, making, and testing model structures or vehicles (e.g., towers, bridges, cars, rockets, airplanes, boats). Other curricula feature lessons and learning activities that capitalize on the knowledge and experience of both male and female students. For instance, in the "Design and Discovery" curriculum, engineering concepts and skills are applied to designing paper clips, improving the caps on tubes of toothpaste, and analyzing bicycle systems. "City Technology" introduces engineering principles in conjunction with testing the design and strength of shopping bags, designing packages, making maps, establishing classroom procedures, analyzing pump dispensers, and building shelves. In the interest of inclusiveness, the "Infinity Project" deliberately focuses on technologies likely to be found in a high school student's backpack (e.g., digital music players, digital camera, cell phone, etc.). Activities in "Designing for Tomorrow" involve the reverse engineering of simple kitchen devices and training cups for small children.

We were interested not just in the implicit or explicit messages conveyed through these curricula, but also in the diversity, or lack of diversity, in the student populations that used these materials. The committee was particularly interested in how many girls and underrepresented minorities had an opportunity to participate. Unfortunately, only one of the curriculum projects we reviewed in depth collects demographic data on student participation.

A program evaluation of PLTW for the 2006–2007 school year showed that the number of African American and Hispanic students in schools that used this curriculum was proportional to the populations in the states in which the schools were located (Walcerz, 2007). However, African American students were slightly underrepresented in PLTW classrooms compared with their numbers in most PLTW schools. Girls were dramatically underrepresented throughout the program; they comprised just 17 percent of all PLTW students that school year.

The number for girls cited above is similar to the percentage of entry-level female college engineering students (NSF, 2005) but is well below the proportion of females in the overall U.S. population, which is slightly more than 50 percent (U.S. Census Bureau, 2005). PTLW is taking steps to increase the program's appeal to women and underrepresented minorities, such as participating in an NSF-funded Engineering Equity Extension Service project[5] and partnering with the National Action Council for Minorities in

---

[5]For information about the project, see *http://www.nae.edu/nae/caseecomnew.nsf/weblinks/ NFOY-75WLB5?OpenDocument.*

Engineering to start 100 academies of engineering under the auspices of the National Academy Foundation.

PROFESSIONAL DEVELOPMENT

As yet, there is no clear description of the knowledge and skills needed to teach engineering to children. Nor do states license or certify teachers of engineering the way they do teachers of science, mathematics, technology, and other subjects. Most instructors who teach engineering in middle and high schools have a background in technology education;[6] a smaller number have backgrounds in science education; and an even smaller number have backgrounds in engineering. Because engineering is a developing area of content for K–12 schools, professional training for teachers in this field is still in its infancy.

Teacher "content knowledge" can be thought of as having three dimensions. First, teachers must know the subject they are teaching, in this case engineering, and its organizing principles. Second, they must have curricular knowledge, that is, an understanding of the materials and programs available to deliver the content. Third, they must have pedagogical content knowledge, which has been defined as "that special amalgam of content and pedagogy that is uniquely the province of teachers, their own special form of professional understanding" (Shulman, 1987).

Building on Shulman's work, Ball et al. (2008) have identified subcategories of subject-matter knowledge and pedagogical-content knowledge that reflect the specialized understanding unique to teaching. First, teachers must have "knowledge of content and students," which means they must be able to predict what students will find interesting, motivating, and difficult and to interpret students' incomplete thinking. Second, teachers need "knowledge of content and teaching," which implies they must be able to sequence particular content for instruction, for example, or evaluate the advantages and disadvantages of various representations of specific ideas.

To get a better understanding of how teachers acquire knowledge and skills to teach engineering to K–12 students, the committee looked into a number of programs that provide pre-service and in-service professional-development programs. Two committee workshops, in October 2007 and February 2008, were substantially devoted to this topic and are summarized in what follows.

---

[6]For example, 67 percent of teachers delivering the Project Lead the Way curriculum have a teaching certificate in technology education (R. Grimsely, PLTW, personal communication, June 16, 2009).

In-Service Programs

Most of the professional-development activities we identified are in-service rather than pre-service programs that provide supplemental education based on specific curricula for teachers already working in the classroom (Table 4-3). One advantage of well-designed, curriculum-focused professional development is that teachers come away with in-depth understanding of the purpose of the materials and first-hand experience with some of the difficulties and successes students might encounter. A disadvantage is that potentially useful and important content or pedagogical knowledge that is not included in the curriculum will be omitted.

Education researchers have identified common characteristics of effective in-service professional development programs for teachers. In a discussion of in-service programs for K–12 science educators, Mundry (2007) identified the following requirements:

- clear and challenging goals for student learning,
- adequate time, follow-up, and continuity,
- coherence with local policy, teachers' goals, and state standards,
- active, research-based learning,
- critical reflection on practice to support a collaborative professional culture, and
- evaluation of teacher and student gains resulting from the professional development.

Mundry notes that professional development sustained over time is more likely to be coherent, have a clear focus, and support active learning than "one-shot" workshops and other limited interventions. Opinions differ on the necessary number of hours, but most experts agree that single experiences are not likely to support teacher competence or confidence (e.g., NCES, 2001).

Research at the NSF-funded National Center for Engineering and Technology Education (NCETE) has focused on identifying the requirements for preparing technology educators to teach engineering. One small, qualitative study identified about a dozen interrelated factors that are important to preparing teachers to introduce engineering design concepts into the K–12 classroom (Asunda and Hill, 2007). A member of the NCETE leadership team told us that professional development planned jointly by engineering and technology education faculty resulted in better outcomes for teachers than professional development planned by either one alone (Hailey et al., 2008).

NCETE also conducted an observational analysis of five professional-development programs, including three (Engineering the Future, Project Lead the Way, The Infinity Project) whose curricula we reviewed (Daugherty and Custer, unpublished). Among the study's findings were that (1) most of the programs were run by the curriculum developers, who rarely had a background in teacher professional development; (2) science, technology, and mathematics teachers have different professional development needs; and (3) hands-on activities were a very common element in the programs, but little instructional time was devoted to metacognitive reflection about either the teacher or student learning involved.

Although not all in-service programs for K–12 engineering teachers have all of the required features listed above, professional-development programs can have a dramatic impact on how widely the curriculum is used. A good example is "A World in Motion," developed by SAE International, which was launched in 1990; the first professional-development component was not added until 2005. Matthew M. Miller, manager of SAE's K–12 education programs, told us at the February 2008 workshop that the use of the curriculum doubled and the number of new classroom volunteers increased almost tenfold once the professional-development program was implemented.

Project Lead the Way (PLTW) has a very organized professional-development effort, which may, in part, explain its rapid growth. PTLW conducts two-week summer institutes, during which prospective PLTW teachers are immersed in the course they plan to teach, including completing all of the hands-on projects. PLTW has agreements with 36 universities to supply engineering faculty who team teach with PLTW master teachers to run the program. According to PLTW, about 7,200 teachers have taken part in the summer training sessions. Teachers who complete the course receive a certificate allowing them to teach the course. Ongoing assistance is available from PLTW through an online Virtual Academy (*www.pltw.org/moodle*).

Other in-service programs run the gamut from one-week summer institutes (e.g., "The Infinity Project") to self-paced coaching provided on a DVD included in the curricular materials for "Building Math"(Table 4-2).

Pre-Service Initiatives

Pre-service training of teachers has some distinct advantages over in-service training. The biggest difference is that teachers have longer exposure

TABLE 4-3 In-Service Professional Development Programs for Teachers of K–12 Engineering

Program/Curriculum	Scope of Training	Target Audience	Training Force	Number of Teachers Reached	Notes
Project Lead the Way	All teachers are required to complete a two-week summer institute	Middle school and high school teachers, mostly technology educators	160 master teachers; 120 affiliate professors	7,200 teachers and 5,000 guidance counselors have been trained in all 50 states	Online Virtual Academy provides ongoing support
Engineering is Elementary	Optional training that varies from two-hour workshops to two-week sessions and semester-long programs	Elementary generalists	Professional development staff at the Boston Museum of Science	5,100 teachers in 28 states and the District of Columbia (as of June 2009)	A memorandum of understanding between the Boston Museum of Science and Valley City State University allows Engineering the Future to be used in VCSU online pre-service technology teacher education

continued

City Technology	Optional training—a one-hour introductory workshop followed by 30-minute workshops on particular units	Elementary generalists, special education teachers, elementary science specialists, secondary math and science teachers, museum educators, after-school program staff, and parents	Authors of the curriculum (City College of New York)	Several thousand teachers and informal educators in about 20 states
Children Designing and Engineering	Required: 30-hour graduate course	Elementary teachers	In Virginia, the training is conducted through George Mason University	1,300 teachers since 1999 in six states, the bulk of whom (800) are participants in Virginia's Children Engineering Program

TABLE 4-3 Continued

Program/Curriculum	Scope of Training	Target Audience	Training Force	Number of Teachers Reached	Notes
Engineering Our Future New Jersey (based on the following curricula: Engineering is Elementary, World in Motion, Engineering the Future)	One- or two-day workshops	Elementary, middle, and high school teachers	Staff at the Stevens Institute of Technology	35 teachers in New Jersey	Planned expansion will reach 2,000 teachers
The Infinity Project	Required one-week summer institute	High school teachers		500 teachers in grades 9–12	Training includes an online discussion board for teachers
Material World Modules	Optional workshops that vary in length	High school teachers			
Engineers of the Future (training based on several different curricula)	Summer institute	High school and middle school technology educators, and elementary teachers		Nearly 700 trained, the majority using the Engineering is Elementary curriculum	Supported by $1.7 million grant from the New York State Education Department

Engineering the Future	Half-day, full-day, and multiple-day sessions in the Boston area and 20 to 40 hour moderated online professional development course	High school teachers		A memorandum of understanding between the Boston Museum of Science and Valley City State University allows Engineering the Future to be used in VCSU online pre-service technology teacher education
Building Math	Training DVD supplied with curriculum materials			
INSPIRES	Two-day workshops	Technology teachers in Maryland		
A World in Motion	One-day workshop	Elementary, middle, and high school teachers	65,000 kits shipped since 1990 (not clear how many teachers trained)	Teachers must agree to work with an engineer who volunteers in the classroom

times to concepts and skills, including math and science skills, necessary to teach engineering. The committee was able to identify just three programs that offer pre-service education to prepare individuals to teach engineering in K–12 classrooms.

Leveraging its model of in-service professional development, PLTW is working toward "infusing" its K–12 curriculum into teacher-preparation programs at nine university partners that already serve as sites for PLTW in-service summer institutes. The infusion of PLTW coursework into existing teacher-preparation curricula must be carefully planned to ensure that it aligns with state licensing requirements (Rogers, 2008). As of early 2009, fewer than 10 teachers had graduated from the new PLTW-infused programs (Richard Grimsley, Project Lead the Way, personal communication, January 5, 2009).

In contrast to PLTW's curriculum-focused approach, in 2002 the College of New Jersey (TCNJ) initiated the Math/Science/Technology (M/S/T) interdisciplinary degree program for aspiring elementary school teachers that requires coursework in all four STEM subjects. The program is a collaborative effort by the schools of engineering, education, and science administered by the Department of Technological Studies in the School of Engineering. The 32-credit program (Box 4-1) now has more than 150 graduates and current majors and is one of the fastest growing majors at TCNJ (Karsniz et al., 2007).

Students who matriculate from the M/S/T program appear to have an appropriate background for teaching engineering. Unfortunately, TCNJ does not track the employment histories of its M/S/T graduates who, according to school officials, are in great demand as science and math teachers (John Karsnitz, TCNJ, personal communication, September 20, 2007). So, at least for now, the TCNJ program does not appear to be contributing to the national supply of engineering teachers.

In 2006, Colorado State University in Fort Collins established a joint major in engineering and education. To the committee's knowledge, this is the only program of its kind in the United States. Students in the program must complete general-education requirements, core engineering requirements, engineering-school electives, and professional education requirements. In the first year, 11 students (70 percent of them female) were enrolled in the program. Graduates will receive an engineering degree and a teaching license (DeMiranda, 2008).

Other models of pre-service engineering education for teachers exist. For example, at Boise State University, students majoring in elementary

BOX 4-1
The M/S/T Major at TCNJ

The M/S/T program provides 10 units of "liberal learning" courses, such as creative design, calculus A, and a natural science. The 12-unit M/S/T academic major has an eight-unit core, which includes courses in multimedia design, structures and mechanics, two additional science courses, and one additional math course (either calculus B or engineering math). Areas of specialization must include four additional units in technology/pre-engineering, mathematics, biology, chemistry, or physics. Specialization is the equivalent of a minor in one of the disciplines and may require that specific courses be included in the core requirements. M/S/T students who major in education must also complete 10 units of professional education courses. Such students meet New Jersey's certification requirements for highly qualified teachers. In addition to primary K–5 certification, M/S/T majors can apply for an endorsement for teaching middle school mathematics or science, if they have completed 15 credits of coursework in the discipline and have passed the appropriate PRAXIS test. They may also receive technology-education certification, if they have completed at least 30 specified credits and passed the appropriate PRAXIS test.

SOURCE: Karsnitz, 2007.

education may enroll in an introductory engineering course offered by the College of Engineering. The course is supplemented by a seminar led by education faculty that considers how engineering projects can be used in the K–12 classroom to meet state teaching standards for math and science as well as reading, writing, and other non-technical subjects (Miller and Smith, 2006).

Through a collaboration with TERC (*www.terc.edu*), Lesley University and Walden University offer an online course, Engineering: From Science to Design, for education master's degree candidates. The course includes independent, hands-on work and group feedback and discussion in facilitated online forums (Sara Lacy, TERC, May 15, 2008).

At least two states have started programs to provide new K–12 teachers with STEM credentials. In California, the University of California, California State University, and state and industry leaders initiated Cal Teach (*http://*

calteach.berkeley.edu/), which recruits students majoring in math, science, and engineering to become K–12 teachers. The goal of Cal Teach is to have 1,000 teachers in place by 2010. A similar effort, UTeach (*http://uteach.utexas. edu/*), was launched in 1997 at the University of Texas at Austin. As of 2007, the program had graduated a total of 480 STEM students, 41 of whom had degrees in engineering in addition to teaching certificates (376 had degrees in the natural sciences) (University of Texas at Austin, 2007). Under the auspices of the National Math and Science Initiative, UTeach has been expanded to 13 additional colleges and universities across the United States.

OBSTACLES FACING PROFESSIONAL DEVELOPMENT PROGRAMS

Based on information provided during the two preliminary workshops and in the research literature, several barriers to professional development programs must be overcome in preparing educators to teach engineering in K–12 classrooms. For instance, teachers who are not familiar with engineering may feel anxious and apprehensive, which can inhibit the effectiveness of professional development programs. Christine Cunningham, the director of professional development for "Engineering is Elementary," described the problem (Cunningham, 2007):

> If most elementary teachers are afraid of teaching science, the notion of teaching engineering is often accompanied by terror. Much of the point of our professional development is to defuse their feelings of ineptitude through engagement.

Similarly, teachers who do not have adequate knowledge of science and, especially, mathematics sometimes have difficulty understanding the material. In addition, some have little, if any, desire to take part in training activities (Diefes-Dux and Duncan, 2007). Reportedly, some teachers also are uncomfortable with the open-endedness of engineering design. "A major challenge in PD for K–12 engineering is to undo the mindset that sees answers as right or wrong, and as complete or incomplete," note Benenson and Neujahr (2007). In a survey of 44 technology teacher-education programs, only 17 percent had completed the mathematics and science courses that would qualify them to teach PLTW courses (McAlister, 2005). McAlister also found that, when a group of 43 technology teachers was presented with two fairly simple problems involving structural load, half of them indicated that they would require additional training before they could teach those problems to students. Only one was able to identify the correct formula for solving one of the problems.

INSPIRES (INcreasing Student Participation, Interest and Recruitment in Engineering & Science), a small-scale professional-development program at the University of Maryland, Baltimore County, relies on engineering faculty to lead some activities. The program leaders note, however, that large numbers of engineering faculty might not be able to participate in such ventures because of their workloads and because of typical university reward structures (Ross and Bayles, 2007). More systemic problems, such as a lack of understanding of program content and learning progressions, may also interfere with the effectiveness of professional-development programs for K–12 teachers of engineering (Hailey et al., 2008).

REFERENCES

Asunda, P. and R. Hill. 2007. Critical features of engineering design in technology education. Journal of Industrial Teacher Education 44(1): 25–48.

Ball, D.L., M.H. Thames, and G. Phelps. 2008. Content Knowledge for Teaching: What Makes It Special? Presented at the National Symposium on Professional Development for Engineering and Technology Education, Dallas, Texas, February 11–13, 2007. Available online at *www.conferences.ilstu.edu/NSA/homepage.html* (accessed May 23, 2008).

Bandura, A., W.H. Freeman, and R. Lightsey. 1999. Self-efficacy: The exercise of control. Journal of Cognitive Psychotherapy 13(2): 158–166.

Benenson, G., and J. L. Neujahr. 2007. Unraveling a Knotty Design Challenge: PD for Engineering K–12. Paper presented at a workshop of the NAE/NRC Committee on K–12 Engineering Education, Washington, D.C., October 22, 2007. Unpublished.

Cunningham, C. 2007. Elementary Teacher Professional Development in Engineering: Lessons Learned from Engineering is Elementary. Paper resented at a workshop of the NAE/NRC Committee on Engineering Education, Washington, D.C., October 22, 2007. Unpublished.

Daugherty, J.L., and R.L. Custer. Unpublished. Engineering-Oriented Professional Development for Secondary Level Teachers: A Multiple Case Study Analysis. Unpublished doctoral dissertation, University of Illinois, Champaign-Urbana.

DeMiranda, M. 2008. K–12 Engineering Education Workshop. Paper presented at a workshop of the NAE/NRC Committee on K–12 Engineering Education, Washington, D.C., February 25, 2008. Unpublished.

Diefes-Dux, H and D. Duncan. 2007. Adapting Engineering is Elementary Professional Development to Encourage Open-Ended Mathematical Modeling. Paper presented at a workshop of the NAE/NRC Committee on K–12 Engineering Education, Washington, D.C., October 22, 2007. Unpublished.

EWEP (Extraordinary Women Engineers Project). 2005. Extraordinary Women Engineers—Final Report, April 2005. Available online at *http://www.eweek.org/site/news/ Eweek/EWE_Needs_Asses.pdf* (accessed December 15, 2008).

Garmire, E. 2002. The engineering design method. The Technology Teacher 62(6): 22–28.

Hailey C., D. Householder, and K. Becker. 2008. Observations about Professional Development. Paper presented at a workshop of the NAE/NRC Committee on K–12 Engineering Education, Washington, D.C., February 25, 2008. Unpublished.

IDSA (Industrial Design Society of America). 2008. ID defined. Available online at *http:// www.idsa.org/absolutenm/templates/?a=89&z=23* (accessed December 15, 2008).

Karsnitz, J., S. O'Brien, and S. Sherman. 2007. M/S/T at TCNJ. Paper presented at a workshop of the NAE/NRC Committee on K–12 Engineering, Washington, D.C., October 22, 2007. Unpublished.

Maple, S.A., and F.K. Stage. 1991. Influences on the choice of math/science major by gender and ethnicity. American Educational Research Journal 28(1): 37-60.

McAlister, B. 2005. Are Technology Education Teachers Prepared to Teach Engineering Design and Analytical Methods? Paper presented at the International Technology Education Association Conference, Session IV: Technology Education and Engineering, Kansas City, Missouri, April 4, 2005.

Melchior, A., F. Cohen, T. Cutter, and T. Leavitt. 2005. More Than Robots: An Evaluation of the FIRST Robotics Competition—Participant and Institutional Impacts. Center for Youth and Communities, Heller School for Social Policy and Management, Brandeis University. Available online at *http://www.usfirst.org/uploadedFiles/Who/Impact/ Brandeis_Studies/FRC_eval_finalrpt.pdf* (accessed August 1, 2008).

Miller, R., and E.B. Smith. 2006. Education by Design: Connecting Engineering and Elementary Education. Paper published as part of the proceedings from The Fourth Annual Hawaii International Conference on Education, January 6–9, 2006, Honolulu. Available online at *http://coen.boisestate.edu/EBarneySmith/Papers/Hawaii_2006.pdf* (accessed January 6, 2009).

Mundry, S. 2007. Professional Development in Science Education: What Works? Presented at the National Symposium on Professional Development for Engineering and Technology Education, Dallas, Texas, February 11–13, 2007. Available online at *www. conferences.ilstu.edu/NSA/homepage.html* (accessed May 23, 2008).

NAE (National Academy of Engineering). 2008. Changing the Conversation: Messages for Improving Public Understanding of Engineering. Committee on Public Understanding of Engineering Messages. Washington, D.C.: The National Academies Press.

NCES (National Center for Education Statistics). 2001. Teacher Preparation and Professional Development: 2000. Available online at *http://nces.ed.gov/surveys/frss/ publications/2001088* (accessed May 23, 2008).

NSF (National Science Foundation). 2005. Science and Engineering Degrees: 1966–2004. Table 47, Engineering degrees awarded, by degree level and sex of recipient: 1996–2004. Available online at *http://www.nsf.gov/statistics/nsf07307/pdf/tab47.pdf* (accessed August 11, 2008).

Prevost, A., M. Nathan, B. Stein, N. Tran, and A. Phelps. 2009. The Integration of mathematics in pre-college engineering: The search for explicit connections. Proceedings of the 2009 American Society for Engineering Education Annual Conference, Austin, Texas, June 14–17, 2009. Available online at *http://sca.asee.org/paper/conference/paperview.cfm?id=11744.*

Rogers, G. 2008. Pre-Service Professional Development for Middle School and High School Teacher of Engineering. Paper presented at a workshop of the NAE/NRC Committee on K–12 Engineering Education, Washington, D.C., February 25, 2008. Unpublished.

Ross, J. M. and T. M. Bayles. 2007. Implementing the INSPIRES Curriculum: The Role of Professional Development. Professional Development of Engineering and Technology: A National Symposium Proceedings. Illinois State University.

SAE (Society of Automotive Engineers). 2009. A World in Motion. Facts. Available online at *http://www.sae.org/exdomains/awim/aboutus/facts.htm* (accessed April 2, 2009).

Shulman, L.S. 1987. Knowledge and teaching: foundations of the new reform. Harvard Educational Review 57(1): 1–22.

TexPREP (Texas Prefreshman Engineering Program). 2003. Program Results—2003 PREP Fact Sheet. Available online at *http://www.prep-usa.org/portal/texprep/generaldetail. asp?ID=107* (accessed January 30, 2009).

University of Texas at Austin. 2007. UTeach, Special Addition, 10th Anniversary Report. Available online at *https://uteach.utexas.edu/download.cfm?DownloadFile=1DE15E0B-9A97-2621-857E36A4D0DFC1EA* (accessed August 13, 2008).

U.S. Census Bureau. 2005. Population Profile of the United States: Dynamic Version. Race and Hispanic Origin in 2005. Available online at *http://www.census.gov/population/ pop-profile/dynamic/RACEHO.pdf* (accessed January 5, 2009).

Walcerz, D. 2007. Report on the Third Year of Implementation of the TrueOutcomes Assessment System for Project Lead the Way. Available online at *http://www.pltw. org/pdfs/AnnualReport-2007-Public-Release.pdf* (accessed August 11, 2008).

Weber, K., and R. Custer. 2005. Gender-based Preferences Toward Technology Education Content, Activities, and Instructional Methods. Available online at *http://scholar.lib. vt.edu/ejournals/JTE/v16n2/weber.html* (accessed December 15, 2008).

Annex

PRE-UNIVERSITY ENGINEERING EDUCATION IN OTHER COUNTRIES[1]

Given the universality of science and technology, the committee felt it appropriate to look into how other nations encourage engineering thinking in pre-college students. However, because of budget and time constraints,

---

[1]This appendix is adapted from a paper written for the committee by Dr. Marc J. DeVries, Eindhoven University, The Netherlands, based on research conducted by Carolyn Williams, a 2007 Christine Mirzayan Science and Technology Policy Graduate Fellow at the National Academy of Engineering.

BOX 4A-1
Selected Countries with
Pre-College Engineering Programs

England/Wales: General Certificate of Education, Engineering
Australia (New South Wales): Higher School Certificate in Engineering
    Studies
Israel: ORT Innovative Science Track in Engineering Sciences
Germany: Junior-Ingenieur-Akademie (Academy for Junior Engineers)
South Africa: Further Education and Training in Electrical Technology
France: Baccalauréat General, Série Scientifique Sciences de
    l'Ingénieur; Baccalauréat Technologique, Série Sciences et
    Technologies Industrielles
Netherlands: Technasium, Research and Design
Colombia: Pequeños Cientificos (Little Scientists)

the committee did not pursue this research and analysis with the same intensity as it had for U.S. efforts. In addition, because of differences in the organization and operation of educational systems in other countries, it was difficult to draw direct comparisons with the situation in the United States. Materials in languages other than English further complicated the analysis, and curricular documents were not always available. In many cases, the curriculum content had to be inferred from a review of sample assessment items. Despite these limitations, the committee was able to identify several important principles.

The committee used a variety of information-gathering techniques, including online searching; telephone interviews; and e-mail requests to professional, corporate, academic, government, and education groups and individuals. Eight programs or projects in eight countries were identified (Box 4A-1), all but one of which (Pequenos Cientificos) were for senior secondary-level students (i.e., grades 10–12). In all probability, these eight initiatives represent only a fraction of these kinds of activities around the world.

The Goals of Pre-College Engineering Education

Two primary purposes were identified for exposing pre-college students to the study of engineering—"mainline" goals (i.e., general education) and "pipeline" goals (i.e., preparation for engineering careers). The majority of programs were in the "pipeline" category. In France, for example, preparation for the academic study of engineering is preceded by a competitive selection process at the pre-college level with the goal of identifying the very best students for continued engineering education. Based on sample exam questions for prospective engineers in Israel, the committee inferred that the emphasis of the ORT engineering sciences program is on preparing students for post-secondary engineering education, rather than on expanding their general education.

Programs in some countries seem to serve both purposes. For example, in England and Wales, the General Certificate of Education, Engineering, has some features in common with the U.K.'s Design and Technology Curriculum, which is designed primarily for general education purposes. At the same time, to receive a General Certificate, students must master a good deal of specific knowledge in engineering domains, thus preparing them for further engineering studies.

Treatment of Engineering Concepts and Domains

The focus on core engineering concepts in international programs varies greatly. The U.K. materials, for example, treat the concepts of systems and control in some detail, while other concepts, such as optimization, are largely absent. The design process is evident, consistent with the influence of the design and technology paradigm. In the Israeli programs, the curriculum and sample exam questions focus on the concept of systems; related ideas, such as control, feedback, and parameters, are also treated in some detail. By contrast, the South African assessment materials have few explicit references to general engineering concepts; instead, they focus on ideas specific to electrical engineering, most of which are scientific rather than engineering concepts (e.g., voltage, current). Exam questions in the French Série de Sciences de l'Ingénieur explicitly refer to engineering concepts, including system analysis, requirements, and optimization.

Overall, the international pre-college engineering programs include a wide range of engineering domains. The U.K. General Certificate of Education, Engineering, reflects the compulsory pre-college design and technology curriculum; thus it explores the traditional disciplines of electrical and mechanical engineering, as well as less traditional areas, such as food technology and biotechnology. The exam questions for Australia's Higher School Certificate in Engineering (HSCE) Studies address issues in telecommunications, transportation, civil engineering, aeronautics, and electronics; the exam also includes a biotechnology module.

In addition to two engineering sciences courses, students pursuing the Israeli ORT curriculum pick a specialization course from one of the following areas: motion systems, biomedical engineering, robotic systems, artificial intelligence, or aerospace engineering. The content of the sample exam for the ORT curriculum, however, appears to focus on computer programming. The French baccalauréat programs cover a variety of engineering domains spread over different 'séries' in the 'bac'. In the engineering series, the focus is on electrical engineering, mechanical engineering, and information science.

Treatment of Science, Technology, and Mathematics

International pre-college engineering initiatives appear to face same challenges as U.S. initiatives, such as teaching students to use math and science to solve or optimize authentic design challenges. In the French curriculum, math and science are integrated, but at a high level of difficulty. Exam questions for the 'Séries de Sciences de l'Ingénieur' describe a technical device that has to meet a given set of requirements, and students are asked to calculate certain variables based on their knowledge of science.

In most instances, however, math and science concepts are treated as separate from technological content. For example, sample assessment items for the Australian HSCE require the application of scientific knowledge and mathematical skills to problems specific to technical devices. Either the technical device is used as a context for asking a question that requires knowledge of science and/or math, or the question is about technology and does not require science or math.

The same separation was evident in exam questions and practical assessment tasks in the South African curriculum. The exam includes questions about abstract situations (e.g., diagrams representing electrical and logical circuits) in which students must make calculations and apply their knowledge of the laws of electricity. The practical assignments are design challenges, but they do not encourage the application of science or math to develop or optimize the design solution.

5

Teaching and Learning Core Engineering Concepts and Skills in Grades K–12

Curriculum initiatives in the K–12 setting that include engineering content and courses (primarily in the context of science) have raised questions about teaching engineering to pre-college students, and especially pre-high school students. In response to these concerns, studies have been undertaken on a number of issues, including determining whether K–12 students, who have limited knowledge of basic mathematical concepts, can learn engineering concepts and skills and whether "positioning engineering design primarily as a tool for science learning runs the risk of misrepresenting . . . engineering as *applied science*" (Leonard, 2004).

Although engineering is rarely taught explicitly in K–12 classrooms in the United States, a growing body of evidence on the teaching and learning of core engineering concepts and skills suggests that elementary students are capable of engaging with this material. The committee commissioned two reviews (Silk and Schunn [2008] and Petrosino, Svihla, and Brophy [2008]) of this growing body of evidence. The relative paucity of research on K–12 students' understanding of engineering concepts and skills places significant limitations on what can be currently claimed. The following review presents our current best understanding of learning trends in this domain, including the challenges inherent in designing engineering instruction for K–12 students.

Deciding on the scope and sequence of teaching engineering-related concepts and skills can be difficult, sometimes even controversial. Like scientists, engineers in different areas of engineering require different sets of specific skills and concepts. The reviewers focused on core concepts and skills that are usually considered essential, defining features of "engineering." Although it is impossible to separate concepts from skills in engineering practice, the research literature tends to treat them separately. Thus, for the sake of simplicity, this chapter follows that dual structure.

The discussion of each skill or concept addresses (1) difficulties encountered by K–12 students in learning that particular concept or skill; (2) the development of students' understanding and cognitive capabilities during their K–12 years; and (3) the experiences and teaching interventions that facilitate an increasingly sophisticated understanding of each concept or skill. Based on the these three issues, the committee identified common principles: (1) the allocation of sufficient classroom time; (2) student engagement in iterative design activities; (3) sequencing of instruction that moves from easier-to-learn concepts to more difficult-to-learn concepts; and (4) the integration of tools (e.g., computer software or computational devices). These principles are discussed in more detail at the end of the chapter.

ENGINEERING CONCEPTS

Engineers generally agree that the prototypical engineering process is design and redesign. However, engineering design is not the same as trial-and-error "gadgeteering." Engineering design involves the following essential components: identifying the problem; specifying requirements of the solution; decomposing the system; generating a solution; testing the solution; sketching and visualizing the solution; modeling and analyzing the solution; evaluating alternative solutions, as necessary; and optimizing the final design. These essential components can be categorized into three type-specific groups of engineering concepts: basic science and math concepts, domain-specific concepts, and concepts common to most areas of engineering. Though this review does not focus on the social aspects of engineering design, engineering design is an inherently social enterprise, since those involved typically are working in teams and must communicate with clients or other stakeholders.

Research on the development of science and math concepts is not discussed in this chapter but has been extensively reviewed in recent studies by the National Research Council (e.g., *Taking Science to School: Learning and Teaching Science in Grades K–8* [Duschl et al., 2007] and *Adding It Up: Helping Children Learn Math* [NRC, 2001]). Very little research has been

TABLE 5-1 Engineering Concepts in the Categories of Systems and Optimization

Systems	Optimization
Structure-behavior-function*	Multiple variables*
Emergent properties*	Trade-offs*
Control/feedback	Requirements
Processes	Resources
Boundaries	Physical laws
Subsystems	Social constraints
Interactions	Cultural norms
	Side effects

*Related empirical research on K–12 students is available on these concepts.

published about the development of domain-specific concepts, some of them closely connected to particular engineering disciplines (e.g., statics), in K–12 students. In fact, with the exception of students who enroll in higher level math and physics courses in high school, very few K–12 students are even exposed to these concepts. Based on Silk and Schunn's (2008) review of relevant literature, which includes national and international content standards in technology education and engineering, the concepts that are common to most areas of engineering include structure-behavior-function (SBF); trade-offs, constraints; optimization; and system, subsystem, and control. The discussion of the concepts is divided into two categories: systems and optimization. As depicted in Table 5-1, the majority of empirical research on systems focuses on the concepts of SBF and emergent properties (i.e., behaviors that emerge from dynamic interactions among system components). Most of the research on optimization is on multiple variables and trade-offs.

Systems

The concept of a system relates to how individual components of an object or process work together to perform a function. The analysis and design of systems is central to engineering, the purpose of which is to modify surroundings to achieve particular purposes. Engineers may focus on the role and performance of individual parts, subsystems, or levels in a system, or they may highlight the boundaries and interactions between a system and its surrounding environment. Thus the concept of a system has many aspects and can serve different purposes in the engineering design process. Thinking in terms of systems involves understanding (1) how individual parts function, (2) how parts relate to each other, and (3) how parts, or combinations of parts, contribute to the function of the system as a whole.

Structure-Behavior-Function

SBF, a framework for representing a system, can be used to describe both natural and designed systems. SBF relates the components (structures) in a system to their purpose (function) in the system and the mechanisms that enable them to perform their functions (behavior). The SBF framework has been used to explain designed physical systems, such as electrical devices (Goel, 1991; Goel and Bhatta, 2004), as well as to represent the process of design as conducted by experienced designers (Gero and Kannengiesser, 2004). Empirical evidence (Gero and Kannengiesser, 2004) suggests that functional considerations actually drive the design process for more experienced designers, who often label the framework FBS to reflect the change in emphasis. For our purposes, we distinguish between the three aspects of design without formally choosing their order of importance.

Researchers have found that young children, and even preverbal infants, seem to have a strong sense of cause-and-effect principles (Bullock et al., 1982; Koslowski, 1996; Leslie, 1984). By the end of the preschool years, most children can use reasoning processes and problem-solving strategies, including evaluating simple if-then rules. Thus they already have developed many capacities when they enter the formal learning environment (Duschl et al., 2007).

Based on a review of the literature, however, the commissioned authors concluded that very young students (second graders) are unlikely to spontaneously consider what causes an effect, the basis for an SBF understanding of a system. Older students (fifth graders) are more likely to consider the cause, but, in general, younger students are much more likely to consider surface features, even when prompted to think about what affected the system under investigation (Silk and Schunn, 2008). Younger students often use a device for its functional purpose without inspecting the elements or components of which the device is made (Rozenblit and Keil, 2002).

For example, Lehrer and Schauble (1998) interviewed second- and fifth-grade students to assess their reasoning about the mechanics of gears. The students were shown increasingly complex combinations of gears on a gearboard that performed no function and gears in familiar machines with a known purpose (e.g., a handheld eggbeater and a 10-speed bicycle). They found that, even though all aspects of the devices could be directly inspected and had no hidden parts, the students' ideas about the structures in the devices and the mechanisms that made them work varied by grade level.

Fifth graders were more likely than second graders to form causal chains of relationships among three or more components in the functional devices. In the function-free context, they were more likely to identify the gear teeth as the important feature that drives the motion of the gears. Interestingly, in the functional context (i.e., the eggbeater), both groups were likely to mention the gear teeth. In this case, the improved performance of the second graders may indicate the importance of context in helping young students to reason about causal mechanisms.

When fifth and sixth graders were compared, students at both grade levels were equally likely to mention that the relative gear size determined the speed of the gears, but sixth graders were more likely to take that idea a step further and actually count and calculate the ratio of gear teeth to velocity. Fifth graders also used this mathematical reasoning when analyzing more complicated combinations of gears, which may have been their way of minimizing the complexity of the task.

The authors of the study caution that, even when the structures of a design are visible, young students may recognize the function of an object without considering how the underlying structures contribute to the performance of that function. In addition, early elementary students appear to lack sophisticated strategies for explicitly articulating causal mechanisms and for using mathematical representations as tools to represent complex causal behaviors. However, when children are provided explicit support for developing mathematical descriptions of natural systems, they can often use them to support their understanding of causal mechanisms (Lehrer et al., 2001).

Studies by Hemlo-Silver and colleagues on differences between adults and students focused on how the understanding of systems in terms of SBF changes over time and with experience (Hmelo-Silver and Pfeffer, 2004; Hmelo-Silver et al., 2004). They found minimal differences between the way pre-service teachers and sixth graders think about structures. However, they found large differences in how they understood functions, and even larger differences in how they understood causal behaviors, which require an appreciation of "connectedness" among elements in a system. The authors suggest that causal behaviors are the most difficult to understand, because they are often dynamic and invisible, whereas functions lead to specific outcomes that are visible.

Silk and Schunn (2008) found that research on elementary and middle-school students (Kolodner et al., 2003; Penner et al., 1997, 1998) suggests that a primary method of advancing students' ideas about SBF was to engage them in designing models, especially successively complex models. Students' first models tend to focus on superficial features and structural features. However, as models are revised and refined, many constructive ideas come into play. In addition, teacher support appears to have a large impact on whether, and how much, model building furthers an understanding of the SBF concept. Teachers' questions that focus attention on design help students set step-wise, pragmatic goals for each revision, which deepens their understanding of SBF.

With considerable teacher support, both early elementary students and middle school students can move toward a conceptual understanding that emphasizes function, just as experienced designers do (Penner et al., 1998). Effective teacher strategies include (1) pointing out limitations of the class models as a whole (e.g., if none of the initial models includes a mechanism for motion, the teacher may suggest that students consider the specific idea of motion in their revisions); (2) providing information when there is no way for students to discover the information on their own (e.g., providing the mathematical concept of median as a way of representing a range of data); and (3) encouraging individual teams of students to pursue specific design challenges that extend their models in general ways (e.g., considering how the function of the object under investigation is similar to and different from a familiar related object). Students whose teachers used these strategies were able to design increasingly complex functional models, including models of the mechanism of motion, and then to develop data representations to support their claims about the performance of their designs.

The importance of teacher input cannot be overemphasized. Unfortunately, teachers who have had little or no experience with formal modeling may not have a deep understanding of the process and thus may not be able to formulate questions to guide students engaged in exploring functional relationships among constituent parts of models. Teachers who have not participated in differentiated, sustained staff development, may also lack underlying training in science and, therefore, may not be able to explain basic natural phenomena.

Another factor that can negatively affect students' conceptual understanding of SFB is the amount of time allocated for design/redesign cycles. In an already crowded curriculum, it may be difficult to set aside enough time for modeling activities that are not merely superficial exercises. So, although the findings about younger students' abilities to develop modeling concepts are encouraging, effective teacher development and making room in a crowded curriculum are paramount concerns.

Emergent Properties

Not all systems can be analyzed in terms of causal behaviors or a direct, linear sequence of events. Another framework for understanding systems is focusing on behaviors that emerge from dynamic interactions among system components. These emergent properties can be global, aggregate, or macro-level behaviors that emerge from local, simple, or micro-level interactions between (or among) individual elements or components of a system. Aggregate behavior is qualitatively distinct from the sum of behaviors of individual components and indicates a complex engineered system, such as highways, the Internet, the power grid, and many others, which are all around us.

Based on their review of the literature, Silk and Schunn (2008) concluded that a major impediment to understanding the concept of emergent properties is the strong, perhaps innate, tendency of individuals to ascribe a central plan or single cause to system behavior (Resnick, 1996). Thus, analyzing emergent properties, which requires thinking on multiple levels of a system, may be particularly difficult for elementary-age students. However, there is not enough research to support that claim, because most of the empirical studies on emergent properties have been with students in middle-school or above. It is possible, however, that the concept of emergent properties is not understood through everyday experiences, even by adults (Resnick, 1996), and may require special support or learning experiences.

In Resnick's study, 12 high school students used StarLogo, a complex systems-modeling program created by Resnick based on the Logo program, in which users specify the behaviors of individuals, then observe how interactions among them give rise to group-level behaviors. Working mostly in pairs, and with considerable help from Resnick, the students developed individualized projects using StarLogo.

For example, one project was a model of traffic flow on a one-lane highway. The behavior of each car was governed by three basic rules: (1) if a car was close ahead, the trailing car slowed down; (2) if no cars were close ahead, the car speeded up until it was going the speed limit; and (3) if a radar trap was detected, the car slowed down.

When traffic jams developed, the students first reasoned that the slow-downs must have been caused by a specific, localizable event or circumstance, which they decided was a speed trap. When they removed the speed trap, effectively eliminating rule 3, they were surprised that traffic jams continued to develop—even if all of the cars started at the same speed. Only when they specified that the cars move at a uniform speed and start from equally spaced positions, did each car accelerate to the speed limit and continue moving at that speed, thus ensuring the smooth flow of traffic.

Thus the randomness of the initial spacing of cars led to the emergent behavior—traffic jams. This result was directly counter to the students' ideas, which Resnick characterized as a *centralized mindset*. Their initial reaction was to assume that a "leader" (e.g., a bird at the head of a flock) or a specific restriction (e.g., a speed trap) was the reason for the emergent behavior.

As Resnick's concept of a centralized mindset suggests, most of the students, in fact most adults, prefer explanations based on a central control, single cause, and predictability. However, as the students tested their simulations with different starting parameters and refined their rules, and as Resnick continued to challenge their assumptions, they began to appreciate decentralized thinking and the concept of emergent properties. Levy and Wilensky (2008) found that in coping with emergent properties, middle school students often negotiated the relation between individual and aggregate levels by inventing an intermediate level involving a collection of individuals. The intermediate level facilitated understanding, because students could still identify individuals while simultaneously viewing how individual interactions produced aggregate behaviors that were not identical to those of the participating individuals. Taken together, these data suggest that once a person understands emergent properties, he or she can begin to reason about decentralized control and multiple causes and, eventually, understand stochastic and equilibration processes.

Resnick's conclusion that, with proper guidance, students can recognize emergent properties is supported by evidence from two studies by Penner (2000, 2001). The goal of these studies was not simply to characterize students' (sixth graders) understanding of emergent properties, but also to investigate ways of supporting the development of their understanding. Penner showed that through simulation, sixth graders were able to consider the idea that macro-level order in a group did not require an explicit, central plan. They learned that order may emerge when individuals follow simple rules in their interactions with each other.

An important precondition for the success of the simulations was proper motivation. The students understood how the simulation was related to the real-world question they were studying in their classroom, and they clearly predicted the results of the simulation.

Besides a centralized mindset, students may also naturally try to understand emergent behavior in terms of what they already know, such as direct causes or material substances. In a series of studies, Chi and her colleagues proposed that some misconceptions about scientific phenomena are difficult to change because they are classified conceptually in an inappropriate ontological category (Chi, 2005; Chi and Roscoe, 2002; Reiner et al., 2000; Slotta and Chi, 2006; Slotta et al., 1995). For example, as children become aware that plants are alive, they tend to overgeneralize the characteristics they associate with living things. Most children believe that plants "eat" or absorb nutrients through their roots, rather than synthesizing sugars in their leaves (Roth, 1984).

In short, these studies suggest that students must first be helped to form a category of emergent properties and then encouraged to restructure their existing understanding to align with their new understanding of emergent properties.

After reviewing the literature on cognitive reasoning, Silk and Schunn concluded that simulations in the classroom context can clarify connections between different levels of a system and help students transition from a strong tendency to attribute behaviors to central plans and/or single causes to a perspective more consistent with the concept of emergent properties. Investigations of how simulations influence the teaching of emergent properties include studies of the effects of life-sized, participatory simulations (e.g., Colella, 2000; Penner, 2001; Resnick and Wilensky, 1998) as well as software environments that help students manipulate complex systems (Resnick, 1996; Wilensky and Reisman, 2006; Wilensky and Resnick, 1999).

Although research indicates that both types of simulations were helpful, software environments tended to be more effective because students could more easily explore, manipulate, and finally understand concepts that spanned levels of a system (Resnick, 1996). Evidence also indicates that making connections between levels of a system explicitly facilitates students' understanding of emergent properties and that dynamic simulations make connections between the levels of a system apparent and thus easier to identify and understand (Frederiksen et al., 1999).

Optimization

The concept of optimization in engineering relates to the stage of the design process in which the functionality or effectiveness of the design is maximized (ITEA, 2000). Real-world designs must always meet multiple, conflicting requirements and are always subject to constraints. Thus optimization necessarily involves trade-offs among different aspects of a design to improve one quality at the expense of another (e.g., range of motion versus mechanical advantage or additional strength versus added material cost). The requirements and constraints may include (1) available resources, (2) cultural and social norms that influence how the qualities of a design are valued, and (3) physical laws that determine how things work. Thus, optimization is a core concept that brings together many related engineering concepts, including trade-offs, requirements, resources, physical laws, social constraints, cultural norms, and side effects.

None of the literature on cognitive development or the learning of science directly addresses the difficulties for K–12 students in understanding the concept of optimization in the context of engineering. Therefore, this discussion is focused on concepts that are relevant to the idea of optimization, although they may be discussed in slightly different terms. For instance, optimization can be thought of as the manipulation of the internal variables of a system or product to maximize the external performance measures of that system or product.

Understanding conceptually how to simultaneously consider the effect of multiple variables on an outcome is essential to optimization. In addition, when variables interact, trade-offs must be considered. Thus making trade-offs is an essential concept in student's understanding of optimization in engineering.

Multiple Variables

The goal of engineering is to design products or processes that result in predictable outcomes within a given set of resource and other constraints. Almost all real-world products or processes are designed based on trade-offs among a large number and wide range of input variables that have been "manipulated" to reach an optimal solution. That manipulation must be based on knowing which variables have a causal effect on the outcome.

People with an interest in introducing engineering concepts to young children may be concerned that children are simply not cognitively ready to work on complex engineering problems that require taking into account many variables and requirements. Overall, cognitive processes gradually improve throughout childhood. These include processing speed, working memory, and executive functioning (Kail, 2004). These general, age-dependent aspects of cognitive functioning can have a significant influence on task performance. However, domain-specific aspects (e.g., task strategies and prior knowledge) are as important, if not more so, in children's learning. Furthermore, considerable evidence supports cognitive load theory (CLT), which argues that the seemingly infinite intellectual capacity of humans is primarily attributable to modifications in long-term memory; short-term memory, at all ages, is tightly constrained to consideration of a maximum of five to seven elements at a time (Sweller and Chandler, 1994). Even well-practiced adults can only process three or four variables simultaneously without compensating for their constraints by some sort of "chunking" or bundling strategy or linear processing (Halford et al., 2005). So, although students' capabilities almost certainly do improve over the course of their years in K–12, many aspects of real-world engineering design are beyond the cognitive processing limitations even of adults.

Based on their review of the literature, Silk and Schunn came to the same conclusion—that the large number of variables involved in most engineering contexts can easily overwhelm the limited cognitive resources of most individuals, adults or students (Halford et al., 2005; Kuhn, 2007; Kuhn et al., 2000; Schauble et al., 1991). They also found that meta-level knowledge about the nature of causality and the goal of testing can organize their thinking about design. In addition, simplifying tasks by focusing on sub-problems and using external representations (physical and mathematical) are effective strategies that can be taught to students in the K–12 setting. In fact, they found that a number of strategies can help young students overcome memory constraints and lead to mature learning, as well as authentic engineering practice. Research shows that these strategies can be learned in classroom settings.

For example, one strategy is to help students build schemas for analyzing multivariable systems, such as the strategy of assuming additive and consistent effects while controlling independent variables. Although these concepts can be explained at the meta-level, evidence suggests that they can be taught to young children by explicit instruction or experimentation (Keselman, 2003).

"Chunking" is another strategy for overcoming memory constraints. Similar to context-specific schemas, chunking involves creating a mental representation of a situation as a discrete element in memory with many aspects hidden underneath it (Chase and Simon, 1973; Miller, 1956). Another strategy—functional decomposition—is a design-specific strategy that can also be used to simplify a system and focus on one part of it. For example, the Wright Brothers used functional decomposition to isolate the effects of different aspects of the plane for testing before they built the entire system (Bradshaw, 1992). A third strategy is to produce physical representations of ideas to help students understand complicated situations. For example, a representation might be in the form of a prototype of the design that makes most aspects of it concrete and visible (Bradshaw, 1992).

Other strategies include "mathematizing," taking notes, and sketching. In mathematizing, conceptual ideas are represented as mathematical relationships. In contrast to prototyping, mathematizing purposely makes only some variables concrete and hides others. Studies by Lehrer and colleagues (2000) have shown a relationship between conceptual change and mathematizing. Note taking (Garcia-Mila and Andersen, 2007) and sketching (Anning, 1997; MacDonald and Gustafson, 2004; MacDonald et al., 2007) can also facilitate learning when working with multivariable systems. Sketching is more abstract than prototyping, more concrete than mathematical or graphic representations, and allows for hiding or deemphasizing irrelevant variables.

In short, Silk and Schunn found that strategies for simplifying tasks by focusing on sub-problems and using external representations (physical and mathematical) are effective learning strategies in the K–12 setting that enable students to construct and evaluate complicated designs in systematic ways.

Trade-offs

Trade-offs are one aspect of all real-world engineering design (Otto and Antonsson, 1991). They are always necessary in optimizing a system, both when considering input variables, which can be manipulated in the design process, and outcome variables, which indicate the quality of the design. A trade-off of an input variable occurs when a modification of the level of that variable impacts the effect of another variable on the outcome of the design. Thus trade-offs are not simply combinations of variables that influence an outcome in an additive way. There can also be cases when variables have opposing impact on an outcome. For example, the goals of controlling costs and producing the most effective product possible are often at odds.

Based on their review of the literature, Silk and Schunn (2008) concluded that, because K–12 students are unlikely to have a normative understanding of interactions among variables in a general sense, they may not easily come to a conceptual understanding of trade-offs. Nevertheless, some research studies (Acredelo et al., 1984; Zohar, 1995) have shown that youngsters may have some kinds of understanding that can be a basis for a more complete grasp of the trade-off concept.

For example, even in well understood physical settings, younger students understand direct relationships before they understand indirect relationships. Thus when considering the relationships between distance, time, and speed, fifth graders are likely to understand that speed is directly related to distance and that time is directly related to distance, but they are not likely to understand that speed and time are indirectly related to each other (Acredelo et al., 1984). Although it is not clear how students transition toward understanding indirect relationships, which are more cognitively demanding, an understanding of direct relationships in a system may be a necessary precondition.

Despite the difficulties of understanding trade-offs, Silk and Schunn concluded that certain classroom strategies can help students to consider trade-offs. One strategy is (1) to use mathematical representations to make connections between variables explicit and then (2) to engage in successive iterations in which variables are considered in isolation and in then in combinations (Schwartz et al., 2005). Mathematical formulas may be one way of conceptually representing trade-offs and thus helping students to consider variables that are indirectly related.

Schwartz and colleagues (2005) have demonstrated the effectiveness of simply encouraging students to represent situations mathematically. In a series of three studies, the first two with fifth graders and the third with fourth graders, they presented students with a balance-scale task (Siegler, 1976) in which they were asked to consider forces over a distance by predicting the outcome of balances that varied in two dimensions—the number of weights on each side and their distance from the fulcrum.

In the first study, they represented the weights as discrete pegs and as beakers of water filled up to different levels. The students in the beaker scenario were more likely to reason only about weight and not to consider the effect of distance. The researchers concluded that these students were less likely to quantify the beakers into discrete values, which made it more difficult to consider both dimensions simultaneously.

In the second study they tested this hypothesis. Students were given only peg problems and then asked to justify their predictions. Some students, however, were asked with a general prompt ("explain you answer"); others were asked to use math ("show your math"). Only 19 percent of the first group ("explain") considered both dimensions in at least one problem; in the second group ("math"), 68 percent considered both dimensions in at least one problem. Students in the first group switched between distance and weight as a justification, especially after receiving feedback on a problem they had predicted incorrectly, but they did not often represent the dimensions simultaneously.

Students in the second group also did better on more complex problems with weights at multiple locations on each side of the scale. Among all students who did consider both dimensions, the students in the second group were also more likely to consider both dimensions on these more challenging transfer problems.

The third study was similar to the second, but no sample justifications or examples of how to count were provided. The students, fourth graders, were less likely to use the multiplicative rule when predicting outcomes. However, the students in the math group did better on more complex problems with weights at multiple locations on each side of the scale; that is, they were more likely to use both dimensions in predicting outcomes.

Schwartz et al. considered these results in the context of extensive developmental research on the balance-scale task (Siegler, 1981), which showed that the reasoning of fifth graders was similar to that of kindergartners when they were presented with a problem that included hard-to-measure, continuous quantities in the form of a beaker. However, these same students performed as well as their peers when the problem included discrete, easy-to-quantify pegs. When they were given explicit instructions, feedback on their predictions, and encouragement to justify their answers mathematically, their reasoning was on a level similar to that of adults. Thus these studies provide compelling evidence that students, when encouraged to use mathematics, can represent physical situations and reason about them, even if they involve variables that are related indirectly.

The results of the studies described above have been supported by subsequent research with younger children. For example, in a study by Lehrer et al. (2000), second graders who were asked to reason about speed and distance were influenced by attempts to create mathematical models of the slope of the ramps they were using to study the movement of cars. In this case, the mathematical models were provided to one group of students, while another group had to invent the mathematical models themselves. The exercise only had positive effects for the second group.

Working on complex mathematical problems requires that students consider multiple paths and options in attempting to design optimal solutions. In another study, high-achieving sixth graders and college undergraduates were asked to develop individual business plans for a dunking booth at a school fair (Vye et al., 1997) using mathematical problem solving. To find possible solutions, college undergraduates were much more likely to consider more than one plan and select among them. But neither group was likely to test their solution against all of the initial constraints.

In a follow-up study, pairs of fifth graders were just as likely as the undergraduates to consider multiple solutions and to consider one or both of the constraints on their expenses. Success in this study was predicated not on the number of goals generated by each pair of students, but by appropriate reasoning and sound execution of the goals. Students who engaged in explanatory reasoning and counterarguments searched more of the "solution space" by monitoring each other, thus increasing their successful problem solving. This study provides some evidence that young students are capable of considering very complex mathematical problems that involve searching for optimal solutions. And, in this case at least, students seemed to benefit from having a partner who challenged them to justify their ideas and to monitor their subsequent actions.

ENGINEERING SKILLS

To understand the engineering process, K–12 students must learn not only engineering concepts, but also necessary skills. In their integrative review of research results on the development of core engineering skills in K–12, the commissioned authors focused on skills related to design and redesign, which are the prototypical engineering processes (Petrosino et al., 2008). The necessary skills include defining the problem, specifying requirements, decomposing systems, generating solutions, drawing and creating representations, and experimenting and testing. Because empirical evidence about how students develop most of these skills is limited, the commissioned authors could only glean evidence on the latter two topics, the development of drawing and representational skills and experimentation and testing skills.

Drawing and Representing

In professional design practice, drawing and representing have several purposes. Doodling commonly facilitates nascent ideas. "Exploded views" not only reveal the assembly of complex devices and their components, but also suggest the functionality of the system and components. Side and top schematics and computer-aided design (CAD) renderings show the aesthetics and scale of a device. Finally, drawings can communicate ideas and constraints (Anning, 1997; King and Fries, 2003; Stacey and Lauche, 2004).

Other forms of representation, such as modeling and "making" are also used in design. Various aspects of making representations are considered part of the design process, as it moves from concept to embodied design. Designers also use gestures and objects in their representations (e.g, they use their bodies to understand and convey their designs, especially inchoate designs). In the discussion that follows, the word "making" is used in relation to incipient design ideas.

From their review of the literature, Petrosino and colleagues (2008) concluded that, for children, drawing tends to be a way of recording significant personal events (Anning, 1997). Unless there is deliberate intervention, children's drawings are unlikely be used for design.

For example, drawing as part of a design activity has been described in an ethnographic study of design implementation for early elementary students in Australia in which students designed, made, and appraised vehicles (Rogers, 2000). After lectures on wheels, young students were shown examples of vehicles and instructed to make, out of simple objects, a vehicle with at least one wheel and then to draw it. The students were then divided into pairs, and each pair was asked to draw a picture of a vehicle to make and then to make it; they received no guidance on either of these steps. The student pairs did not directly compare their vehicles, although the teacher provided some comments.

This example highlights a number of missed opportunities and pitfalls. First, the teacher did not explain the differences between a design drawing and other types of drawings, and the students obviously did not understand the difference. This was apparent from the drawings themselves, which included details such as people and roads that were not related to the task at hand, and in the absence of details regarding the materials the vehicle would be made from. Also, conversations among students while drawing their vehicles did not focus on details such as what the car should be built from.

Second, because of the lack of connection between the design (drawing) phase and the making-and-appraising phase, students understood design as a linear, rather than iterative process, in which drawing served little or no purpose. In fact, the drawings had little correlation to the vehicles the students made (Rogers, 2000).

Third, although not noted by Rogers, Petrosino et al. suggested that the teacher could have drawn students' attention to the connection between design and the constructed vehicles by showing examples of vehicles before asking them to make drawings. Similar results in studies of elementary students also showed a lack of innate connection between a drawing and design (Anning, 1994; Samuel, 1991; Williams, 2000). In addition, young students have difficulty creating design drawings, which involve "graphical conventions of representing scale, spatial orientation and overlap" that are unfamiliar to them (Anning, 1994).

Other kinds of representation, such as models, without intervention, may preserve only structural and superficial features. Penner et al. (1997) conducted a study in which lower level elementary school students were asked to design functional models of elbows. Prior to the modeling activity, when students discussed the purpose of a model, the recurring criteria was physical resemblance. However, after a discussion of how models differ from real things, the students began to understand the functional differences between a simple, representational drawing and a model. The children, who worked in pairs, had access to a variety of everyday materials to make their models.

At first, the children tended to see models as small, superficial copies of the thing itself. Initially, the models were copies of the form of an elbow, but they did not perform the functions of an elbow. Although some of the models could flex, the flexure was unrestrained in direction. Discussion with the children revealed that they did not isolate the motion of the elbow and that they inferred a greater range of motion based on the pivot of the shoulder. After experimenting with real elbow movements, the students made new models. This time, the models incorporated constraints but also included more nonfunctional, but physically similar, details, such as representations of veins.

Johnsey (1995) conducted a study of pre-K through fifth-grade students in the United Kingdom to investigate the role of making in design. Eight case studies of students who tried to create designs with little or no teacher intervention revealed how children think about representations. Johnsey found that making representations played a role early in the design process; that it supported other design process skills, such as clarifying, specifying, and researching; and that it occurred in tandem with planning, generating, and modeling. The activity could generally be considered a make-evaluate-make cycle.

Making also encourages the development of a common design language among children. When students begin building well before they finalize their design (a divergence from professional design), they gain experience in moving between the actual and the possible. They develop norms and vocabulary appropriate to their designs as they need them, rather than imposing them from the beginning of the activity (Roth, 2001). Representations are particularly effective in collaborative situations (Arias et al., 2000). One of the benefits of design activities is that thinking and acting become inextricably connected. In fact, with continued iterations, designs become "tools to think with" (Roth, 1996).

The reviews of the literature by the commissioned authors show that, although schoolchildren do not naturally use drawings and representations effectively in the design process, some classroom practices can have a positive impact on the way they use them. Allowing young children to play with the construction materials they will use can lead to better design drawings, particularly when children also participate in a discussion of how their drawings will be used. Comparing drawings done before and after design can help determine the usefulness of the initial drawing (Claire, 1991; Pace and Larson, 1992).

Drawing and representing are useful methods of eliciting nascent ideas, but design representations tend to be highly specific and do not easily lead to abstraction or transference to other situations (Gick and Holyoak, 1980). Nevertheless, repeated experiences related to a single complex concept can encourage abstraction, and students' representations do evolve and improve over the course of the dynamic design process (Spiro et al., 1991). Iterations of a full design cycle can improve learning and challenge students to "translate experiential knowledge into abstract rational form" (Hill and Smith, 1998).

For young children, a preliminary to drawing may be investigation and exploration of materials. In one study, lower elementary students were allowed to play with a limited selection of materials and explore their possibilities before being asked to draw and then make a figure from those materials (Samuel, 1991). To support their drawings, they were supplied with notes about the materials and instructions, such as drawing top and side views rather than perspective views.

Another study (Fleer, 1999) in which children who were asked to draw designs of forts they had constructed led to an interesting observation about plan-view versus side-view drawings. The point of view tended to correlate with the drawing position of the child. If the fort was on the desk, the drawing tended to be a side view; it the model was on the floor, the drawing tended to be a plan view.

For young students who may not know what engineering is, contextualizing their design activity by using simple, familiar objects can be productive.

Solomon and Hall (1996) explain that drawing ability may be accelerated when students learn the various roles a drawing may play. Craft skills improve with familiarization via direct experience with the tools and materials to be used. Improvement in craft skills leads to improvement in spatial ability, including visual and haptic shape recognition, as well as manipulation and translation between two and three dimensions (Solomon and Hall, 1996).

In their review, Lehrer and Schauble (2006) pointed out various methods of instruction that evidence shows support modeling. First, informed decisions about the sequencing and timing of introducing new and more difficult forms of modeling are critical to support student learning. Second, involving students in group activities is essential to helping students understand and appropriate the inquiry processes, emphasize the development and use of different forms of representation, and capitalize on the cyclical nature of modeling. Third, modeling approaches only develop when inquiry is a priority in the classroom. Fourth, nuanced forms of modeling require a long-term effort and are more likely to develop in students who build on successively complex experiences with modeling. Finally, although this is not usually done in traditional classrooms, critiquing and discussing their own models and those of other students can support students' understanding of engineering design.

Experimenting and Testing

In professional practice, engineering designers use experimentation and testing to determine the level of optimization of a design and whether all of the requirements have been met. This step may be done with full or partial prototypes or with virtual models using finite elements analysis. Unlike scientific experimentation, the purpose of which is to identify causal relationships through a process that does not involve optimization and trade-offs, engineering experimentation and testing are iterative processes with multiple steps, including modeling and analysis (Schauble et al., 1991). The differences can be attributed to the similar but different purposes of engineering and science.

As described in Chapter 2, scientists ask questions about the world around us, whereas engineers modify the world to adapt it to our needs. Scientific inquiry is concerned with what is, while engineering design is focused on what can be. Models may be used by both, but the nature and purpose of models in science and engineering are different due to differences between scientific inquiry and engineering design. Understanding these differences is critical to understanding potential learning outcomes when engineering is used to teach science, especially because children's engagement in engineering experimentation is done, necessarily, without modeling, analysis, or mathematical optimization, which engineers use with experimentation.

In their review of the literature, the commissioned authors explained that inquiry commonly involves experimentation with multiple variables (Petrosino et al., 2008). However, when middle school students are presented with an activity in which they manipulate variables that contribute to flooding, for example, they tend to focus on outcomes and do not immediately experiment in an analytical way (Kuhn et al., 2000). Rather than isolating variables, they tend to change many at once and attribute the good or bad outcome to *all* variables, even those that had been determined to be good in prior experiments. Although many students progress toward altering one variable at a time, many others consistently alter multiple variables. Kuhn et al. suggest that students with "additive mental models of causality" are able to transition to a multivariate model, while those with "co-occurrence models of causality" are resistant this transition.

To address this issue, students in Kuhn's experimental group were presented with a scenario in which they argued about the effect of one variable. All of the students had participated in the flood activity described above, but more students in the experimenting group made valid inferences. An analysis of a meta-level test demonstrated that the experimenting students developed both implicit and explicit understanding, whereas the larger, control group developed only an implicit understanding and could not justify their responses (Kuhn et al., 2000). This study highlights the importance of attending to a student's experimental strategies.

Experimentation has been posited as a critical prerequisite to learning in design, including posing and solving problems (Childress and Rhodes, 2008; ITEA, 2000). In a study on the effects of experimentation on problem solving, fifth and sixth graders completed two experimentation tasks (Schauble et al., 1991). The first task was to design a canal with optimal water depth for boats traveling at a given speed. This task can be accomplished with no understanding of the causes of buoyancy and still be a complicated problem to solve. Thus although solving this problem requires some characteristic engineering processes, it is more akin to gadgeteering than engineering. The second task was to explore why boats float. This buoyancy task required that students engage in scientific experimentation, including manipulating variables (volume, mass, and position) as they measured the buoyancy using a spring. Although these tasks had some common principles, they required different problem-solving strategies.

Prior to the activities, the students were read a framing statement either about what scientists do or what engineers do to provide a context for their problem solving. After completing the activities, the students were asked to reconstruct what they had learned. Their answers revealed that they approached the two tasks differently, depending on how the task had been framed. When the tasks had been framed as exploring why boats float, students undertook a broader exploration of variables and a more thorough investigation of each variable, even of variables that seemed to be irrelevant to the goal.

The group that completed the water-depth task first showed greater improvement in making valid inferences than the group that completed the buoyancy task first. Despite the framing procedure, the water-depth task led to more inferences based on less evidence, and these inferences were more commonly related to causal variables. The buoyancy task tended to lead to inferences related to both causal and exclusive variables, which are critical to the formation of disconfirming evidence.

This example reveals some of the challenges in using design to teach science. However, the design in the study just described is unlike professional design, in that the design goals are created by the designers themselves, as opposed to being developed by a client or external source (Petrosino et al., 2008). Working within the constrains of the goals provided by a client or external source can have a significant impact on the design process.

Testing is necessary to determine if design requirements have been met. In elementary school classrooms, testing or evaluations are usually done by the teacher, but in professional settings, testing is done by the designer. Teacher evaluations of students' designs can be taken as personal criticism, even when couched as a question, such as "How can this design be improved?" It is recommended, therefore, that teachers evaluate student designs via comparisons to the design drawing, which facilitates metacognition, or via comparison to the original design goals, which is a common practice in professional design and can lead to further optimization. Evaluation also helps to promote the utility of the design drawings (Solomon and Hall, 1996).

Solomon and Hall (1996) suggest that design activities in K–12 classrooms should include a careful description of the customer who commissioned the design. In most studies, the teacher is the customer, which, because of the teacher's power position, can render the evaluation stage challenging and less than fruitful. Children may perform better when designing for themselves, their families, their community, or a historical or fictional character. The last two may also provide opportunities to contextualize design problems in interdisciplinary ways by tapping into other subjects taught in the class-room. Over-specification, which can cause students to feel less involved in the activity, can also interfere with K–12 design experimentation. Students per-form best when the focus is not on any one student's work and when they have an opportunity to negotiate ideas in a group (Solomon and Hall, 1996).

Kolodner's learning-by-design (1997), which builds on case-based reasoning (Schank, 1999; Williams, 1992) and problem-based learning (Barrows, 1986), involves iterations of increasing complexity. In a study of Kolodner's program, Vattam and Kolodner (2006) addressed two challenges in teaching science via design. The first challenge, facilitating students' scientific understanding during design, was addressed by incorporating an explanation tool. In this scaffolding technique, students were prompted to explain the science behind their designs. A focus on the relationships between structures, behaviors, and functions, discussed above, also helped students connect science to design.

The second challenge, coping with time, material, and environmental constraints in the classroom, can be addressed through simulation-based design. The virtual design world enables students to isolate and test their designs before building a prototype in the real world. The ability to test and model at a smaller focal length encourages experimentation that leads to an understanding of the science behind the design (Vattam and Kolodner, 2006).

LESSONS LEARNED

Cognitive development research distinguishes between general devel-opmental constraints (i.e., limitations related to the development of the mind) and knowledge constraints (i.e., limitations based on an individual's experiences and how he/she processes them). Researchers and others dis-agree about the extent to which these constraints exist, and, if they exist at all, which limitations have a greater impact in different domains of learn-ing (Kuhn, 1997; Metz, 1995, 1997). Regardless of the reasons for cognitive development (architecture or experience), the demonstrated success of a number of the interventions reviewed here, even with students in early elementary grades, clearly shows that certain experiences can support rela-tively sophisticated understanding of engineering concepts and development of engineering skills.

As this chapter makes clear, there are significant gaps in our under-standing of how K–12 students learn and might best be taught engineering concepts and skills. At the same time, the research that has been conducted provides some important clues about effective approaches to curriculum development and classroom practice. Based on the reviews of the literature in this chapter, we suggest the following guidelines for the incorporation of core engineering concepts (systems and optimization) and skills (representation and experimentation) in K–12 education:

1. allocating sufficient classroom time for students to develop core concepts through immersion in extended design activities;
2. encouraging iterative, purposeful revisions of student designs; and
3. sequencing instruction to build from the easiest-to-learn aspects of core concepts to the more difficult-to-learn aspects.

Sufficient Classroom Time for Extended Design Activities

In every successful intervention we reviewed, significant learning resulted only after an extended time for design activities in a meaningful context. Core engineering ideas and skills cannot be developed in a single class period. These ideas and skills must be developed and elaborated through extended investigations that give students time to engage in the full engineering process of design and redesign. Studies show that design activities are an appropriate context for introducing these core ideas and skills because they retain students' interest and invite increasingly sophisticated ways of understanding.

Iterative, Purposeful Revisions of Designs, Ideas, and Models

The second important idea is that iterative, purposeful modeling appears to be central to helping students to a more sophisticated understanding of the salient idea or skill. Modeling can take the form of a physical design or a conceptual, graphical, mathematical, or diagrammatic design. The models help students answer particular questions based on their analysis of previous designs, and as iterations continue, the questions become increasingly specific and operationally defined, and thus increasingly purposeful. As models are developed, revised, and refined over time, students begin to understand ideas in deeper ways. Ethnographic studies of engineers engaged in design work reveals that modeling is the most prevalent and challenging form of activity (Gainsburg, 2006; Neressian et al., 2003; Nersessian and Patton, in press).

Unfortunately, design in K–12 settings usually allows for only a single iteration of a design, which barely begins to reveal conceptual difficulties and design challenges that require further investigation. For modeling to be used productively in the classroom, mathematics education must allow for the development of spatial visualization and related design skills, and algebraic reasoning.

The teacher's role is crucial in shaping students' questions and directing their revisions. Although it may be tempting to allow students to direct their modeling themselves, the successful interventions reviewed here highlight the importance of the teacher providing explicit guidance and developing activities for investigating and negotiating contested claims. These strategies support students' progress toward increasingly sophisticated understanding and representations. In addition, the iteration of cycles based on the teacher's questioning of students' ideas and suggesting of resources for students to consider is essential to focusing attention on the core idea.

Sequencing Instruction from Easier to More Difficult Ideas

The third important idea is that knowledge builds on itself. Thus a simple understanding of an idea is likely to precede a more complex understanding in predictable ways. This applies to learning both engineering concepts and engineering skills. Although this may seem obvious, the purpose of drawing attention to this principle is to encourage the reader to focus on specifying cognitive developmental trajectories for particular concepts.

Common trajectories in the development of expertise can be identified in any domain of knowledge. Once these are specified, a logical sequence of experiences can be developed to build that knowledge over time. For instance, the commissioned authors found that structure was often easier for students to understand than behaviors or functions. Therefore, beginning an activity at the structural level may provide a basis for moving toward an understanding of the more difficult concepts of behavior and function.

Of course, the learning progressions, types of ideas, and depth of exploration of those ideas must be adapted for different grade levels (Duschl et al., 2007). Unfortunately, the literature on teaching core engineering concepts is not sufficient for us to make specific recommendations at this time. In general, however, our findings indicate that with a well thought out instructional sequence and sufficient time and support students can make the transition from a novice level of conceptual understanding and ability to a more sophisticated level. This is true even for students in the elementary grades.

REFERENCES

Acredelo, C., A. Adams, and J. Schmid. 1984. On the understanding of the relationships between speed, duration, and distance. Child Development 55(6): 2151–2159.

Anning, A. 1994. Dilemmas and opportunities of a new curriculum: design and technology with young children. International Journal of Technology and Design Education 4(2): 155–177.

Anning, A. 1997. Drawing out ideas: graphicacy and young children. International Journal of Technology and Design Education 7(3): 219–239.

Arias, E., H. Eden, G. Fischer, A. Gorman, and E. Scharff . 2000. Transcending the individual human mind—creating shared understanding through collaborative design. ACM Transactions on Computer-Human Interaction 7(1): 84–113.

Barrows, H.S. 1986. A taxonomy of problem-based learning methods. Medical Education 20(6): 481–486.

Bradshaw, G. 1992. The Airplane and the Logic of Invention. Pp. 239–250 in Cognitive Models of Science, edited by R.N. Giere. Minneapolis, Minn.: University of Minnesota Press.

Bullock, M., R. Gelman, and R. Baillargeon. 1982. The Development of Causal Reasoning. Pp. 209–254 in The Developmental Psychology of Time, edited by W.J. Friedman. New York: Academic Press.

Chase, W.G., and H.A. Simon. 1973. Perception in chess. Cognitive Psychology 4: 55–81.

Chi, M.T.H. 2005. Commonsense conceptions of emergent processes: why some misconceptions are robust. Journal of the Learning Sciences 14(2): 161–199.

Chi, M.T.H., and R.D. Roscoe. 2002. The Processes and Challenges of Conceptual Change. Pp. 3–27 in Reconsidering Conceptual Change: Issues in Theory and Practice, edited by M. Limon and L. Mason. Netherlands: Kluwer Academic Publishers.

Childress, V.W., and C. Rhodes. 2008. Engineering outcomes for grades 9–12. The Technology Teacher 67(7): 5–12.

Claire, H. 1991. A child centered technology curriculum—a primary school case study. Design and Technology Teaching 24: 17–22.

Colella, V. 2000. Participatory simulations: building collaborative understanding through immersive dynamic modeling. Journal of the Learning Sciences 9(4): 471–500.

Duschl, R.A., H.A. Schweingruber, and A.W. Shouse, eds. 2007. Taking Science to School: Learning and Teaching Science in Grades K–8. Committee on Science Learning, Kindergarten Through Eighth Grade. Washington, D.C.: The National Academies Press.

Fleer, M. 1999. The science of technology: young children working technologically. International Journal of Technology and Design Education 9(3): 269–291.

Frederiksen, J.R., B.Y. White, and J. Gutwill. 1999. Dynamic mental models in learning science: the importance of constructing derivational linkages among models. Journal of Research in Science Teaching 36(7): 806–836.

Gainsburg, J. 2006. The mathematical modeling of structural engineers. Mathematical Thinking and Learning 8: 3–36.

Garcia-Mila, M., and C. Andersen. 2007. Developmental change in notetaking during scientific inquiry. International Journal of Science Education 29(8): 1035–1058.

Gero, J.S., and U. Kannengiesser. 2004. The situated function-behavior-structure framework. Design Studies 25(4): 373–391.

Gick, M.L., and K.J. Holyoak. 1980. Analogical problem solving. Cognitive Psychology 12(3): 306–355.

Goel, A. 1991. A Model-Based Approach to Case Adaptation. Pp. 143–148 in Proceedings of the Thirteenth Annual Conference of the Cognitive Science Society. Wheat Ridge, Colo.: Cognitive Science Society.

Goel, A., and S. Bhatta. 2004. Use of design patterns in analogy-based design. Advanced Engineering Informatics 18(2): 85–94.

Halford, G.S., R. Baker, J.E. McCredden, and J.D. Bain. 2005. How many variables can humans process? Psychological Science 16(1): 70–76.

Hill, A.M., and H. Smith. 1998. Practice meets theory in technology education: a case of authentic learning in the high school setting. Journal of Technology Education 9(2): 29–45.

Hmelo-Silver, C.E., S. Marathe, and L. Liu. 2007. Fish swim, rocks sit, and lungs breathe: expert-novice understanding of complex systems. Journal of the Learning Sciences 16(3): 307–331.

Hmelo-Silver, C.E., and M.G. Pfeffer. 2004. Comparing expert and novice understanding of a complex system from the perspective of structures, behaviors, and functions. Cognitive Science 28(1): 127–138.

ITEA (International Technology Education Association). 2000. Standards for Technological Literacy: Content for the Study of Technology. Reston, Va.: International Technology Education Association.

Johnsey, R. 1995. The Place of the Process Skill Making in Design and Technology: Lessons from Research into the Way Primary Children Design and Make. Pp. 15–20 in IDATER95: International Conference on Design and Technology Educational Research and Curriculum Development, Loughborough University of Technology, Loughborough, U.K.

Kail, R.V. 2004. Cognitive development includes global and domain-specific processes. Merrill-Palmer Quarterly 50(4): 445–455.

Keselman, A. 2003. Supporting inquiry learning by promoting normative understanding of multivariable causality. Journal of Research in Science Teaching 40(9): 898–921.

King, P.H., and R.C. Fries. 2003. Design of Biomedical Devices and Systems. Boca Raton, Fla.: CRC Press.

Kolodner, J.L. 1997. Educational implications of analogy: a view from case-based reasoning. American Psychologist 52(1): 57–66.

Kolodner, J.L., P.J. Camp, D. Crismond, B. Fasse, J. Gray, J. Holbrook, S. Puntambekar, and M. Ryan. 2003. Problem-based learning meets case-based reasoning in the middle-school science classroom: putting learning-by-design into practice. Journal of the Learning Sciences 12(4): 495–547.

Koslowski, B. 1996. Theory and evidence: The development of scientific reasoning. Cambridge, Mass.: MIT Press.

Kuhn, D. 1997. Constraints or guideposts? Developmental psychology and science education. Review of Educational Research 67(1): 141–150.

Kuhn, D. 2007. Reasoning about multiple variables: control of variables is not the only challenge. Science Education 91(5): 710–726.

Kuhn, D., J. Black, A. Keselman, and D. Kaplan. 2000. The development of cognitive skills to support inquiry learning. Cognition and Instruction 18(4): 495–523.

Lehrer, R., and L. Schauble. 1998. Reasoning about structure and function: children's conceptions of gears. Journal of Research in Science Teaching 35(1): 3–25.

Lehrer, R., and L. Schauble. 2006. Cultivating model-based reasoning in science education. Pp. 371–388 in Cambridge Handbook of the Learning Sciences, edited by K. Sawyer. Cambridge, Mass.: Cambridge University Press.

Lehrer, R., L. Schauble, S. Carpenter, and D.E. Penner. 2000. The Inter-related Development of Inscriptions and Conceptual Understanding. Pp. 325–360 in Symbolizing and Communicating in Mathematics Classrooms: Perspectives on Discourse, Tools, and Instructional Design, edited by P. Cobb, E. Yackel, and K. McClain. Mahwah, N.J.: Lawrence Erlbaum Associates.

Lehrer, R., L. Schauble, D. Strom, and M. Pligge. 2001. Similarity of Form and Substance: Modeling Material Kind. Pp. 39–74 in Cognition and Instruction: 25 Years of Progress, edited by D. Klahr and S. Carver. Mahwah, N.J.: Lawrence Erlbaum Associates.

Leonard, M. 2004. Toward Epistemologically Authentic Engineering Design Activities in the Science Classroom. Paper presented at National Association for Research in Science Teaching. Vancouver, B.C., April 2004.

Leslie, A.M. 1984. Spatiotemporal continuity and the perception of causality in infants. Perception 13(3): 287–305.

Levy, S.T. and U. Wilensky. 2008. Inventing a "mid-level" to make ends meet: reasoning through the levels of complexity. Cognition & Instruction 26(1): 1–47.

MacDonald, D., and B. Gustafson. 2004. The role of design drawing among children engaged in a parachute building activity. Journal of Technology Education 16(1): 55–71.

MacDonald, D., B.J. Gustafson, and S. Gentilini. 2007. Enhancing children's drawing in design technology planning and making. Research in Science and Technological Education 25(1): 59–75.

Metz, K.E. 1995. Reassessment of developmental constraints on children's science instruction. Review of Educational Research 65(2): 93–127.

Metz, K.E. 1997. On the complex relation between cognitive developmental research and children's science curricula. Review of Educational Research 67(1): 151–163.

Miller, G.A. 1956. The magical number seven, plus or minus two: some limits on our capacity for processing information. Psychological Review 63(2): 81–97.

Nersessian, N. J., and C. Patton. In press. Model-based reasoning in interdisciplinary engineering: Cases from biomedical engineering research laboratories. Handbook of the Philosophy of Technology & Engineering Sceinces, A.W. M. Meijers, ed., Springer.

Nersessian, N. J., E. Kurz-Milcke, W.C. Newsletter, and J. Davies. 2003. Research laboratories as evolving distributed cognitive systems. Pp. 857-862 in Proceedings of the Twenty-Fifth Annual Conference of the Cognitive Science Society, R. Alterman and D. Kirsh, Eds. Mahwah, NJ: Erlbaum.

NRC (National Research Council). 2001. Adding It Up: Helping Children Learn Math. Washington, D.C.: National Academy Press.

Otto, K.N., and E.K. Antonsson. 1991. Trade-off strategies in engineering design. Research in Engineering Design 3(2): 87–103.

Pace, G., and C. Larson. 1992. On design. Science and Children 29: 12–15.

Penner, D.E. 2000. Explaining systems: investigating middle school students' understanding of emergent phenomena. Journal of Research in Science Teaching 37(8): 784–806.

Penner, D.E. 2001. Complexity, emergence, and synthetic models in science education. Pp. 177–208 in Designing for science: Implications from everyday, classroom, and professional settings, edited by K. Crowley, C.D. Schunn, and T. Okada. Mahwah, N.J.: Lawrence Erlbaum Associates.

Penner, D.E., N.D. Giles, R. Lehrer, and L. Schauble. 1997. Building functional models: designing an elbow. Journal of Research in Science Teaching 34(2): 125–143.

Penner, D.E., R. Lehrer, and L. Schauble. 1998. From physical models to biomechanics: a design-based modeling approach. Journal of the Learning Sciences 7(3/4): 429–449.

Petrosino, A.J., V. Svihla, and S. Brophy. 2008. Engineering Skills for Understanding and Improving K–12 Engineering Education in the United States. Presented at the National Academy of Engineering/National Research Council workshop on K–12 Engineering Education. Washington, D.C.

Reiner, M., J.D. Slotta, M.T.H. Chi, and L.B. Resnick. 2000. Naive physics reasoning: a commitment to substance-based conceptions. Cognition and Instruction 18(1): 1–34.

Resnick, M. 1996. Beyond the centralized mindset. Journal of the Learning Sciences 5(1): 1–22.

Resnick, M., and U. Wilensky. 1998. Diving into complexity: developing probabilistic decentralized thinking through role-playing activities. Journal of the Learning Sciences 7(2): 153–172.

Rogers, G. 2000. The wheels of the bus: children designing in an early years classroom. Research in Science & Technological Education 18(1): 127–136.

Roth. K. 1984. Using Classroom Observations to Improve Science Teaching and Curriculum Materials. In Observing Science Classrooms: Perspective from Research and Practice, edited by C.W. Anderson. Columbus, Ohio: Education Resources Information Center.

Roth, W.M. 1996. Art and artifact of children's designing: a situated cognition perspective. Journal of the Learning Sciences 5(2): 129–166.

Roth, W.M. 2001. Learning science through technological design. Journal of Research in Science Teaching 38(7): 768–790.

Rozenblit, L., and F. Keil. 2002. The misunderstood limits of folk science: an illusion of explanatory depth. Cognitive Science 26(5): 521–562.

Samuel, G.C. 1991. 'They can never make what they draw'—producing a realistic, appropriate and achievable design at key stages 1 and 2. Paper presented at the IDATER 91: International conference on design and technology educational research and curriculum development, Loughborough, U.K.

Schank, R.C. 1999. Dynamic Memory Revisited. Cambridge, U.K.: Cambridge University Press.

Schauble, L., L.E. Klopfer, and K. Raghavan. 1991. Students' transition from an engineering model to a science model of experimentation. Journal of Research in Science Teaching 28(9): 859–882.

Schwartz, D.L., T. Martin, and J. Pfaffman. 2005. How mathematics propels the development of physical knowledge. Journal of Cognition and Development 6(1): 65–88.

Siegler, R.S. 1976. Three aspects of cognitive development. Cognitive Psychology 8: 481–520.

Siegler, R.S. 1981. Developmental sequences within and between concepts. Monographs of the Society for Research in Child Development 46(2).

Silk, E.M., and C. Schunn. 2008. Core Concepts in Engineering as a Basis for Understanding and Improving K–12 Engineering Education in the United States. Paper presented at the National Academy of Engineering/National Research Council workshop on K–12 Engineering Education, Washington, D.C.

Slotta, J.D., and M.T.H. Chi. 2006. Helping students understand challenging topics in science through ontology training. Cognition and Instruction 24(2): 261–289.

Slotta, J.D., M.T.H. Chi, and E. Joram. 1995. Assessing students' misclassifications of physics concepts: an ontological basis for conceptual change. Cognition and Instruction 13(3): 373–400.

Solomon, J., and S. Hall. 1996. An inquiry into progression in primary technology: a role for teaching. International Journal of Technology and Design Education 6(3): 263–282.

Spiro, R.J., P.J. Feltovich, M.J. Jacobson, and R.L. Coulson. 1991. Cognitive flexibility, constructivism, and hypertext: random access instruction for advanced knowledge acquisition in ill-structured domains. Educational Technology 31(5): 24–33.

Stacey, M., and K. Lauche. 2004. Thinking and Representing in Design. Pp. 198–229 in Design Process Improvement—A Review of Current Practice. London: Springer.

Sweller, J., and P. Chandler. 1994. Why some material is difficult to learn. Cognition and Instruction 12(3): 185–233.

Vattam, S.S., and J.L. Kolodner. 2006. Design-based Science Learning: Important Challenges and How Technology Can Make a Difference. Pp. 799–805 in Proceedings of the 7th International Conference on Learning Sciences, Indiana University, Bloomington, June 27–July 6, 2006.

Vye, N.J., S.R. Goldman, J.F. Voss, C. Hmelo, and S. Williams. 1997. Complex mathematical problem solving by individuals and dyads. Cognition and Instruction 15(4): 435–484.

Wilensky, U., and K. Reisman. 2006. Thinking like a wolf, a sheep, or a firefly: learning biology through constructing and testing computational theories—an embodied modeling approach. Cognition and Instruction 24(2): 171–209.

Wilensky, U., and M. Resnick. 1999. Thinking in levels: a dynamic systems approach to making sense of the world. Journal of Science Education and Technology 8(1): 3–19.

Williams, P.J. 2000. Design: the only methodology of technology. Journal of Technology Education 11(2): 48–60.

Williams, S.M. 1992. Putting case-based instruction into context: examples from legal and medical education. Journal of the Learning Sciences 2(4): 367–427.

Zohar, A. 1995. Reasoning about interactions between variables. Journal of Research in Science Teaching 32(10): 1039–1063.

6

Findings and Recommendations

In comparison to K–12 education in science, mathematics, and technology, K–12 engineering education is still in its infancy in the United States. Nevertheless, we have enough examples of practice to begin to take the measure of this developing academic area. Although more and better impact studies will be necessary in the future, the available evidence shows that engaging elementary and secondary students in learning engineering ideas and practices is not only possible, but can lead to positive learning outcomes.

It is equally clear, however, that the potential effectiveness of K–12 engineering education has been limited by a number of factors, such as challenges associated with curriculum and professional development, difficulties in reconciling this new content with existing curricula in other subjects, the influences of standards-based education reform and accountability,[1] and the absence of teacher certification requirements and pre-service teacher preparation programs. Despite these challenges, it is the committee's judgment, supported by data gathered during the two years of this project, that much can be gained by working to improve the quality and increase the availability of K–12 engineering education.

---

[1]An ongoing study at the National Academy of Engineering is examining the potential value and feasibility of developing content standards for K–12 engineering education. Information about the project can be viewed at *http://www8.nationalacademies.org/cp/projectview.aspx?key=48942*.

Although improving teaching and learning in this nascent area is important, the committee is even more interested in seeing engineering education become a catalyst for improved learning in the other STEM subjects. Despite all of the concerns by policy makers, educators, and people in industry about the quality of U.S. K–12 STEM education, the role of technology education and engineering education have hardly been mentioned. In fact, the STEM acronym has become shorthand for science and mathematics education only, and even these subjects typically are treated as separate entities.

Finding 1. As STEM education is currently structured and implemented, it does not reflect the natural interconnectedness of the four STEM components in the real world of research and technology development.[2]

The committee believes that the disconnects between STEM subjects has not only impeded efforts to stimulate student interest and improve performance in science and mathematics, but has also inhibited the development of technological and scientific literacy, which are essential to informed citizens in the twenty-first century.

Finding 2. There is considerable potential value, related to student motivation and achievement, in increasing the presence of technology and, especially, engineering in STEM education in the United States in ways that address the current lack of integration in STEM teaching and learning.

In the rest of this chapter, we present the committee's recommendations and remaining findings. Because of the numerous unanswered questions about K–12 engineering education, the findings outnumber the recommendations, which are largely focused on research. We turn our attention first to "defining" engineering in the context of K–12 education. Next we address the scope, nature, and impacts of current efforts to teach engineering to pre-college students in the United States. The following section deals with policy and program issues associated with K–12 engineering education. The chapter concludes with a discussion of fully integrated STEM education.

---

[2]See, for example, Almeida et al., 2008; Gogate and Kabadi, 2009; and Hood et al., 2008.

GENERAL PRINCIPLES FOR K–12 ENGINEERING EDUCATION

One goal of this project was to clarify the place and "look" of engineering in K–12 classrooms in the United States. Chapter 4 goes a long way toward meeting that goal, but, based on our review of curricular materials, some of what now passes for engineering education is not aligned with generally accepted ideas of the discipline of engineering. We do not mean to suggest that K–12 students should be treated like little engineers or that engineering education in K–12 classrooms should resemble in scope or rigor the post-secondary engineering curriculum. However, we do mean to suggest that in any K–12 school subject for which there is a professional counterpart there must be a conceptual connection to post-secondary studies and to the practice of that profession in the real world.

The absence of standards or an agreed-upon framework for organizing and sequencing the essential knowledge and skills to be developed through engineering education at the elementary and secondary school levels limits our ability to develop a comprehensive definition of K–12 engineering education. Nevertheless, over the course of the committee's deliberations, general principles emerged based on our knowledge of engineering and technology, our review of K–12 engineering curricula, and key documents, such as the *Standards for Technological Literacy: Content for the Study of Technology* (ITEA, 2000).

Principle 1. K–12 engineering education should emphasize engineering design.

The design process, the engineering approach to identifying and solving problems, is (1) highly iterative; (2) open to the idea that a problem may have many possible solutions; (3) a meaningful context for learning scientific, mathematical; and technological concepts; and (4) a stimulus to systems thinking, modeling, and analysis. In all of these ways, engineering design is a potentially useful pedagogical strategy.

Principle 2. K–12 engineering education should incorporate important and developmentally appropriate mathematics, science, and technology knowledge and skills.

Certain science concepts as well as the use of scientific inquiry methods can support engineering design activities. Similarly, certain mathematical concepts and computational methods can support engineering design, especially in service of analysis and modeling. Technology and technology concepts can illustrate the outcomes of engineering design, provide opportunities for "reverse engineering" activities, and encourage the consideration of social, environmental, and other impacts of engineering design decisions. Testing and measurement technologies, such as thermometers and oscilloscopes; software for data acquisition and management; computational and visualization tools, such as graphing calculators and CAD/CAM (i.e., computer design) programs; and the Internet should be used, as appropriate, to support engineering design, particularly at the high school level.

Principle 3. K–12 engineering education should promote engineering habits of mind.

Engineering "habits of mind"[3] align with what many believe are essential skills for citizens in the twenty-first century.[4] These include (1) systems thinking, (2) creativity, (3) optimism, (4) collaboration, (5) communication, and (6) attention to ethical considerations. Systems thinking equips students to recognize essential interconnections in the technological world and to appreciate that systems may have unexpected effects that cannot be predicted from the behavior of individual subsystems. Creativity is inherent in the engineering design process. Optimism reflects a world view in which possibilities and opportunities can be found in every challenge and an understanding that every technology can be improved. Engineering is a "team sport"; collaboration leverages the perspectives, knowledge, and capabilities of team members to address a design challenge. Communication is essential to effective collaboration, to understanding the particular wants and needs of a "customer," and to explaining and justifying the final design solution. Ethical considerations draw attention to the impacts of engineering on people and the environment; ethical considerations include possible unintended consequences of a technology, the potential disproportionate advantages or disadvantages of a technology for certain groups or individuals, and other issues.

These principles, particularly Principle 3, should be considered aspirational rather than a reflection of what is present in current K–12 engineering education efforts or, indeed, in post-secondary engineering education.

THE SCOPE OF K–12 ENGINEERING EDUCATION

Because of the lack of reliable data, it is impossible to gauge how many U.S. K–12 students have been exposed to engineering-related coursework.

---

[3]The committee has adopted the term "habits of mind," as used by the American Association for the Advancement of Science in *Science for All Americans* (1990), to refer to the values, attitudes, and thinking skills associated with engineering.

[4]See, for example, The Partnership for 21st Century Skills, *www.21stcenturyskills.org.*

However, because a number of curriculum projects track the use of their materials, we can derive an indirect measure. With a few notable exceptions (e.g., ECCP, 1971), the first formal K–12 engineering programs in the United States emerged in the early 1990s. Since that time, the committee estimates that no more than 6 million K–12 students have had any kind of formal engineering education. By contrast, the estimated enrollment in 2008 for grades pre-K–12 for U.S. public and private schools was nearly 56 million (DOEd, 2008).

Another measure of the scale of K–12 engineering education is the number of teachers involved. Once again, no reliable data are available on this measure. However, most curricular projects include teacher professional development programs or activities and collect information about the individuals who participate in the training. Based on these and related data, the committee estimates that some 18,000 teachers have received pre- or in-service training to teach engineering-related coursework. This estimate does not take into account the nature, duration, or quality of the training, factors that markedly influence whether a participating teacher continues to teach engineering. By comparison, U.S. public and private middle and high schools employ roughly 276,000 mathematics teachers, 247,000 science teachers,[5] and 25,000 to 35,000 technology education teachers[6] (Dugger, 2007; NCES, 2007).

Finding 3. K–12 engineering education in the United States is supported by a relatively small number of curricular and teacher professional development initiatives.

K–12 curricular initiatives have been developed independently, often have different goals, and have been created by individuals with very different backgrounds and perspectives. In addition, the treatment of engineering concepts, engineering design, and relationships among engineering and other STEM subjects varies greatly. For these reasons, it is difficult to compare directly their strengths and weaknesses.

Finding 4. Even though engineering education is a small slice of the K–12 educational pie, activity in this arena has increased significantly, from almost no curricula or programs 15 years ago to several dozen today.

---

[5]The figures for science and mathematics teachers do not include the over 1 million public and private school elementary school generalists, who are frequently responsible for teaching both subjects.

[6]Variations in research methodologies over the years have resulted in some uncertainty about the exact number of technology education teachers working in the United States.

At this point, it is impossible to predict whether this upward trend will continue, flatten out, or reverse itself. The committee believes that the future of K–12 engineering education will depend at least in part on whether engineering becomes a catalyst for integrated STEM education. (This idea is discussed more fully at the end of this chapter.)

Through the course of the project, the committee has come to appreciate the important role that technology education has played in the development of K–12 engineering education. Indeed, evidence suggests that technology educators form the bulk of the teaching force for engineering in K–12 classrooms, and many curricula intended to convey engineering concepts and skills have been developed in part or whole by those in the field. Given its historical hands-on, project-based emphasis and the more recent focus on technological literacy, it is not surprising technology education has gravitated toward engineering.

IMPACTS OF K–12 ENGINEERING EDUCATION

Finding 5. While having considerable inherent value, the most intriguing possible benefit of K–12 engineering education relates to improved student learning and achievement in mathematics and science and enhanced interest in these subjects because of their relevance to real-world problem solving. However, the limited amount of reliable data does not provide a basis for unqualified claims of impact.

Even fewer quality data are available on the impacts of K–12 engineering education on student engagement, technological literacy, understanding of engineering, and interest in engineering as a possible career. The paucity of data reflects a modest, unsystematic effort to measure, or even define, learning and other outcomes. Before engineering education can become a mainstream component of K–12 education, this information gap must be filled. Without better data, policy makers, teachers, parents, and others with a stake in the education of children will have no basis for making sound decisions.

RECOMMENDATION 1. Foundations and federal agencies with an interest in K–12 engineering education should support long-term research to confirm and refine the findings of smaller studies on the impacts of engineering education on student learning in STEM subjects, student engagement and retention, understanding of engineering, career aspirations, and technological literacy. In addition to looking at impact, researchers should attempt to ascertain, from a learning sciences perspective, how curricular materials are being used by teachers in the classroom.

RECOMMENDATION 2. Funders of new efforts to develop and implement curricula for K–12 engineering education should include a research component that will provide a basis for analyzing how design ideas and practices develop in students over time and determining the classroom conditions necessary to support this development. After a solid analytic foundation has been established, a rigorous evaluation should be undertaken to determine what works and why.

THE NATURE OF K–12 ENGINEERING EDUCATION

Finding 6. Based on reviews of the research literature and curricular materials, the committee finds no widely accepted vision of the nature of K–12 engineering education.[7]

A lack of consensus does not reflect disagreements among the visions of K–12 engineering education. Rather, it represents ad hoc development and that no major effort has been made to define the content of K–12 engineering education in a rigorous way.

Curriculum Content

Our curriculum review revealed that the central activity of engineering—engineering design—is a dominant feature of most of the curricular and professional-development activities we examined. Both curriculum developers and providers of professional development programs seem to understand engineering design as an iterative, problem-solving process in which multiple solutions are possible. However, the treatment of key ideas in engineering, many closely related to engineering design, is much more uneven and, in some cases, shows a lack of understanding on the part of curriculum developers. Some concepts, such as systems, are generally well explained and appropriately used to support student learning, but others, such as optimization, modeling, and analysis, are incompletely developed or presented in ways that do not reflect their role in engineering practice.

---

[7]This finding appears to apply also to the non-U.S. pre-college engineering education initiatives considered in this project (see Chapter 4).

One reason for these shortcomings is the absence of a clear articulation of the engineering knowledge, skills, and habits of mind that are most important, how they relate to and build on each other, and how and when (i.e., at what age) they should be introduced to students. As far as the committee knows, no one has attempted to develop a rigorous, systematic specification of age-appropriate learning progressions. A handful of states, most notably Massachusetts (Massachusetts Department of Education, 2006), has developed K–12 curriculum "frameworks" that include a modest degree of engineering content. The majority of state-developed learning goals, however, do not consider engineering at all.

Finding 7. The variability and unevenness in the curricula we reviewed can be attributed largely to the lack of specificity and the lack of a consensus on learning outcomes and progressions.

One approach to addressing this problem might be to develop content standards for K–12 engineering education. After discussing this idea several times, most committee members concluded that, although a thoughtful, authoritative parsing of engineering content appropriate for K–12 would lead to more coherence in teaching and learning, another layer of academic requirements in the current standards-laden U.S. education system would surely meet with strong resistance. A study by the National Academy of Engineering is already under way on the value and feasibility of developing standards for K–12 engineering education, and the results of that study could provide valuable guidance on this important issue.

Curriculum Connections

Finding 8. Existing curricula do not fully exploit the natural connections between engineering and the other three STEM subjects.

The three most important types of interconnection—(1) scientific investigation and engineering design, (2) mathematical analysis and modeling, and (3) technological literacy and K–12 engineering education—are described below.

Scientific Investigation and Engineering Design

Scientific investigation and engineering design are closely related activities that can be mutually reinforcing. Both are methods of solving problems, both must be conducted within constraints, and both require creative thinking, communication, and collaboration. In the curricula we reviewed, we found instances in which scientific inquiry was used to explore the interface between science and technology and, less often, to generate data that could then be used to inform engineering design decisions. We also found numerous instances in which engineering design was used to provide contextualized opportunities for science learning.

A more systematic linkage between engineering design and scientific inquiry to improve learning in both domains has intriguing possibilities. One option, which was evident in several of the curricula we reviewed, is to use engineering as a pedagogical strategy for laboratory activities.

Mathematical Analysis and Modeling

Although mathematical analysis and modeling are essential to engineering design, very few of the curricula or professional development initiatives reviewed by the committee used mathematics in ways that support modeling and analysis. There may be many reasons for this. Curriculum developers may be unfamiliar with how mathematics is used in engineering design or may not understand mathematics learning progressions. Curriculum developers may have concerns about students' mathematical understanding and skills and may be afraid that poor performance would be a barrier to exposing students to engineering material.

Despite the paucity of mathematics in most curricula, the committee believes that K–12 engineering education could contribute to improvements in students' understanding and performance on certain areas of mathematics. For example, numerical manipulations required for measurements and analyses associated with engineering design may, through exposure and repetition, increase students' confidence in their mathematical abilities. In addition, specific concepts, such as ratio and proportion, fractions, and decimals, are useful for a variety of engineering design projects. Understanding these concepts is closely linked to success in algebra, which is a gatekeeper course for advancement in STEM education (NMAP, 2008).

RECOMMENDATION 3. The National Science Foundation and/or U.S. Department of Education should fund research to determine how science inquiry and mathematical reasoning can be connected to engineering design in K–12 curricula and teacher professional development. The research should be attentive to grade-level differences in classroom environment and student cognitive development and cover the following specific areas:

- the most important concepts, skills, and habits of mind in science and mathematics that can be taught effectively using an engineering design approach;
- the circumstances under which students learn important science and mathematics concepts, skills, and habits of mind through an engineering-design approach as well or better than through science or mathematics instruction;
- how engineering design can be used as a pedagogical strategy in science and mathematics instruction; and
- the implications for professional development of using engineering design as a pedagogical tool for supporting science and mathematics learning.

Technological Literacy and K–12 Engineering Education

Technology in K–12 engineering education has primarily been used to illustrate the products of engineering and provide a context for thinking about engineering design. However, using engineering to explore ideas consistent with other elements of technological literacy, such as the nature and history of technology and the cultural, social, economic, and political dimensions of technology development are less prevalent.

A number of concepts important to understanding the nature of technology, such as systems, optimization, and trade-offs, are salient to engineering design. The way technology has influenced the course of human affairs provides a natural bridge to other K–12 subjects, such as social studies and history. For students to have an appreciation of the value and limits of engineering, they should have an understanding of the nontechnical dimensions of technology, such as an awareness that all technologies can have unintended consequences and that the decisions to develop and use a technology necessarily involve ethical considerations.

The committee believes that the value of K–12 engineering curricula and of professional development for teachers of K–12 engineering would be increased by stronger connections to technological literacy, as described in such documents as the *Standards for Technological Literacy: Content for the Study of Technology* (ITEA, 2000).

Professional Development Programs

Finding 9. As reflected in the near absence of pre-service education as well as the small number of teachers who have experienced in-service professional development, teacher preparation for K–12 engineering is far less developed than for other STEM subjects.

Nearly all teacher in-service initiatives for K–12 engineering education are associated with a few curriculum projects. Many of these professional development initiatives lack one or more of the characteristics known to lead to teacher learning, such as professional development that lasts for a week or longer, ongoing in-classroom or online support following formal training, and opportunities for continuing education. No active pre-service initiatives seem likely to contribute significantly to the supply of qualified engineering teachers in the near future. Indeed, the qualifications for an engineering educator at the K–12 level have not even been defined. Thus, although graduates of a handful of teacher-preparation programs have strong backgrounds in STEM subjects, including engineering, few if any of them appear to end up teaching K–12 engineering classes.

The reader should keep in mind the important differences between elementary and secondary schools and between teachers in these two branches of the K–12 education system. At the elementary level, separate courses for individual subjects and teachers with special credentials, for example, a licensed "engineering teacher," are very rare. At the secondary level, teacher specialization is more common. Thus approaches to professional development vary depending on grade level.

According to input from the workshops and public comments on the committee's project summary report, many K–12 teachers are unfamiliar with engineering, do not have content knowledge in science, and have relatively little preparation for teaching mathematics. All of these factors are certain to make in-service professional development for engineering education less effective. Furthermore, no accepted model for professional development for K–12 engineering has yet been developed. However, based on research in other domains, such as mathematics and science, we can get a good idea of successful approaches to preparing teachers in engineering.

Current K–12 engineering teachers come predominantly from the ranks of technology educators. Only a few science and math teachers teach engineering; even fewer engineers have become K–12 teachers. The lack of certification or licensing for "engineering" teachers, which is an issue at the secondary school level, reflects the relative newness of the field and uncertainties about the knowledge and pedagogical skills engineering teachers need to be competent. Over the long term, it is not clear where future engineering teachers for K–12 will come from, which could delay the acceptance of K–12 engineering education as a mainstream component of the school curriculum.

RECOMMENDATION 4. The American Society of Engineering Education (ASEE), through its Division of K–12 and Pre-College Education, should begin a national dialogue on preparing K–12 engineering teachers to address the very different needs and circumstances of elementary and secondary teachers and the pros and cons of establishing a formal credentialing process. Participants in the dialogue should include leaders in K–12 teacher education in mathematics, science, and technology; schools of education and engineering; state departments of education; teacher licensing and certification groups; and STEM program accreditors. ASEE should consult with the National Center for Engineering and Technology Education, which has conducted research on this topic.

Diversity

Finding 10. Based on evaluations, anecdotal reports, and our own observations, lack of diversity is a serious issue for K–12 engineering education.

As was noted in Chapter 2, the lack of diversity in post-secondary engineering education and the engineering workforce in the United States has been well documented The diversity problem in K–12 engineering is manifested in two ways. First, the number of girls and underrepresented minorities who participate in K–12 engineering education initiatives does not correspond to their proportion of the general population. Second, with a handful of exceptions, curricular materials do not portray engineering in ways likely to be meaningful to students from a broad range of ethnic and cultural backgrounds. Such students often have life experiences and technological interests different from those of the curriculum developers or of the majority culture.

For K–12 engineering education to yield the benefits its supporters claim for it, access and participation will have to be broadened considerably, if only because, according to predictions, the U.S. population will shift to "majority minority" by midcentury (U.S. Census Bureau, 2008). Thus ensuring that a wide range of K–12 students have an opportunity to experience engineering education will require reaching out to diverse groups and may lead, in the long run, to a more diverse technical workforce, which some have argued will be more capable of anticipating and addressing the technological needs of a diverse society and a global marketplace (Page, 2007).

Attracting girls and minority students to K–12 engineering education will require pro-active efforts by curriculum developers, teachers, providers of professional development, and supporters of these efforts. These efforts could include more effective communication about the work of engineers and how it contributes to human welfare. As part of a recent project at the National Academy of Engineering, messages for improving public understanding of engineering were developed and tested for their effectiveness and appeal to young people of all backgrounds (NAE, 2008). Tests on teens and adults, including large samples of African Americans and Hispanics, showed that the most effective messages stress the beneficial impacts of engineering on people and the environment.

RECOMMENDATION 5. Given the demographic trends in the United States and the challenges of attracting girls, African Americans, Hispanics, and some Asian subpopulations to engineering studies, K–12 engineering curricula should be developed with special attention to features which appeal to students from these underrepresented groups, and programs that promote K–12 engineering education should be strategic in their outreach to these populations. Both curriculum developers and outreach organizations should take advantage of recent market research that suggests effective ways of communicating about engineering to the public.

POLICY AND PROGRAM ISSUES

Many questions remain to be answered about the best way to deliver engineering education in the K–12 classroom and its potential on a variety of parameters of interest, such as science and mathematics learning, technological literacy, and student interest in engineering as a career. Despite these uncertainties, engineering is already being taught in K–12 schools scattered around the country, and, the trend appears to be upward. Given this situation, it is important that we consider the best way to provide guidance and support to encourage this trend.

An underlying question for policy makers is how engineering concepts, skills, and habits of mind should be introduced into the curriculum. There are at least three options along a continuum in terms of ease of implementation—ad hoc infusion, stand-alone courses, and interconnected STEM education.

- Ad hoc infusion, the introduction, or infusion, of engineering ideas and activities (i.e., design projects) into existing science, mathematics, and technology curricula is the most direct and least complicated option, because implementation requires no significant changes in school structure. The main requirements would be (1) willingness on the part of teachers and (2) access to instructional materials. Ideally, teachers would also have a modicum of engineering pedagogical content knowledge to deliver the new material effectively. The ad hoc option is probably most useful for providing an introductory exposure to engineering ideas rather than a deep understanding of engineering principles and skills.
- Stand-alone courses for engineering, an option required for implementing many of the curricula reviewed for this project, presents considerably more challenges for teachers and schools. In high schools, the new material could be offered as an elective. If that is not possible, it would either have to replace existing classes or content, perhaps a science or technology course, or the school day would have to be reconfigured—perhaps lengthened—to accommodate a new course(s) without eliminating existing curriculum. Stand-alone courses would also require teacher professional development and approval at various levels (e.g., state department of education, school board). This option has the potential advantage of providing a more in-depth exposure to engineering.
- Fully interconnected STEM education, that is, using engineering concepts and skills to leverage the natural connections between STEM subjects, would almost certainly require changes in the structure and practices of schools. Research would be necessary to develop and test curricula, assessments, and approaches to teacher professional development. New interconnected STEM programs or "pilot schools" might be established to test changes before they are widely adopted.

The three options just described, as well as others that are not described here, are not mutually exclusive. Indeed, the committee believes that implementation of K–12 engineering education must be flexible because no single approach is likely to be acceptable or feasible in every district or school. To illustrate the need for flexibility, three case studies of schools that have made engineering a significant part of their curricula can be found in the annex to this chapter.

Broader inclusion of engineering studies in the K–12 classroom also will be influenced by state education standards, which often determine the content of state assessments and, to a lesser extent, curriculum used in the classroom. Forty states have adopted the technological literacy standards developed by the International Technology Education Association, which contain a number of learning goals related to engineering design (Dugger, 2007). However, only 12 states require students to take coursework in technology education as a requirement of graduation.

It is worth noting that the No Child Left Behind Act of 2001 (P.L 107-110) puts considerable pressure on schools and teachers to prepare K–12 students to take annual assessments in mathematics, reading/language arts, and science,[8] and these assessments are based on state learning standards. Thus NCLB currently provides little impetus for teaching engineering.

Plans for implementing changes to include engineering in a school curriculum at any level must take into account places and populations (e.g., small rural schools, urban schools with high proportions of students of low socio-economic status, etc.) with a limited capacity to access engineering-education resources.

Another important element of implementation is the "technical core" of education, that is, what actually happens in the classroom between the teacher, the student, and the content (Elmore, 2000). In many respects, this is where real change and improvements in teacher practice and student learning occur. However, it is also very difficult for reformers to gain access, because schools have structures and traditions to isolate this core from the effects of change. One way to gain access might be to work toward "coherence," that is, to create educational systems in which standards, curricula, professional development, and student assessments are aligned and school leadership supports the need for change. A recent report from the National Science Board (NSB, 2007) calls for more coordination among stakeholders

---

[8]Unlike in mathematics and reading, scores from the science assessments are not used to judge states' progress toward so-called Adequate Yearly Progress, a measure of the proportion of children who are meeting or exceeding specified achievement levels.

in STEM education and urges the development of national STEM content guidelines and student assessments as part of an effort to encourage "horizontal coordination and coherence." Although the current situation for K–12 engineering shows little evidence of coherence, working toward greater coherence is an important, long-term objective.

The committee believes that, ideally, all K–12 students in the United States should have the option of experiencing some form of formal engineering studies. We are a long way from that situation now.

RECOMMENDATION 6. Philanthropic foundations or federal agencies with an interest in STEM education and school reform should fund research to identify models of implementation for K–12 engineering education that embody the principles of coherence and can guide decision making that will work for widely variable American school systems. The research should explicitly address school populations that do not currently have access to engineering studies and take into account the different needs and circumstances of elementary and secondary school populations.

K–12 engineering also has policy and program implications for the articulation between high school and college. If K–12 engineering education emphasizes design activities, then two- and four-year post-secondary institutions may have to place early emphasis on design projects to avoid "turning off" students who expect that experience in their first year. Schools of engineering and other post-secondary institutions may also have to improve interactions among science, mathematics, and technology departments to accommodate the expectations of students who have experienced interconnected STEM education in high school.

Finally, the need for qualified teachers to teach engineering in K–12 classrooms raises a number of policy and program issues. Putting aside the uncertain definition of "qualified" in this context, it is not clear that solutions are available that can be funded, accommodated in the current structure of schools, and sustained. A variety of traditional and alternative mechanisms should be evaluated as part of the initiative suggested in Recommendation 4.

INTEGRATED STEM EDUCATION

Perhaps the most compelling argument for K–12 engineering education can be made if it is not thought of as a topic unto itself, but rather as part of integrated STEM education (Box 6-1). After all, in the real world engineering is not performed in isolation—it inevitably involves science, technology, and mathematics. The question is why these subjects should be isolated in schools. This same issue was raised by Project 2061 of the American Association for the Advancement of Science more than 15 years ago, long before the STEM acronym appeared on the scene (AAAS, 1993, pp. 321–322).

By "science," Project 2061 means basic and applied natural and social science, basic and applied mathematics, and engineering and technology, and their interconnections—which is to say the scientific enterprise as a whole. The basic point is that the ideas and practice of science, mathematics, and technology are so closely intertwined that we do not see how education in any one of them can be undertaken well in isolation from the others.

BOX 6-1
"Integrated" STEM Education

The committee chose to use the word "integrated" to describe its vision for STEM education, in part because this term is in wide use already within the education community. The modest literature that examines efforts at integration in STEM education mostly concerns science and mathematics (e.g., Berlin and Lee, 2005; Pang and Good, 2000) and, occasionally, science and technology (e.g., Geraedts et al., 2006). Integration suggests connections on at least one and perhaps many levels, including curriculum, professional development, instruction, and standards, in concert with supporting policies at the school, district, or state level. A major barrier to discerning which integration approaches may be effective and why is that researchers and practitioners appear to have no common definition of what integration means (Hurley, 2001). In addition, some types of integration may have higher barriers to implementation than others (e.g., Czerniak et al., 1999). For example, integration may require a high level of teacher content and pedagogical content knowledge in multiple STEM fields. Other models of integration, with lower barriers to implementation, might rely on content specialists in individual STEM disciplines to introduce students to key concepts in those areas. Some concepts would be reinforced or elaborated through connections to other subjects. For example, the design process could be taught by a biology teacher in the context of biomimicry or by a physics teacher exploring assistive technologies. Schools could facilitate this kind of integration by co-locating STEM teaching areas, identifying STEM "teams," providing time for STEM teachers to coordinate lesson plans, and encouraging STEM teams to redesign existing activities to emphasize connections.

Finding 11. Although the term "STEM education" is used in national education policy, it is not implemented in a way that reflects the interdependence of the four STEM subjects.

Although the committee did not target K–12 STEM education initiatives specifically, based on the personal experience and judgment of committee members, the great majority of efforts to promote STEM education in the United States to date focus on either science or mathematics (generally not both) and rarely include engineering or technology (beyond the use of computers). By contrast, the committee's vision of STEM education in U.S. K–12 schools includes all students graduating from high school with a level of "STEM literacy" sufficient to (1) ensure their success in employment, post-secondary education, or both, and (2) prepare them to be competent, capable citizens in a technology-dependent, democratic society. (The three school case studies described in the annex to this chapter represent varying degrees of STEM integration.) Engineering education, because of its natural connections to science, mathematics, and technology, might serve as a catalyst for achieving this vision. The committee was not asked to determine the qualities that would characterize a STEM-literate person, but making such a determination would be a worthwhile exercise.

RECOMMENDATION 7. The National Science Foundation should support research to characterize, or define, "STEM literacy," including how such literacy might develop over the course of a student's K–12 school experience. Researchers should consider not only core knowledge and skills in science, technology, engineering, and mathematics, but also the "big ideas" that link the four subject areas.

Pursuing a goal of STEM literacy in K–12 will require a paradigm shift by teachers, administrators, textbook publishers, and policy makers, as well as by scientists, technologists, engineers, and mathematicians involved in K–12 education. Standards of learning, instructional materials, teacher professional development, and student assessments will have to be re-examined and, possibly, updated, revised, and coordinated. Professional societies will have to rethink their outreach activities to K–12 schools in light of STEM literacy. Colleges and universities will have to cope with student expectations that may run counter to traditional departmental stovepipe conceptions of courses, disciplines, and degrees.

Why do we suggest such a comprehensive change? First, the committee believes that STEM-literate students would be better prepared for life in the twenty-first century and better able to make career decisions or pursue post-secondary education. Second, interconnected STEM education could improve teaching and learning in all four subjects by reducing excessive expectations for K–12 STEM teaching and learning. This does not mean that teaching should be "dumbed down," but rather that teaching and learning in fewer key STEM areas should be deepened and that more time should be spent on the development of a set of STEM skills that includes engineering design and scientific inquiry.

A FINAL WORD

In the course our efforts to understand and assess the potential of engineering education for K–12 students, the committee underwent an epiphany of sorts. To put it simply, for engineering education to become more than an afterthought in elementary and secondary schools in this country, STEM education as a whole must be reconsidered. The teaching of STEM subjects must move away from its current siloed structure, which may limit student interest and performance, toward a more interconnected whole. The committee did not plan to come to this conclusion but reached this point after much thought and deliberation.

We feel confident that our instincts are correct, but other organizations and individuals will have to translate our findings and recommendations into action. Meaningful improvements in the learning and teaching of engineering and movement toward integrated STEM education will not come easily or quickly. Progress will be measured in decades, rather than months or years. The changes will require a sustained commitment of financial resources, the support of policy makers and other leaders, and the efforts of many individuals both in and outside of K–12 schools. Despite these challenges, the committee is hopeful that the changes will be made. The potential for enriching and improving K–12 STEM education is real, and engineering education can be the catalyst.

REFERENCES

AAAS (American Association for the Advancement of Science). 1990. Science for All Americans. New York: Oxford University Press.

AAAS. 1993. Benchmarks for Science Literacy. New York: Oxford University Press.

Almeida, H.A., P.J. Bartolo, and J.C. Ferreira. 2008. Mechanical behaviour and vascularisation analysis of tissue engineering scaffolds. Pp. 73–80 in Proceedings of the 3rd International Conference on Advanced Research in Virtual and Rapid Prototyping: Virtual and Rapid Manufacturing Advanced Research Virtual and Rapid Prototyping.

Berlin, D.F., and H. Lee. 2005. Integrating science and mathematics education: historical analysis. School Science and Mathematics 105(1): 15–24.

Czerniak, C.M., W.B. Weber, Jr., A. Sandmann, and J. Ahern. 1999. A literature review of science and mathematics integration. School Science and Mathematics 99(8): 421–430.

DOEd (U.S. Department of Education). 2008. National Center for Education Statistics. Digest of Education Statistics, 2007 (NCES 2008-022), Table 3. Available online at *http://nces.ed.gov/fastfacts/display.asp?id=65* (October 1, 2008).

Dugger, W.E., Jr. 2007. The status of technology education in the United States: a triennial report of the findings from the states. The Technology Teacher 67(1): 14–21.

ECCP (Engineering Concepts Curriculum Project). 1971. The Man-Made World. New York: McGraw Hill.

Elmore, R.F. 2000. Building a New Structure for School Leadership. Washington, D.C.: The Albert Shanker Institute.

Geraedts, C., K.T. Boersma, and H.M.C. Eijkelhof. 2006. Towards coherent science and technology education. Journal of Curriculum Studies 38(3): 307–325.

Gogate, P. R., and A. M. Kabadi. 2009. A review of applications of cavitation in biochemical engineering/biotechnology. Biochemical Engineering Journal 44(1): 60–72.

Hood, L., L. Rowen, D.J. Galas, and J.D. Aitchison. 2008. Systems biology at the Institute for Systems Biology. Briefings in Functional Genomics and Proteomics 7(4): 239–248.

Hurley, M.M. 2001. Reviewing integrated science and mathematics: the search for evidence and definitions from new perspectives. School Science and Mathematics 101(5): 259–268.

ITEA (International Technology Education Association). 2000. Standards for Technological Literacy: Content for the Study of Technology. Reston, Va.: ITEA.

Massachusetts Department of Education. 2006. Massachusetts Science and Technology/Engineering Curriculum Framework. Available online at *http://www.doe.mass.edu/frameworks/scitech/1006.doc* (accessed April 2, 2009).

NAE (National Academy of Engineering). 2008. Changing the Conversation: Messages for Improving Public Understanding of Engineering. Washington, D.C.: The National Academies Press.

NCES (National Center for Education Statistics). 2009. Teacher Attrition and Mobility: Results from the 2004-05 Teacher Follow-Up Survey. First Look. Table 2 and Table 3. U.S. Department of Education. Available online at *http://nces.ed.gov/pubs2007/2007307.pdf* (January 29, 2009).

NMAP (National Mathematics Advisory Panel). 2008. Foundations for Success: The Final Report of the National Mathematics Advisory Panel. Washington, D.C.: U.S. Department of Education. Available online at *http://www.ed.gov/about/bdscomm/list/mathpanel/report/final-report.pdf* (January 6, 2009).

NSB (National Science Board). 2007. National Action Plan for Addressing the Critical Needs of the U.S. Science, Technology, Engineering, and Mathematics Education System. NSB 07-114. Arlington, Va.: National Science Foundation.

Page, S.E. 2007. The Difference: How the Power of Diversity Creates Better Groups, Firms, Schools, and Societies. Princeton, N.J.: Princeton University Press.

Pang, J., and R. Good. 2000. A review of the integration of science and mathematics: implications for further research. School Science and Mathematics 100(2): 73–82.

U.S. Census Bureau. 2008. An older and more diverse nation by midcentury. Press release, Aug. 14, 2008, U.S. Census Bureau News. Available online at *http://www.census.gov/Press-Release/www/releases/archives/population/012496.html* (November 6, 2008).

Annex

THREE CASE STUDIES

High Tech High

At High Tech High in San Diego, engineering instruction is integrated not only with the other STEM subjects (science, technology, and mathematics), but also with many other subjects, including art, writing, and literature. High Tech High is a compelling example of how engineering can be woven into the fabric of a high-school curriculum.

High Tech High was founded in 2000 by a group of San Diego educators and business leaders as a charter high school. Since then, it has grown to include five high schools, two middle schools, and one affiliated elementary school. The goal of High Tech High is to provide students with personalized, project-based instruction (High Tech High, 2008a). Teachers work closely with students, adapting class content to individual learners. Students take only four subjects per semester, instead of the usual six or seven, to ensure that the curriculum remains focused. The school has no sports teams, no marching band—just academics.

Class sizes are small—generally 20 to 25 students—as is the student body. In 2008, the eight schools that make up High Tech High had a total of 2,500 students; even the oldest and largest of the eight, Gary and Jerri-Ann Jacobs High Tech High, had only 490 students in grades 9 through 12 (High Tech High, 2008b).

The success of High Tech High in teaching students from diverse backgrounds has been widely reported (e.g., Murphy, 2004). Students are selected by lottery from a pool of applicants from all over San Diego County; no aptitude tests or assessments are required for admission. Yet every high school student graduates, and every one of the graduates has been accepted to a college, 80 percent to four-year colleges and universities (High Tech High,

2008a). About 35 percent of High Tech High graduates so far have been the first in their families to attend college, some the first to finish high school. Colleges attended include Stanford, University of California at Berkeley, Massachusetts Institute of Technology, Yale, Dartmouth, Georgetown, Northwestern, and Rensselaer Polytechnic Institute. More than 30 percent of High Tech High alumni enter a science, engineering, or mathematics field, compared with a national average of 17 percent (High Tech High, 2008c).

Engineering has been taught at High Tech High almost since its inception. Near the end of the inaugural 2000–2001 school year, David Berggren was hired to be an engineering instructor starting in the fall of 2001. Like a number of other teachers at the school, Berggren did not have a traditional teaching background. He studied engineering at the California Maritime Academy, where he earned a B.S. in marine engineering technology with a minor in computer science; he then worked for several years on factory fishing trawlers in the Bering Sea. In 2000 and 2001, he worked with his father to build, from scratch, a 58-foot steel salmon-fishing boat, which was delivered to its owners in Alaska in May 2001. By that time, looking for something different to do, Berggren had applied for the teaching position at High Tech High and had been accepted.

With no formal training on how to teach engineering to high school students—indeed, with no background in education at all—Berggren turned to the Project Lead the Way (PLTW) program, which, he says, was a "lifesaver." PLTW provides a variety of well developed modules and courses that can be taught as is to engineering students. Berggren found that by using PLTW, he was able to focus his attention on aspects of teaching other than course development. For his first course, on the principles of engineering, he used PLTW's course materials. As he became more comfortable and familiar with the materials and with teaching, he began modifying PLTW material to suit his students' needs and his own ideas of the best way to teach the subject.

Berggren found himself teaching different areas of engineering, depending on the students' interests and on the other teachers with whom he was collaborating at the time. To do this, he had to ask himself exactly what his students should be learning about engineering. "Over the years, it's something I really struggled with—what is common across the different fields of engineering." Ultimately, he says, he decided that the most important thing was for the students to learn and be able to use the design process. "I feel like this design process is not only common to all areas of engineering, but it's something that can be applied to all areas of life," he says.

In the past few years, Berggren has been teaching engineering design principles to seniors at High Tech High who must all complete a senior project (a large, complex project, sometimes combined with a few small projects to help them get started). Berggren is one of six teachers teaching these seniors; the others are an art teacher, a multimedia teacher, a physics teacher, and two English teachers. The students rotate through four of them, two each semester, so that one group of students may take, for example, art and physics in the fall and English and engineering in the spring. Each semester course is actually a double course that takes up half the day; by the end of the year students have taken a full-year equivalent of art, physics, English, and engineering. "In the past we let the seniors choose their disciplines," Berggren says, "but we decided we wanted to expose them to as much as possible." Now the school decides which of the four classes each senior will take. "We're constantly changing," Berggren says, "trying new things."

Whenever possible, the senior-project teachers collaborate so no matter which courses a particular student takes in a given semester, he or she will be taught with an emphasis on various connections and common subjects. This is easier to do for some pairings than others, Berggren notes. When he was paired with the art teacher, for instance, they worked on creating pots. In the spring 2008, he was paired with an English literature teacher, and they did mostly separate things.

Over the years, Berggren says, he has found that the most difficult thing for students working on a senior project with an engineering component has been to identify the problem that had to be solved. So, before the 2007–2008 school year, he traveled to Purdue University to be trained in their Engineering Projects in Community Service (EPICS) program. EPICS students work in design teams to solve problems for nonprofit organizations in the local community (Coyle et al., 2005). Originally developed for students in college engineering classes, EPICS is now being tested in 15 to 20 high schools around the country, including High Tech High.

Today, instead of students trying to come up with a design problem on their own, Berggren has them begin by researching nonprofit organizations in the community. Once a group of students decides on a nonprofit they would like to work with, they set up a meeting with members of that organization to discuss what they can design to help the organization run better or to do things it can't do. "The students identify a problem, research it, see what's been done, come up with solutions, settle on a design, build it, test it, and deliver it to the organization," Berggren says. "They have a real customer—it's not me telling them what to do. And it gives them more 'buy in' because they are selecting the organization."

In one case, Berggren describes how his students worked with the local chapter of United Cerebral Palsy to design a specialized paper holder for a woman with visual problems. To keep her place on a line of words as she was typing, she had an assistant move a bar along the paper for her. The students created a motor-driven system "that allows her to move the bar up and down herself," Berggren says. "She was just beaming with excitement and joy, and the students were really excited. They felt they had really done something to change this person's life."

In addition to PLTW and EPICS, Berggren also works with US FIRST, an organization started by the inventor Dean Kamen to inspire young people's interest in science and engineering (FIRST is an acronym for For Inspiration and Recognition of Science and Technology). US FIRST sponsors and organizes robotics competitions in which teams of students have six weeks to solve a particular problem using a standard parts kit and a common set of rules (US FIRST, 2008).

Berggren sponsors a team for his students as an extracurricular activity. About 30 students participate, including students from other schools in the High Tech High system. Besides designing and building their robot, the students also make presentations at schools, conferences, and local fairs. US FIRST expects the team to run itself as a corporation, Berggren says, with the goal of learning how engineering is done in the real world. Many late nights and weekends are spent working, he says. "I do it because you see what the kids get out of it."

The kids also get much out of the High Tech High engineering classes, he says, especially "an understanding of and an interest in engineering." Of the 80 students in his engineering classes over the course of a year, he estimates that about 15 to 20 percent pursue engineering in college. And, he says, at least a few of them tell him something along the lines of, "I had no idea what this was, it never crossed my radar screen, but now I want to go on to college and study engineering."

REFERENCES

Coyle, E.J., L H. Jamieson, and W.C. Oakes. 2005. EPICS: Engineering Projects in Community Service. International Journal of Engineering Education 21(1):139-150. Also available online at *http://epics.ecn.purdue.edu/about/papers/IJEE1549.pdf* (accessed May 26, 2008).

High Tech High. 2008a. About High Tech High. Available online at *http://www.hightechhigh.org/about/* (accessed May 23, 2008).

High Tech High. 2008b. The Gary and Jerri-Ann Jacobs High Tech High. Available online at *http://www.hightechhigh.org/schools/HTH/* (accessed May 23, 2008).

High Tech High. 2008c. Results. Available online at *http://www.hightechhigh.org/about/ results.php* (accessed May 23, 2008).

Murphy, V. 2004. Where everyone can overachieve. Forbes, October 11, 2004. Also available online at *http://www.forbes.com/forbes/2004/1011/080_print.html* (accessed May 23, 2008).

US FIRST. 2008. What is FRC? Available online at *http://www.usfirst.org/what/default. aspx?id=366* (accessed May 26, 2008).

Texarkana ISD K–16 Engineering Collaborative

Texarkana Independent School District (TISD) and Texas A&M University-Texarkana have forged a powerful partnership. Working together, they are building a pipeline for students well versed in science, technology, engineering, and math (STEM) education from kindergarten through college. This model, the first of its kind in the country, may turn out to be one that can be replicated in other school districts.

The planning for the program, officially called the Texas A&M University-Texarkana—Texarkana ISD K–16 Engineering Collaborative—began in January 2005, when a blue-ribbon committee of TISD had its first meeting. Members of the committee included parents, community and business leaders, and school district representatives. The purpose of the meeting was to review the school district's facilities and programs and determine how to improve its STEM program. This committee had a strong incentive—a need for more engineers at the local level to support businesses, such as International Paper, Domtar Paper Mill, and Alcoa.

As plans for the K–16 vertically aligned program evolved, the planning committee received good news. The family of Josh Morriss, Jr., donated land near the Texas A&M-Texarkana campus for the new K–5 elementary school. The first piece of the K–16 pipeline, this school, called the Martha and Josh Morriss Mathematics and Engineering Elementary School, focuses on math, science, and engineering.

The new school opened its doors in the fall of 2007, with Principal Rick Sandlin at the helm. Students apply to attend the school and are selected on a first-come-first-served basis. The school's first cohort of 396 students has about 23 percent African American, Hispanic, Asian, and American Indian students and 15 percent from low-income households. No matter where the students live or what their backgrounds are, they are all expected to live up to the school's high standards.

The planning team of TISD decided to develop its own engineering curriculum working with faculty from Texas A&M to design K–5 learning units that would be age-appropriate, hands-on, and conceptually based. The units are also aligned with the Texas Essential Knowledge and Skills (TEKS) curriculum, so students will be prepared for the state exams given each year.

The school day begins with engineering. Students work on units covering many topics, such as problem solving, architecture, weather and space, bioengineering, forces of motion, robotics, and engineering structures. "Our goal is to teach as much engineering as we can," explains Sandlin. "We teach the engineering process of 'imagine, plan, design, improve, and share' in the engineering program, as well as throughout the curriculum." At the end of many of the six-week units, students participate in an Engineering Encounter, a presentation for parents and community members to showcase what they have learned. The event also serves as an embedded assessment.

Just as students are held to high standards, so too are teachers. Every teacher in the school must have a master's degree and either Texas Master Mathematics Teacher Certification or Texas Master Technology Teacher Certification, both of which can be obtained through programs at Texas A&M. For teachers who do not yet have a master's degree, the district pays for coursework if the teacher makes a commitment to stay at the school for four years.

In addition to educational requirements, teachers also must take two courses in curriculum design and curriculum delivery designed by Texas A&M faculty specifically for this program. Throughout the school year, the school curriculum coach works with teachers by conducting weekly planning sessions. "We're working on raising the bar in the way we teach engineering," says Principal Sandlin.

By all accounts, these efforts have paid off. In the first year of the program, 98 percent of the students in grades 3 through 5 scored high enough on the state exam to meet the standards in math. Fifth-grade students also take a science assessment test, and 98 percent of them also met those standards. Perhaps even more important, the students clearly enjoy the program. Even though the academics are difficult, most students opt to stay at the school. Of the 396 kids admitted in the first year, only 25 left. The school is already at capacity for the upcoming school year.

In the fall of 2008, the district expanded the engineering program to include the sixth grade. Creating a "school within a school" at Texas Middle School, the district is adding two STEM-related components. The first is a modular program called Synergistic Technologies, a series of science and technology units with an emphasis on problem solving. Working in pairs, students use a combination of hands-on activities and technology to explore a range of topics, including biotechnology, heat and energy, and light and lasers. The modules encourage students to work independently, with the teacher acting as a guide and facilitator.

To prepare for the new academy structure at the middle-school level, all sixth grade teachers participated in a training program in the summer of 2008. The program included an accelerated version of the curriculum design and curriculum delivery courses designed for Morriss Elementary School teachers and is meant to prepare the sixth grade teachers to use inquiry-based, hands-on instructional methods. "If the modules work well in sixth grade, we may consider using them in the seventh and eighth grades, which will be added over the next couple of years," explains Ronnie Thompson, assistant superintendent for school improvement.

The second addition to the middle school program is an accelerated math course for sixth graders, which introduces the main concepts of algebra. This course gives students the background they need to take Algebra I in seventh grade.

By taking the elementary engineering program and the new STEM offerings in middle school, students will be prepared to take the engineering courses already in place at the district high school. As part of the partnership with Texas A&M, a faculty member teaches two electrical engineering courses on the high school campus. Students who take these courses receive both high school and college credit. Other engineering courses at the high school level include AutoCAD and upper level math courses, including statistics and calculus.

"We want to see the program all the way through," says Thompson. "Over the next several years, we will be collecting longitudinal data to determine how many of the 66 kids per grade from the new elementary school program stay with engineering through high school and beyond. While building a strong engineering pipeline, we also want to build a model program that gives all students a strong foundation in math and science."

Denver School of Science and Technology

When the Denver School of Science and Technology (DSST) opened its doors in 2004, it had two goals: (1) to serve an economically and socially diverse population and (2) to ensure that this population succeeded in the school's rigorous science, technology, and engineering curriculum. Since then, DSST has come a long way toward realizing those goals. A college preparatory charter school in the Denver Public School (DPS) system, DSST selects students by lottery. Adding one grade a year, the school now serves all four high school grades; the sixth grade (in middle school) was added in fall 2008. Of the 425 high school students, about 34 percent are African American; 24 percent are Hispanic; and 34 percent are white. About 45 percent are girls, and 46 percent come from low-income households.

"We are a diverse school for a reason," explains Bill Kurtz, who heads the school. "You are going to be living and working with people who are different from you. Part of our goal in this school is to say, 'We have people from all backgrounds, and we are about demonstrating that a community of people can use that difference as a strength.'" Indeed, a close-knit community is integral to the school's culture, which emphasizes hard work and success. But DSST does not expect students to meet these high standards alone. Many mechanisms are in place to ensure that none of them slips through the cracks.

The school day begins with a school-wide meeting to give students and faculty an opportunity to share problems, successes, and issues of concern. Each student is also part of a small bi-weekly advisory class that offers help and support on a smaller scale and closely connects each student with an adult in the school. If students come to school with homework uncompleted, they must stay after school that day to finish it. Tutoring also is available after school. These strategies exemplify how all members of the school live by its core values of respect, responsibility, integrity, courage, curiosity, and doing your best.

Students also exemplify the school's values by working hard to master the rigorous curriculum. The engineering curriculum was designed by University of Colorado, Boulder, professors and DSST teachers. The goal is to interest students in the possibility of studying engineering in college. Although the emphasis in ninth and tenth grade is on building a strong foundation in the liberal arts, students performing at grade level in mathematics and reading can begin taking engineering electives in ninth grade. These design-based courses range from fashion engineering to biomimicry.

In their senior year, students can choose to focus on a physics/engineering program or a biochemistry/biotechnology program. Among the seniors who graduated in 2008, two-thirds opted to specialize in engineering. Those students took both an engineering course and an advanced physics course, which included how physics can be applied to engineering design.

Academic expectations at the school are high. To graduate, all students must pass pre-calculus and complete five core lab-based science courses (physics, chemistry, biology, earth science, and physics/engineering or biochemistry/biotechnology), four years of college preparatory language arts, three years of Spanish, and two electives. "The culture of our school stresses engineering and applied math and science degree paths and careers more than any other school I have seen," says Mark Heffron, head of the math department, who has two engineering degrees. "Engineering is often stressed as a reason for learning something in a math or science class."

Another way DSST strives to make the curriculum relevant to students' lives is through an internship program. All high school juniors must complete a 10-week internship, which involves "going to work" for about eight hours a week. Ideally, the students work with a mentor who evaluates their progress and is in regular contact with the school. Throughout the internship, students keep a journal and complete other projects as assigned.

Students can choose either an engineering- or science-based internship; 10 to 15 percent opt for an engineering internship. HDR, Inc, is an engineering and architecture firm that often works with students from DSST. According to Terry Heffron, project manager at the company, "We have students analyzing bridge plans, calculating quantities of concrete needed, and figuring out the linear feet of pipe. By the end of the internship, some students have even progressed to the point where they are doing reinforced-concrete design and preliminary wall layouts. They learn very fast."

During senior year, each student is expected to complete a senior project, which includes an extensive research paper and a work product, such as building a solar car, running a conference, creating a presentation, or producing a film. Again, about 10 to 15 percent choose to complete an engineering-related project.

Through DSST's partnership with the University of Colorado at Boulder, one DSST engineering teacher has been trained directly by university professors; in addition, university engineering faculty teach some engineering courses. Mark Heffron, who teaches math and engineering electives and was a structural engineer before becoming a teacher, brings real-world experience directly to the classroom.

Although the school is still quite new, its scores on standardized math tests are the best in DPS. DSST's first class of ninth graders received the highest scores on the Colorado Student Assessment Program (CSAP) math exams, with 55 percent scoring at the proficient or advanced levels, compared to 17 percent in DPS and 38 percent statewide. Sixty-four percent of DSST tenth graders scored at the proficient or advanced level, compared to 18 percent in DPS and 31 percent statewide. For two consecutive years, the ninth grade classes have been one of the top two math classes in DPS.

Perhaps even more gratifying than the specific results on test scores has been DSST's rating on a statewide measure that evaluates not only what students know now but how much they have progressed since entering high school. On this key measurement, DSST showed the top growth rate in DPS.

The school's own statistics help explain why. Of the 132 students in DSST's first freshman class, 100 did not pass a proficiency exam and had to attend a three-week summer academy; not all of the kids from this first group stayed with their class. Some left the program altogether, and 15 were held back a year. The 79 students who stayed with their class and persevered are now among the top achievers in DPS, and all 79 have been accepted to four-year colleges or universities. Of these 79 students, 50 percent are the first in their families to reach this milestone. One-quarter of 2008 DSST graduates went on to study engineering in college, and all seniors in the class of 2009 have been accepted into four-year colleges.

Although this is good news for many students, DSST still faces a serious problem. The level of readiness of students coming to DSST hasn't changed significantly in the past three years. About 75 percent of students who take the post-admission proficiency exam continue to need intensive remediation, and some just cannot catch up in four years. This problem is what motivated DSST to open a middle school in the fall of 2008. "We realized that we have to start working with the students sooner," says DSST founder David Greenberg. "By the time they enter high school, they've had eight years of poor education, and for many, it's almost impossible to catch up. We want to help even more kids succeed, and we think that adding grades 6 through 8 to our program will be the most effective approach."

DSST has accomplished much in its first four years, mostly by plain hard work. But the school also had many advantages. An initial challenge grant from the Bill and Melinda Gates Foundation, contributions from corporate, foundation, and philanthropic donors, and a DPS construction bond enabled DSST to build a state-of-the art building that is inviting to students and conducive to learning. "We held focus groups to find out what the kids wanted," says Greenberg. "Girls wanted nooks where they could peel off into small groups. They wanted bright colors and soft furniture. We did all we could to build a 'cool school.'"

In addition, the exposed ductwork and heating and ventilating systems offer a ready-made engineering lesson. The school also is wireless, making it possible to provide each student with a laptop that works in any part of the building. The new $8 million Morgridge Middle School is the first school in the district built according to guidelines for "green" buildings.

Although other urban schools may not have all of these advantages, they can still learn much from DSST's example. One state has already initiated a project inspired by DSST. The Texas High School Project, a consortium of the Texas Education Agency, the Bill & Melinda Gates Foundation, and the Michael and Susan Dell Foundation, has chosen DSST as one of its best-practices models. The project is creating 35 public STEM (science, technology, engineering and math) secondary schools.

"People ask about how expensive our model is," says Greenberg. "It probably costs about 10 percent more per year than a conventional urban public school. But think about it. We had more minority kids [from DSST] going to the University of Colorado than any other school in the state. We also scored fifth highest in Colorado on the ACT exam. DPS, on the other hand, has a 50 percent drop-out rate. So which model is really more expensive?"

Appendix A

Committee Biographies

Linda P.B. Katehi (*chair*) is chancellor of the University of California, Davis. Previously, she served as provost and vice chancellor for academic affairs at the University of Illinois at Urbana-Champaign; the John Edwardson Dean of Engineering and professor of electrical and computer engineering at Purdue University; and associate dean for academic affairs and graduate education in the College of Engineering and professor of electrical engineering and computer science at the University of Michigan. Professor Katehi led the effort to establish the Purdue School of Engineering Education, the first department at a U.S. university focused explicitly on engineering education, particularly on K–12 engineering curricula, standards, and teacher education. The author or coauthor of 10 book chapters, she has published more than 600 articles in refereed journals and symposia proceedings and owns 16 patents. She is a member of the National Academy of Engineering (NAE), a fellow and board member of the American Association for the Advancement of Science, chair of the Nominations Committees for the National Medal of Science and National Medal of Technology and Innovation, and a member of the Kauffman National Panel for Entrepreneurship. She is currently a member of a number of NAE/National Academy of Sciences committees and the Advisory Committee for Harvard Radcliffe College and a member of the Engineering Advisory Committees for Caltech, the University of Washington, and the University of California, Los Angeles.

Lynn Basham received her B.S. in 1977 and M.S. in 1985 from the University of Southern Mississippi and completed her doctoral work in 2006 at Louisiana State University. As a state specialist for technology education at the Virginia Department of Education, she is responsible for curriculum projects and the development of new initiatives. Ms. Basham has received many professional honors and has been active in professional organizations throughout her career. From 2000 to 2002, she was Region 2 representative for the International Technology Education Association (ITEA) Board of Directors and was recently president of the ITEA Council for Supervisors (CS). She was awarded the ITEA-CS Distinguished Service Award in 2004 and the ITEA-CS Outstanding State Supervisor Award in 1992 and 2001. Ms. Basham is also a member of the Mississippi Valley Technology Teacher Education Conference, a member and past president of the Southeastern Technology Education Conference, and a member of the Association for Career and Technical Education, American Association for Training and Development, and American Society for Curriculum Development. She is currently working on the U.S. Department of Energy Real World Design Challenge.

M. David Burghardt is a professor of engineering, a licensed professional engineer in New York, and a Chartered Engineer in the United Kingdom. He is also co-director of the Hofstra University Center for Technological Literacy (CTL), which he established in 1989, and the author of 11 books on engineering and secondary-school technology education. Since 1993, through CTL, he has won seven major National Science Foundation grants for work on improving technological literacy. Dr. Burghardt's particular interest is in how engineering design can promote student learning in mathematics and science, especially for lower performing students. In addition to developing engineering courses at the university level, he was co-creator of a master's degree program for in-service teachers, which now has more than 300 graduates.

Kathleen Conn, assistant professor at Neumann College in the Division of Human Services, is a scientist, educator, and former school administrator. She earned her Ph.D. in physics/biology at Bryn Mawr College, completed postdoctoral work at Lankenau Medical Research Center in Philadelphia, and took her legal training at Widener University School of Law. She was a participant and leader in the Thayer School of Engineering (Dartmouth College) "Engineering Concepts in the High School Classroom" Program, which trains mathematics and science teachers to use problem-solving approaches. Dr. Conn has been a delegate to international conferences on physics education and a member of the Advisory Council for the Mechanical Universe High School Adaptation (MUHSA) and the Comprehensive Conceptual Curriculum for Physics (C3P), two pre-college physics curriculum projects sponsored by the National Science Foundation. She is also an adjunct professor at Widener University School of Law, Wilmington, Delaware.

Alan G. Gomez, an instructor at the University of Wisconsin College of Engineering, and an engineering instructor and career and technical education coordinator for the Sun Prairie Area School District. He received his B.S. in Technology Education from the University of Wisconsin-Stout in 1995, his M.S. in Industrial/Technology Education from Stout in 2004, and a Ph.D. in Industrial and Systems Engineering from the University of Wisconsin-Madison in 2008. He has written a National Foundations of Technology curriculum and a National Introduction to Engineering curriculum for the International Technology Education Association Center to Advance the Teaching of Technology and Science. A member of the team writing technology education standards for the state of Wisconsin, he has published materials in professional journals and in the *Proceedings of the American Society for Engineering Education*. Dr. Gomez is principal author of *Engineering Your Future: A Project-Based Introduction to Engineering* and *Survey of Engineering*.

Craig Kesselheim is currently senior associate for the Great Schools Partnership in Maine, where he not only assists and consults with secondary schools on reform initiatives, but also directs a three-year math science partnership of three public schools, a career and technical school, and a community college. Previous positions include director of curriculum and staff development for Maine School Union 98; principal of Tremont Consolidated School (K–8) in Bass Harbor, Maine; assistant professor of biology at the University of Central Arkansas; and science facilitator for the Maine Mathematics and Science Alliance. Dr. Kesselheim earned his B.A. from College of the Atlantic and an M.A.T. from Bridgewater State College. He earned his Ph.D. in science education from the University of Maine in 1997.

Michael C. Lach, officer of high school teaching and learning, oversees curriculum and instruction in 120 high schools in the Chicago School System. Mr. Lach began teaching high school biology and general science at Alceé

Fortier Senior High School in New Orleans in 1990 as a charter member of Teach for America. After three years, he became director of program design for Teach for America, where he developed a portfolio-based alternative-certification system that was adopted by several states. He subsequently returned to teaching science, first in New York and then in Chicago. In 1995, Radio Shack named him one of the Top 100 Technology Teachers; the same year he was named Illinois Physics Teacher of the Year. As an Albert Einstein Distinguished Educator Fellow, he was advisor to Congressman Vernon Ehlers (R-MI) on science, technology, and education. He was also lead curriculum developer of "Investigations in Environmental Science" (It's About Time, Inc.), and has written extensively about science teaching and learning for *The Science Teacher*, *The American Biology Teacher*, *Scientific American*, and other publications. He earned a bachelor's degree in physics from Carleton College and master's degrees from Columbia University and Northeastern Illinois University.

Richard Lehrer is professor of science education in the Peabody College of Teaching and Learning at Vanderbilt University. Previously, at the University of Wisconsin, Madison, he was associate director of the National Center for Improving Student Learning and Achievement in Mathematics and Science. He collaborates with teachers to develop, implement, and assess modeling of mathematics and sciences in the elementary grades and works with engineers and science educators at City College of New York to conduct studies of engineering design in the elementary grades. A former high school science teacher, he has pioneered classroom research on using cognitive technologies as tools for teaching mathematics, science, and literacy. He was a member of the National Research Council Committee on the Foundations of Assessment and Systems for State Science Assessment.

Deborah McGriff has worked for almost four decades to transform the lives of underserved urban school students. Currently, she is president of the Education Industry Association, an association of providers of education services; a member of the Advisory Board of the National Council on Teacher Quality; a founder and national board member of the Black Alliance for Educational Options; and a member of the Advisory Board of the Program on Education Policy and Governance at the Harvard University John F. Kennedy School of Government. She is also a partner at NewSchools Venture Fund, where she works on investment strategy and quality teaching. In 1993, after years of working as an administrator for public school systems in Detroit, Cambridge, Massachusetts, Milwaukee, and New York, she became the first public school superintendent to join EdisonLearning (formerly Edison Schools), where she held numerous positions, including president of Edison Teachers College and executive vice president of charter schools. She has a bachelor's degree in education with a minor in history from Norfolk State University, a master's degree in education, with a specialization in ready pedagogy from Queens College of the City University of New York, and a doctorate in administration, policy, and urban education from Fordham University.

Roland (Rollie) J. Otto is Director of Education Outreach and the Global Teacher Academy for the Berkeley Center for Cosmological Physics at the University of California, Berkeley. From 1988 to 2006, he was head of the Center for Science and Engineering Education at the Lawrence Berkeley National Laboratory, and from 1995 to 1998, he was executive director of the California Science Project, a statewide teacher professional-development network. From 1986 to 1988, he was assistant director of the Lawrence Hall of Science at the University of California, Berkeley. In 2001–2002, Dr. Otto was a member of the Science Subject Matter Committee, California Commission for Teacher Credentialing, which establishes subject-matter content standards for science teachers. He was also principle writer and advisor for the California Science Framework Committee (2000-2001) and chair of the Content Review Panel for the science instructional-materials adoption process (1999). He has a Ph.D. in nuclear/physical chemistry from Purdue and a B.S. in chemistry from Valparaiso University. He did his postgraduate work with Nobelist Glenn T. Seaborg.

Richard J. Schaar, an executive advisor at Texas Instruments (TI), recently retired from his post as a senior vice president of TI, where he was math and science education policy advisor for the corporation. Under his guidance, TI developed educator-support services, including technology training, to increase teachers' confidence and ability to integrate technology education into their classrooms. Dr. Schaar served on the National Science Foundation (NSF) Advisory Committee of the Directorate for Education and Human Resources and chaired the Subcommittee on the Instructional Workforce. He extended TI's commitment to education by partnering with NSF on educational initiatives, including serving as the leading corporate sponsor of the Urban Systemic Programs, Model Institutions for Excellence, and the Superintendents' Coalition. Under his leadership, TI supports an executive director for the Benjamin Banneker Association and helped establish the Dorothy Strong Scholarship for Professional Development. He holds a B.S. from Purdue University, an M.B.A. from the University of Illinois, and a Ph.D. in applied mathematics from the University of Chicago. Dr. Schaar has also received a Woodrow Wilson Fellowship and an NSF Graduate Research Fellowship.

Mark Schroll joined the Kern Family Foundation in August, 2007, where he is program coordinator for engineering and innovation programs, including Project Lead the Way (PLTW). As a member of the original staff of the Science Academy of South Texas, he co-authored and implemented PLTW, a unique four-year pre-engineering curriculum, and later worked to implement a PLTW program at his school. From 2001 to 2007 he was a PLTW teacher trainer for two courses, Digital Electronics and Engineering Design and Development. Drawing on his experience with pre-engineering curricula and instruction, he collaborates with grant-management staff on the application-review and grant-monitoring processes. He also works closely with grantees to develop networks of strong partnerships and sustainability plans.

Christian D. Schunn is an associate professor of psychology and a research scientist in the Learning Research and Development Center at the University of Pittsburgh. His basic research involves studying experts and novices in complex domains, such as science, engineering, submarining, and weather forecasting, to develop theoretical and computational models of cognition underlying expert performance and the difficulties of developing expert-like performance. His applied research involves developing and evaluating tools and curricula to help novices achieve expert performance. Dr. Schunn has developed design-based learning curricula for middle and high school science classrooms that have been found to be more successful than existing hands-on and textbook science curricula at teaching basic science concepts and scientific reasoning skills and stimulating interest in engineering, science, and technology careers. He received his Ph.D. from Carnegie Mellon University in 1995.

Jacquelyn F. Sullivan, associate dean for student cultivation, College of Engineering and Applied Science, University of Colorado (UC) at Boulder, heads the college diversity, recruitment, and retention programs. A founding co-director of the Integrated Teaching and Learning Program and Laboratory, Dr. Sullivan was a driving force behind this hands-on K–16 learning initiative, which now serves more than 4,000 undergraduate engineering students annually. For this work, she was a co-recipient of the 2008 Bernard M. Gordon Prize for Innovation in Engineering and Technology Education from the National Academy of Engineering, and in 2005, she received the inaugural Lifetime Achievement Award from the K–12 Division of the American Society of Engineering Education. She also directs the TEAMS Program (Tomorrow's Engineering—creAte. iMagine. Succeed), funded by the National Science Foundation, and was a co-developer of a retention-building First-Year Engineering Projects course at UC Boulder. Dr. Sullivan is a founding board member of the Denver School of Science and Technology, a public, urban high school that incorporates science, engineering, and technology into a humanities-rich setting focused on student achievement. Her articles have appeared in *Science, The Bridge*, and many other publications. She received her Ph.D. in environmental health physics and toxicology from Purdue University and has 14 years of engineering experience in the energy and software industries and nine years of experience as director of a water resources and environmental engineering research center.

Robin Willner is vice president, Global Community Initiatives, for IBM, which she joined in 1994 to design and implement Reinventing Education, a $90 million philanthropic initiative that promotes K–12 school reform through grant partnerships with school districts and states to develop new applications of technology to overcome common barriers to school improvement and raise the level of student achievement. She also oversees a range of philanthropic and volunteer programs and was project manager for the 2001, 1999, and 1996 National Education Summits, which were co-hosted by IBM. She was instrumental in the initial planning and start-up of Achieve Inc., a national education organization for standards-based reform. Prior to joining IBM, Ms. Willner was executive director for strategic planning/research and development for the New York City Public Schools. She is a member of the boards of directors of the National Center for Educational Accountability, Grantmakers for Education, and Center for Education Policy in Washington, D.C. She was a member of the U.S. Department of Education Expert Panel on Educational Technology from 1999 to 2000. She graduated from Columbia University with a degree in urban affairs.

Appendix B

Curriculum Projects—
Descriptive Summaries

The Academy of Engineering

The Academy of Engineering (AOE) is a mobile engineering laboratory that combines hands-on activities with either Fischertechnik® or LEGO® manipulatives to teach students science, technology, engineering, math, architecture, communications, and robotics. According to the company, AOE includes hundreds of hours of course work and activities. Versions appropriate to elementary, middle, and high school are available. The program also includes online teacher training, student assessment and support, and a virtual online community that includes quarterly engineering challenges, and at-home extension activities. The curriculum is comprised of four volumes of real-world mechanical engineering projects that naturally embed mathematics, design, technology literacy, communications, and science. The volumes address simple machines, power transfer, gear trains, and principles of robotics and each book provides enough materials to cover an entire semester.

Developer: PCS Edventures Inc.
Website: http://edventures.com/imssc/nsimssc/
To Obtain Materials: Contact Sales and Product Information at 800/429-3110 or sales@pcsedu.com

Children Designing & Engineering

Children Designing & Engineering was a collaboration between the College of New Jersey's Department of Technological Studies, the New Jersey Chamber of Commerce, and the Institute of Electrical and Electronics Engineers. With funding from the National Science Foundation, the project developed contextual learning units for children in grades K–2 and 3–5. Each unit is framed in the context of a prominent New Jersey business (i.e., Six Flags Wild Safari, Lucent Technologies, Marcal Paper, Public Service Electric and Water, Elizabethtown Water, Johnson & Johnson, Ocean Spray). They are designed to run from four to six weeks (or 15 to 22 hours), and they begin with a design challenge that must be addressed in the final week. The subsequent instruction enables students to develop a solution to the challenge by engaging them in researching topics, generating ideas, planning courses of action, making things, and testing and presenting their designs. Addressing these challenges requires students to apply concepts and skills from mathematics, science, technology, and other academic subjects.

Developer: The College of New Jersey
Contact: Alison Goeke
E-mail: goeke2@tcnj.edu
To obtain materials: Materials out of print.

DTEACh

DTEACh (Design Technology and Engineering for America's Children) is a product of the Cockrell School of Engineering at The University of Texas at Austin. It began in 1992 as a grassroots science, technology, engineering, and mathematics teacher education project for elementary school teachers. In 2000, DTEACh began partnering with National Instruments to offer robotics and automation workshops using LEGO MINDSTORMS. Over the past eight years, the program has helped hundreds of Central Texas educators integrate cutting-edge technology into the classroom through the DTEACh Robotics and Automation Summer Institutes. Participants learn to use the engineering design process to more effectively teach state-mandated science and math standards. Mentors from the engineering community held these teachers use LEGO MINDSTORMS to engage their students in learning that integrates core STEM subjects while incorporating 21st century skills. DTeach has one published curriculum, for grades 3–4, on automation and control.

Developer: Cockrell School of Engineering, The University of Texas at Austin
Website: www.engr.utexas.edu/dteach
Contact: Cheryl Farmer
E-mail: cheryl.farmer@mail.utexas.edu
To obtain materials: The curriculum on automation and control can be downloaded at http://www.engr.utexas.edu/dteach/resources/DTEACh_Robotics_3-5.pdf

Engineering: An Introduction for High School

Engineering: An Introduction for High School is an open-source high school "flexbook" created using software developed by the CK–12 Foundation by engineering and education faculty at Arizona State University. The flexbook format allows the book to be customized for multiple audiences. The text can be updated, expanded, and repurposed as necessary to support specific standards and classroom needs. The current draft has four content chapters that cover the nature of engineering, engineering and society, engineering design, and the connection between engineering, science, and mathematics.

Developer: Faculty at Arizona State University
Contact: Darryl Morrell
E-mail: DARRYL.MORRELL@asu.edu
To obtain materials: http://flexbooks.ck12.org

Engineering by Design™

Engineering byDesign™ (EbD) is a national model program developed by the ITEA-CATTS (International Technology Education Association-Center to Advance the Teaching of Technology and Science) Consortium in consultation with the ITEA Technology Education Advisory Council, ITEA institutional members, and the mathematics, science, and engineering communities. At the K–5 grades, the program provides content that can be integrated with other school subjects. In grades 6–12, the program offers nine discrete courses, ranging in length from 18 weeks to 36 weeks. Engineering by Design™ is built on the constructivist model, and students in the program learn concepts and principles in an authentic, problem-based environment. A network of technology teachers (EbD™ Network) has been selected to collaborate and conduct action research (through eTIDEonline™ and the EbD Online Assessment & Design Challenge) in order to better understand the complexities of student learning and to help all students succeed and be prepared for the global society in which they will grow up.

Developer: International Technology Education Association
Website: http://www.iteaconnect.org/EbD/ebd.htm
Contact: Barry Burke
E-mail: bburke@iteaconnect.org
Materials available to members of the ITEA-CATTS Consortium.

Engineering Your Future: A Project-Based Introduction to Engineering
Engineering Your Future: A Project-Based Introduction to Engineering is a
high-school level, project-based introduction to engineering. The 19-chapter
text includes information related to the history of technology and engineering; engineers and the engineering profession; the big ideas in engineering,
including systems, optimization, problem solving, design, and modeling;
technology, society, and ethics; and fundamental mathematical and physics
concepts used in mechanical and electrical engineering. There are 43 case
studies that engage students in various types of learning activities. An
instructor's guide can also be purchased.

Developers: Alan Gomez, William Oakes, Les Leone
Contact: Al Gomez
E-mail: aggomez@spasd.k12.wi.us
To obtain materials: Great Lakes Press, Paul Bruner (paul@glpbooks.com)
or 800-837-0201

Engineers of the Future
Engineers of the Future is a set of eight middle and high school courses modeled on the design and technology curriculum of the United Kingdom and intended for use by technology education teachers in the United States. The course are (1) Introduction to Design, Engineering and Technology for Middle School; (2) Foundations of Design, Innovation, Engineering and Technology for High School; (3) Engineering Design and Product Development for MS and HS; (4) Exploring our Designed World; (5) Pro/Desktop Designing and Modeling for MS or HS; (6) Pro Engineering and Prototyping for HS; (7) Introduction to Biotechnology and Bioengineering; and (8) Introduction to Digital Electronics and Control Systems. According to the developers, the courses and accompanying professional development experiences are meant to complement and enhance the delivery of integrated STEM education. The courses were piloted in New York in 2007. Partners in the effort include Buffalo State College, Technology Department; the New York State Education Department; PTC Corporation; and the MIT Consortium.

Developer: Buffalo State College, Technology Department
Website: http://www.buffalostate.edu/technology/eof.xml
Contact: Steve Macho
E-mail: machos@buffalostate.edu

Exploring Designing and Engineering

Exploring Designing and Engineering (ED&E)™, initially funded by the New Jersey Commission on Higher Education, offers teacher professional development and instructional materials that are contextual, problem-based, and authentic. Six-week units for grades 6-8 focus on science and technology integration in "Pack It Up, Ship It Out"; "Community by Design"; "Materials & Processes," and "The Big Thrill—Dream It, Plan It, Build It." High School units include "Digital DJ," "Ready, Set, Sail," "Xtreme Automata" and the "Capstone Course" for advanced students. *Design and Engineering with ProDESKTOP*, ED&E's classroom text, guides students through the skills of computer-aided design and visualization used in the ED&E units. Over 500 New Jersey teachers have taken ED&E workshops since 2000, with nearly 15,000 students now participating in design and engineering activities statewide.

Developer: The College of New Jersey, Center for Mathematics, Science, Technology and Pre-Engineering
Website: http://njtqe-r.grant.tcnj.edu/index.htm
Contact: John Karsnitz
E-mail: karsnitz@tcnj.edu

The Infinity Project (Middle School)

The Infinity Project introduced its middle school (grades 6–8) engineering curriculum in fall 2008. It consists of six three-week modules developed in partnership with engineering professors at Southern Methodist University and middle school educators. Modules can be grouped together and offered as a standalone course or individually incorporated into existing math, science, or technology classes. Additional modules spanning the disciplines of electrical, mechanical, civil, environmental, and biomedical engineering will be introduced in fall 2009.

The initial six modules are:

- Introduction to Engineering Design
- Rocketry—Achieving Liftoff I
- Rocketry—Achieving Liftoff II
- Robots from Concept to Completion
- Sound Engineering—Making Great Sounds
- Engineering in the Natural World

Schools must apply to become an Infinity Project school and offer the middle school engineering curriculum. Once accepted into the program, teachers attend week-long training during the summer. Professional development materials include instructor notes, homework solutions, sample test questions, a daily lesson plan guide, PowerPoint chapter lectures, and online support.

Developer: The Infinity Project, Southern Methodist University
Contact: Dianna McAtee
E-mail: dmcatee@infinity-project.org

Insights: An Inquiry-Based Elementary School Science Curriculum (Structures Module)

Insights: An Inquiry-Based Elementary School Science Curriculum was developed by a coalition of science curriculum specialists at Education Development Center, Inc. and teams of elementary school teachers from Baltimore, Boston, Cleveland, Los Angeles, New York, Montgomery County (Maryland), and San Francisco school districts. Each module was pilot tested by team teachers, revised, field tested on a larger scale, and revised a second time before publication. The Center for the Study of Testing, Evaluation, and Educational Policy (CSTEEP) at Boston College provided evaluation and assessment specialists for the project. In the Structures Module, sixth grade students begin to develop an understanding of some of the basic principles that answer the question, Why do structures stand up? They look at structures in the school neighborhood, observing the variety in size, shape, material, and function. They build their own structures, using straws, index cards, and other materials. As they build, students explore some of the basic concepts of standing structures, such as live load, dead load, tension and compression, the role of shapes, and trusses. By comparing their structures with those in their community, students learn how structure and design are influenced by function, materials, and aesthetics. The last activity in the module challenges students to design and construct a unique piece of playground equipment.

Developer: Center for Science Education, Education Development Center, Inc.
Website: http://cse.edc.org/curriculum/insightsElem/
Contact: Karen Worth
E-mail: kworth@edc.org
To obtain materials: Kendall/Hunt Publishing Company, 800-542-6657, ext. 1042, or orders@kendallhunt.com

INSPIRES: INcreasing Student Participation, Interest and Recruitment in Engineering and Science

INSPIRES is a collaborative project between the University of Maryland Baltimore County and University of Maryland School of Medicine. It is funded through a grant from the National Science Foundation. The curriculum has five units:

- Engineering in Health Care
- Engineering and Flight
- Engineering and the Environment
- Engineering in Communications and Information Technology
- Engineering Energy Solutions

INSPIRES aims to provide students with hands-on experiences and inquiry-based learning with "real world" engineering design exercises. The materials target the ITEA Standards for Technological Literacy as well as national standards in science and mathematics. In addition, the project includes in-service training with curriculum and professional development opportunities for technology education teachers prior to classroom use. A specific objective is to increase the involvement of women and other underrepresented groups in engineering and technology by providing role modes in the classroom and developing case studies that encourage interest and participation by all groups.

Developers: UMBC and UMSM
Contact: Julia Ross
E-mail: jross@umbc.edu

Learning by Design

Learning by Design is a project-based inquiry approach to science for middle school students (grades six through eight). This initiative is housed at the Georgia Institute of Technology and funded by the National Science Foundation, the BellSouth Foundation, the James S. McDonnell Foundation, and the Robert W. Woodruff Foundation. The thrust of the project is to help students "learn science content deeply" in conjunction with developing the "skills and understanding needed to undertake solution of complex, ill-structured problems." Students study science in the context of addressing design challenges that help them make connections between their experiences, science concepts and skills, and the world around them. During the design process, they practice designing and running experiments, analyzing data and drawing conclusions, making informed decisions and justifying them with evidence, working collaboratively in a team, and communicating ideas and experiences to others. Each unit requires students to "publicly describe to their peers what they've done and how they've been reasoning, allowing the teacher and their peers to hear their reasoning and help them around hurdles." The units of instruction center on designing parachutes, erosion management systems, model vehicles, lifting devices, and subway tunnels.

Developer: Georgia Institute of Technology
Website: http://www.cc.gatech.edu/projects/lbd/home.html
Contact: Janet Kolodner
E-mail: jlk@cc.gatech.edu

LEGO® Engineering

LEGO Engineering, a collaboration between the Tufts Center for Engineering Education Outreach and LEGO Education, offers five fully developed curriculum modules based on LEGO design projects. Each module consists of a set of class sessions, with each session building upon previous learning. Modules include lesson plans, teacher resource documents, student handouts, and assessment materials. Four of the modules are designed for grades 3–5: Design a Musical Instrument: The Science of Sound, Design a Model House: The Properties of Materials, Design an Animal Model: Animal Studies, and Design a People Mover: Simple Machines. The fifth module, Robotics: Assistive Devices for the Future, is intended for grades 6–8. All five modules were developed with funding from the National Science Foundation. The LEGO Engineering website also contains a number of discrete Lego design activities, sequences of these activities, and video tutorials (podcasts).

Developers: Center for Engineering Educational Outreach, Tufts University, and LEGO Education
Website: www.legoengineering.com
Contact: Merredith Portsmore
E-mail: merredith@legoengineering.com
To obtain materials: Curriculum resources are downloadable for free from the LEGO Engineering website.

Principles of Engineering

Principles of Engineering (PoE) was a major curriculum project developed under the auspices of the New York State Education Department in 1989, field tested in 65 school districts across New York State from 1989 to 1992, and revised in 1995. PoE was a one-year high school course targeted to students in grades 11 and 12 who had completed two years of Regents level mathematics and two years of Regents level science, preferably including physics. The course included a set of hands-on, laboratory-based case studies and was taught in a laboratory setting, providing students access to tools and materials for individual, small-group, and large-group projects. The case studies addressed auto safety, ergonomics of communication technology, machine automation, structural design, and designing for people with disabilities. Engineering concepts addressed in the course included design, modeling, systems, optimization, technology-society interactions, and engineering ethics. After field testing, a National Science Foundation grant provided funding to disseminate the course nationally through a series of professional development workshops. Teachers from 20 states participated in these workshops.

Developer: New York State Department of Education
Contact: Michael Hacker
E-mail: Michael.Hacker@hofstra.edu
To obtain materials: This curriculum is out of print.

TeachEngineering.org

TeachEngineering.org is a collaborative project between faculty, students and teachers associated with five universities and the American Society for Engineering Education, with funding from the NSF National Science Digital Library. TeachEngineering.org is a searchable, web-based digital library collection populated with standards-based engineering curricula for use by K–12 teachers and engineering faculty to make applied science and math (engineering) come alive in K–12 settings. The collection provides access to a growing curricular resource of multi-week units, lessons, activities and living labs. Materials on the site are organized according to 43 subject areas, each containing related curricular units, lessons, and activities. The site allows users to determine the extent to which a given unit, lesson, or activity is consistent with individual state or national-level educational standards. Initiated by the merging of K–12 engineering curricula created by four universities, the collection continues to grow and evolve over time with new additions from other universities, and input from teachers who use the curricula in their classrooms.

Developer: Multi-university collaboration, ASEE
Website: http://www.teachengineering.org/
Contact: Jackie Sullivan
Email: jacquelyn.sullivan@colorado.edu
To obtain materials: Materials downloadable free from the website.

TECH-Know

The TECH-Know curriculum was developed by North Carolina State University and is a standards-based curriculum adapted from 20 technology-based problems issued by the Technology Student Association (TSA). There are 10 units each for middle and high school classrooms. The following topics are covered in the middle school units:

- Agricultural/Biotechnology
- Cyberspace Pursuit
- Dragster Design Challenge
- Environmental Challenge
- Flight Challenge
- Mechanical Challenge
- Structural Challenge
- Transportation Challenge
- Medical Technology Challenge
- Digital Photography

The following topics are covered in the middle school units:

- Desktop Publishing
- Film/Video Technology
- Manufacturing Prototype
- Radio Controlled Vehicle Transportation
- SciVis
- Structural Engineering
- System Control Technology
- Technology Challenge
- Medical Technologies
- Agricultural and Biotechnologies

Developer: North Carolina State University
Website: http://www.ncsu.edu/techknow/aboutproject.html
Contact: Jerianne Taylor or Rosanne White
Contact e-mail: taylorjs@appstate.edu; rwhite@tsaweb.org
To obtain materials: Materials out of print.

Technology Education: Learning by Design
Technology Education: Learning by Design is a middle school textbook developed by the Center for Technological Literacy at Hofstra University. The text uses the "informed design" approach, which encourages research, inquiry, and analysis; fosters student and teacher discourse; and cultivates language proficiency. The book contains seven units:

- The Nature of Technology
- Design for a Technological World
- Materials, Manufacturing, and Construction
- Communication and Information Technology
- Energy, Power, and Transportation
- Biological and Chemical Technology
- The Future of Technology in Society

Also available are a student activity guide, annotated teacher's edition, teacher's resource binder, test bank with ExamView CD-ROM, and a technology timeline poster.

Developer: Center for Technological Literacy, Hofstra University
Contact: David Burghardt
E-mail: M.D.Burghardt@hofstra.edu
To obtain materials: Pearson Prentice Hall, k12cs@custhelp.com or 800/848-9500

What is Engineering?

What is Engineering? originated as an introduction to engineering class offered to first semester freshmen at Johns Hopkins University (JHU). JHU adapted the course so it could be taught as a summer program aimed at rising high school juniors and seniors as well as incoming college freshmen. The class is an intensive four-week experience where students actively participate in hands-on team activities including laboratory experiments and virtual Internet-based simulations while attending college-level lectures related to these activities. Field trips to local companies that employ engineers and informational sessions on college and career choices are integrated into the course schedule. The curriculum links math, science, and engineering concepts to practical problems as a means of teaching students the essential problem-solving skills required to be a successful engineer. Students may earn college credit from JHU for participating in the class. Course locations include Maryland, California, New Mexico, and Pennsylvania. In California, several of Engineering Innovations' sites are offered in partnership with MESA (Mathematics Engineering Science Achievement) program.

Developer: Johns Hopkins University, Whiting School of Engineering
Contact: Lindsay Carroll (Program Manager) or Michael Karweit (Academic Director)
E-mail: lindsay.carroll@jhu.edu or mjk@jhu.edu
To obtain materials: http://engineering-innovation.jhu.edu

A World in Motion® (High School)

A World In Motion® (High School), developed by SAE International, is an activities-based curriculum focused on electricity and electronics. Student teams conduct in-depth experiments involving transistors and semi-conductors, analog integrated circuits, and digital integrated circuits. As with other World in Motion® curricula, the high school program requires teachers to work with a volunteer classroom mentor from a science, engineering or technical profession. World in Motion® has the goal of increasing student interest in math and science. SAE International provides the AWIM curriculum and materials at no cost to classroom teachers who complete a Statement of Partnership.

Developer: SAE International
Website: http://www.sae.org/exdomains/awim/
Contact: Matt Miller
E-Mail: matt.miller@sae.org
To obtain materials: AWIM hotline, 1-800-457-2946

Appendix C

Curriculum Projects—Detailed Analyses

Appendix C is reproduced on the CD (inside back cover) and in the PDF available online at http://www.nap/edu/catalog.php?record_id=12635.

Index